In-Place Object Server

In-Place Server
Interfaces

IOleInPlaceObject
IOleInPlaceActiveObject

Container In-Place Interfaces
Used by In-Place Server

IOleInPlaceSite

In-Place Architecture

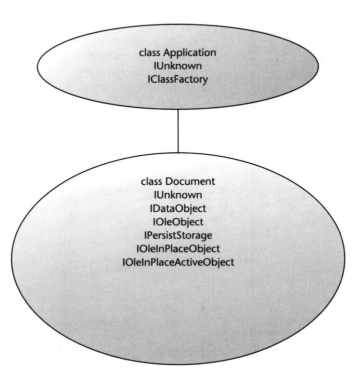

class Application
IUnknown
IClassFactory

class Document
IUnknown
IDataObject
IOleObject
IPersistStorage
IOleInPlaceObject
IOleInPlaceActiveObject

FOR EVERY COMPUTER QUESTION,
THERE IS A SYBEX BOOK THAT HAS THE ANSWER

Each computer user learns in a different way. Some need thorough, methodical explanations, while others are too busy for details. At Sybex we bring nearly 20 years of experience to developing the book that's right for you. Whatever your needs, we can help you get the most from your software and hardware, at a pace that's comfortable for you.

We start beginners out right. You will learn by seeing and doing with our **Quick & Easy** series: friendly, colorful guidebooks with screen-by-screen illustrations. For hardware novices, the **Your First** series offers valuable purchasing advice and installation support.

Often recognized for excellence in national book reviews, our **Mastering** and **Understanding** titles are designed for the intermediate to advanced user, without leaving the beginner behind. A **Mastering** or **Understanding** book provides the most detailed reference available. Add one of our pocket-sized **Instant Reference** titles for a complete guidance system. Programmers will find that the new **Developer's Handbook** series provides a higher-end user's perspective on developing innovative and original code.

With the breathtaking advances common in computing today comes an ever increasing demand to remain technologically up-to-date. In many of our books, we provide the added value of software, on disks or CDs. Sybex remains your source for information on software development, operating systems, networking, and every kind of desktop application. We even have books for kids. Sybex can help smooth your travels on the **Internet** and provide **Strategies and Secrets** to your favorite computer games.

As you read this book, take note of its quality. Sybex publishes books written by experts—authors chosen for their extensive topical knowledge. In fact, many are professionals working in the computer software field. In addition, each manuscript is thoroughly reviewed by our technical, editorial, and production personnel for accuracy and ease-of-use before you ever see it—our guarantee that you'll buy a quality Sybex book every time.

To manage your hardware headaches and optimize your software potential, ask for a Sybex book.

FOR MORE INFORMATION, PLEASE CONTACT:

Sybex Inc.
2021 Challenger Drive
Alameda, CA 94501
Tel: (510) 523-8233 • (800) 227-2346
Fax: (510) 523-2373

SYBEX

Let us hear from you.

Talk to SYBEX authors, editors and fellow forum members.

Get tips, hints and advice online.

Download magazine articles, book art, and shareware.

MASTERING
OLE 2

Bryan Waters

SYBEX®

San Francisco • Paris • Düsseldorf • Soest

Acquisitions Editor: Joanne Cuthbertson
Developmental Editors: Gary Masters and Jane Reh
Editor: Dusty Bernard
Project Editor: Kristen Vanberg-Wolff
Technical Editor: Amrik Dhillon
Book Designer: Suzanne Albertson
Production Artist: Lucie Zivny
Technical Artist: John Corrigan
Screen Graphics Manager: Aldo X. Bermudez
Desktop Publishing Specialist: Stephanie Hollier
Production Coordinator: Kate Westrich
Indexer: Matthew Spence
Cover Designer: Design Site
Cover Photographer: Mark Johann
Cover Photo Art Direction: Ingalls + Associates

Library of Congress Card Number: 94-65376

ISBN: 0-7821-1467-9

Manufactured in the United States of America

10 9 8 7 6 5 4 3 2 1

Warranty

SYBEX warrants the enclosed disk to be free of physical defects for a period of ninety (90) days after purchase. If you discover a defect in the disk during this warranty period, you can obtain a replacement disk at no charge by sending the defective disk, postage prepaid, with proof of purchase to:

SYBEX Inc.
Customer Service Department
2021 Challenger Drive
Alameda, CA 94501
(800) 227-2346
Fax: (510) 523-2373

After the 90-day period, you can obtain a replacement disk by sending us the defective disk, proof of purchase, and a check or money order for $10, payable to SYBEX.

Disclaimer

SYBEX makes no warranty or representation, either express or implied, with respect to this medium or its contents, its quality, performance, merchantability, or fitness for a particular purpose. In no event will SYBEX, its distributors, or dealers be liable for direct, indirect, special, incidental, or consequential damages arising out of the use of or inability to use the medium or its contents even if advised of the possibility of such damage.

The exclusion of implied warranties is not permitted by some states. Therefore, the above exclusion may not apply to you. This warranty provides you with specific legal rights; there may be other rights that you may have that vary from state to state.

Copy Protection

None of the programs on the disk is copy-protected. However, in all cases, reselling or making copies of these programs without authorization is expressly forbidden.

To my son Jarratt Devereaux Waters

ACKNOWLEDGMENTS

I would like to thank my family for putting up with me during the time I spent writing this book. At Sybex a special thanks goes to Rudolph Langer for supporting my book, and to Gary Masters, Kris Vanberg-Wolff, Jane Reh, Dusty Bernard, Amrik Dhillon, Barbara Gordon, and all the others who put so much effort into getting this book ready for publication. And at Microsoft Corporation, thanks go to Mary Kirtland and Tony Williams for their assistance.

CONTENTS AT A GLANCE

TABLE OF CONTENTS

APPENDICES   **331**

INTRODUCTION

OLE, or object linking and embedding, is in a unique position. This is the first time a technology has been created to solve a problem that any number of independent developers have already been trying to solve, yet it has these same developers completely baffled and confused as to how to use it. I am not entirely sure why this is the case, although I can hazard some guesses.

First, the scope of OLE includes solutions for more than just a few simple problems. Second, it is usually explained and presented in a very simple context so that when the details are finally exposed, it is overwhelming, which has the effect of placing a beleaguered developer on the defensive. Finally, it comes from Microsoft, and everything that comes from Microsoft is evil…right? The first two theories I will address; the third you will have to work out for yourself!

OLE was originally developed to solve the problem of how to make it easy for the user to share the Graph program and its data among Microsoft's various productivity tools, such as PowerPoint, Word, and Excel. How many developers out there have had the problem of trying to implement tools to be easily shared among multiple applications in an intuitive manner? I thought so. OLE 1, although it had some major weaknesses, solved this problem. But in OLE 1, the problem was so specifically defined that although it worked, it could not be expanded easily to handle the obvious extensions to the technology. Some basic architectural issues had to be solved to deal with the problems of OLE 1. The designers of OLE 2 realized that these problems were of a general nature, and they solved them by developing a surprisingly simple architecture called the Component Object Model, or COM.

This is where it starts to become obvious why a lot of developers are confused about OLE. Although OLE and the COM are two separate technologies (yes, one is built on the other), the COM solves a much more basic problem than OLE. It provides the developer with the toolkit to create objects that multiple processes can use. It addresses the issues of RPC, memory allocation, parameter and argument manipulation rules, error handling, class registration, and more. All of these areas have nothing at all to do with OLE. OLE just happens to require the ability to create and manage objects across process boundaries.

OLE, on the other hand, is almost nothing more than a specification. There are two pieces to this specification: the container specification for the application that contains and links to OLE objects, and the server specification for creating the objects themselves. Although the specification itself is not actually divided in this manner, this is how it ends up being used. Creating the basic container or the basic server is almost trivial after you understand the concepts.

So here is a challenge to you, the reader: forget everything you've heard about OLE being hard, overly complex, and difficult to implement, and start trying to imagine how you would have designed the technology if you were building it yourself. You may just find that it is a simple, obvious, yet elegant technology with some great features. So good luck, and have fun building the next generation of software using the COM and OLE.

—Bryan Waters

P.S. Included with this book for your convenience is a disk containing the OLE Publisher and OLE Draw applications, along with the source code presented in this book.

PART 1

Designing Your Application

This section presents the fundamental information you need to build OLE applications. It includes a detailed exploration of the Component Object Model, or COM, as well as important design issues you need to understand when building objects.

Chapter 1 provides an introduction to the concepts and features included in OLE 2.

Chapter 2 presents a detailed discussion of the COM.

Chapter 3 walks through the process of actually building a component object.

CHAPTER

ONE

Introduction to OLE 2

- Differences between OLE 1 and OLE 2

- OLE 2 features

- The future of object linking and embedding

Object linking and embedding (OLE) is a technology originally introduced in 1990 as the result of a joint effort by Microsoft and several other software vendors to facilitate the integration of data from multiple applications to create richer documents. OLE 1 was a logical extension of the clipboard, allowing applications to paste data objects from the clipboard regardless of the format. When the user needed to edit or otherwise manipulate the object, the application would "ask" the object's application to provide the needed service. OLE 1 accomplished this by setting a standard format for the data objects that encapsulated a cached representation of the object, information about the object's server application, and the data that made up the object itself. Since each data object had knowledge of its creator, OLE 1 was a simple piece of technology that allowed the user to double-click an embedded object and cause the server application to be launched (see Figure 1.1). The aspect of OLE that made all of this more interesting was the user interface issues that one "bumped" into by having the client and server applications running at the same time.

FIGURE 1.1:

Example of OLE 1-style editing

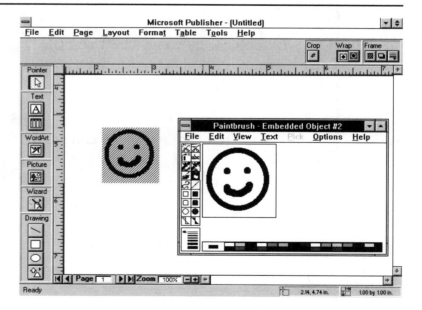

OLE 2 Features

While maintaining backward compatibility with version 1, OLE 2 introduces a rich set of new features, such as in-place editing, drag-and-drop, and application automation.

In-Place Editing

In-place editing allows users to edit embedded data objects in the context of the client application. This fosters the feeling of working within the document instead of struggling with multiple incompatible applications. When activating an object in place, the server negotiates with the client for space for its menus and tool palettes (See Figures 1.2 and 1.3).

FIGURE 1.2:

OLE 2 container with embedded object

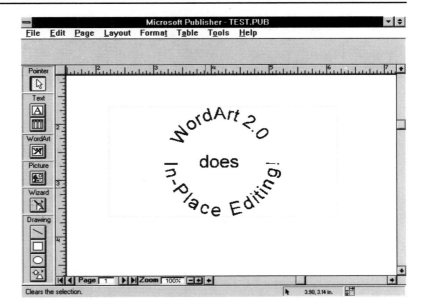

FIGURE 1.3:

Embedded object edited in place

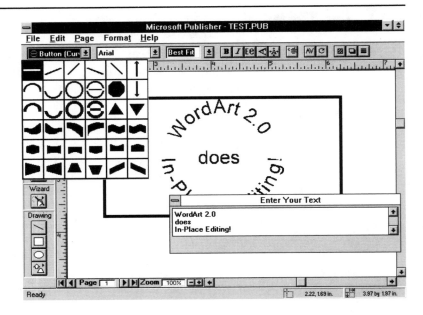

Drag-and-Drop

Although users now had the flexibility to embed and link objects from multiple applications, the only way they could do so was with the clipboard. This fostered the belief that OLE was nothing more than an extension of the clipboard. Of course, the clipboard was an important part of the process, but the main idea was to share objects.

OLE 2 provides a new way of sharing objects, with the addition of drag-and-drop. This technique allows the user to click and drag objects from one application to another and embed, copy, link, or move them.

Automation

Automation is the ultimate extension of the idea of encapsulating applications and their data. OLE automation allows applications to be completely driven by scripts or macros. When this feature was built into OLE, the decision was made not to create a standard macro language. This allows end users to select the macro or script language they are most comfortable with. Also, the trend towards having embedded languages in major applications opens the possibility of meta-applications that are completely customized to end users' needs. For example, you might have a WordBasic macro that loads the company accounting system and runs the end-of-quarter processing, extracts the relevant data, builds an Excel chart, and embeds the chart and the data into a preformatted report in Word. This sort of procedure has been performed within applications for some time, but it has never been able to include external applications.

End-user customization and add-on modules to programmable applications are only the beginning. Automation will really flourish when the operating system and its utilities are fully programmable. A whole new class of setup, debugging, and troubleshooting tools could be built. The potential scope of automation is just beginning to be recognized.

Other Features

OLE 2's other enhancements and features include version management, more flexible link tracking, and support for multiple platforms.

Object servers can now embed version information so they can intelligently handle scenarios in which an object is out of date with respect to the currently installed version of its server. This ability will also allow object servers with similar functionality to handle conversions from foreign objects.

The link tracking for OLE 2 is much more robust than in OLE 1 and can recover more gracefully from broken link situations. OLE 1 stored links as absolute path references to the file that contained the linked data. OLE 2 stores the absolute path name as well as a relative path. Storing both types of path names allows the container to maintain the link between the container's data file and the link document even if both are moved to another drive with the same relative locations. However, the link would still be broken if the file is renamed.

Figure 1.4 illustrates the way a linked object is referenced in OLE 2. If both files were moved to another location, as long as the file PICTURE.BMP resided in a GRAPH-ICS subdirectory relative to the location of the file LETTER.DOC, the link would still be valid. However, it still cannot automatically track a moving link; this will happen when OLE becomes a more integral part of the operating system.

FIGURE 1.4:

Linked word processor document with graphic

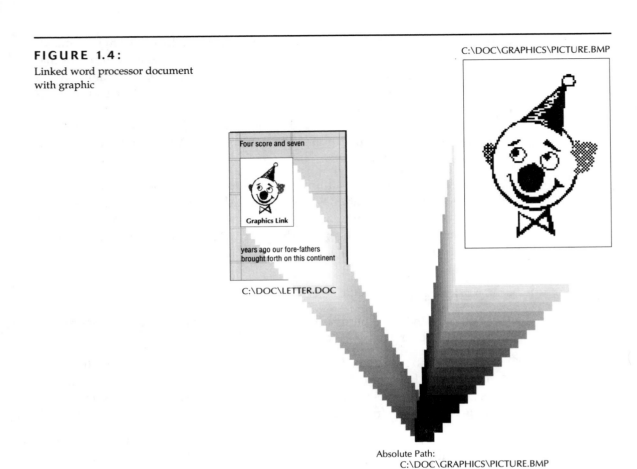

C:\DOC\GRAPHICS\PICTURE.BMP

Four score and seven

Graphics Link

years ago our fore-fathers brought forth on this continent

C:\DOC\LETTER.DOC

Absolute Path:
C:\DOC\GRAPHICS\PICTURE.BMP
Relative Path:
GRAPHICS\PICTURE.BMP

The platforms supported by OLE 2 include Windows 3.1, Windows NT, and the Macintosh. Microsoft is actively pursuing a port to UNIX systems. The support includes similar feature sets on all these platforms, as well as binary compatibility with the compound file storage formats.

Containers and Object Servers

This chapter has referred to the applications involved in OLE-related negotiations as the client and server applications. In OLE 2 terms, the client application, which is the application containing linked and embedded data, is called a *container*, whereas the server, which handles all container requests for a specific type of data, is typically referred to as an *object server*.

What Is the Future of OLE?

In the future it will become more and more difficult to find applications that do not support OLE. End users are already using OLE 1, even though they may not be aware of it. The upcoming releases of the Chicago and Cairo versions of Windows and Windows NT will include OLE as an integral part of the operating system and the system utilities. Microsoft is also adding OLE support to its existing applications, at a furious pace. Applications that include the appropriate level of support for OLE will be in the unique position of having new features appear after installation on an end user's system.

Also, Microsoft has recently announced a major feature to be added to OLE called OLE Controls (or OCX). OLE controls will allow developers to easily add sophisticated features, such as spreadsheet controls, in a fashion similar to VBX controls. OCX is being positioned as a replacement for VBX controls.

Summary

Version 2 of Microsoft's object linking and embedding technology is a major advancement over version 1. It includes a variety of new features, including in-place editing and automation, as well as a completely new architecture that not only allows OLE to be extended indefinitely but also provides a powerful design paradigm for developers. In this book we will show you how to harness this technology for your benefit.

CHAPTER
TWO

The Component Object Model

- Types of object servers

- Using interfaces

- Reference counting

- Using GUIDs

- Creating and using objects

- Registration database

- Memory Management

- Error handling

The design of OLE 1 simply did not allow for the features that were planned for version 2. To develop OLE 2, Microsoft had to rethink the entire architecture of object linking and embedding. This new architecture is the Component Object Model (COM), which provides not only the framework for implementing OLE but also an architecture for designing a whole new class of software. The COM is an object-oriented architecture that defines how small, well-defined pieces of software called *components* can coexist and interact richly on the system. As a result, larger, more sophisticated systems can be built by combining groups of components. OLE is built completely using the COM. The flexibility provided by the COM allows developers to define and build new systems of plug–n–play components.

The COM is composed of a specification and the COMPOBJ.DLL dynamic-link library, which work together to coordinate the interaction between objects and their consumers (any software that uses the objects). Creating an architecture that allows software components from many different developers to interact in a sophisticated manner requires attention to a lot of details about how the different pieces will communicate.

Objects and Object Servers

The COM defines objects as *smart data,* or data that knows how to manipulate and manage itself. An object can be created and used by one or more client tasks. The object knows at any given moment how many clients have a live reference to it, so that when all clients are through with the object, it can delete itself. The object defines a set of interfaces through which clients can communicate with it. Each interface is composed of a collection of methods that allow the client to perform specific actions or request data from the object.

Object servers are simply the software portion of the object. They provide a mechanism for the system to create the objects for the classes supported by the server. It is also the object server's job to manage all instantiated objects.

Types of Servers

The COM has two distinct types of object servers. These types are defined by the difference between implementing a component object as a dynamic-link library and as an executable. A DLL server is called an in-process server, and the EXE server is called a local server.

Local Servers

Local servers are implemented as executable programs. Because of this, the link from the client program to the server must use an RPC (remote-procedure call) link. An object handler runs in the client program's process space and forwards calls to the object across the process boundary to the actual object that exists in the server's process space (see Figure 2.1). The handler acts as a proxy for the actual object. In almost all cases, the client program does not know the difference between an in-process object and a remote object (local server object). (For more details on the differences between in-process servers and local servers, see Part IV.)

FIGURE 2.1:
Local server

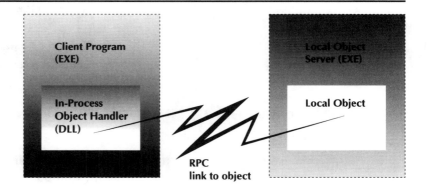

Because of the problem of crossing process boundaries, implementing local servers can be a complicated task. Fortunately, most of the RPC details for the objects you will implement for supporting OLE are taken care of by OLE itself. However, we will still discuss how the connection to a remote object takes place, if for no other reason than to understand how the underlying mechanics of the system work.

In-Process Servers

An *in-process server* runs in the same process context as the client. When a program uses a dynamic-link library (see Figure 2.2), the DLL shares the same task context as the program. This includes sharing file handles, global memory allocations, and some other information. Since in-process servers are implemented as dynamic-link libraries, they run in their client program's context.

Designing an object as an in-process server simplifies the development effort since the RPC connection is not needed. The object's consumer makes calls directly to the object's methods.

FIGURE 2.2:

In-process server

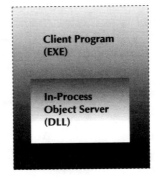

Communicating through Interfaces

An *interface* is the mechanism by which your applications talk to objects. To obtain a new interface pointer, you can use the Component Object Model routines to create a new object and return an interface pointer for the object (see Figure 2.3). Because all interfaces are based on an interface called IUnknown, you can also query an interface for a pointer to another interface for the same object.

FIGURE 2.3:

Conceptual diagram of an object

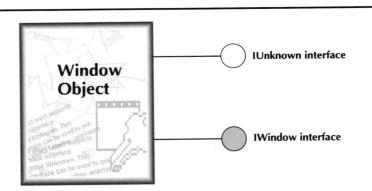

The IUnknown Interface

All objects must support a base interface called IUnknown. This interface can be used to ask the object for other interfaces. Not only does an object have to support the IUnknown interface as a discrete interface, but all other interfaces supported by the object must also support the IUnknown methods. The IUnknown methods are listed in Table 2.1.

TABLE 2.1: I Unknown Interface

Method	Description
HRESULT QueryInterface (iid, ppvInterface)	Queries the object for the interface specified by the iid parameter. The interface is returned in the ppvInterface parameter
ULONG AddRef()	Adds a reference to the object. This keeps the object from being deleted while being used. It should be released with the Release() method when no longer needed
ULONG Release()	Releases the object. This actually decrements the reference count, allowing the object to delete itself when the reference count reaches 0

Calling the IUnknown::QueryInterface() is the primary method of obtaining a specific interface pointer. You call QueryInterface() with an interface ID; if the call is successful, it returns a pointer to the interface you requested.

```
HRESULT hErr ;
LPUNKNOWN lpWindow ;
hErr = lpUnk->QueryInterface( IID_IWindow,
                    (LPVOID *)&lpWindow );
if( SUCCEEDED( hErr ) ) {
    // IWindow interface was obtained
}else{
    // Object does not support IWindow
}
```

In this example the variable lpUnk points to an IUnknown interface for an object. We use lpUnk to call QueryInterface() to obtain a pointer to the IWindow interface in

lpWindow. If we wanted to obtain a third interface, we could call QueryInter-
face() from either lpUnk or lpWindow. If you call QueryInterface() for an interface that is not supported by the object, then the error E_NOINTERFACE is returned.
(See the section "Error Handling" later in this chapter for a detailed discussion of
the subject.)

All interfaces specified by OLE have their IDs defined in the OLEGUID.H header
file that comes with the OLE 2 SDK. The naming convention for these interfaces is
IID_Iinterfacename. Also, OLE defines a pointer type to each variable using the
naming convention LPINTERFACE, where INTERFACE is the name of the interface.
Some of the major OLE 2 interfaces are listed in Table 2.2 with their IDs and pointer
types.

TABLE 2.2: Major OLE Interfaces, IDs, and Pointer Types

Interface	Interface ID	Pointer Type
IClassFactory	IID_IClassFactory	LPCLASSFACTORY
IDataObject	IID_IDataObject	LPDATAOBJECT
IDispatch	IID_IDispatch	LPDISPATCH
IDropSource	IID_IDropSource	LPDROPSOURCE
IDropTarget	IID_IDropTarget	LPDROPTARGET
IMalloc	IID_IMalloc	LPMALLOC
IOleCache	IID_IOleCache	LPOLECACHE
IOleClientSite	IID_IOleClientSite	LPOLECLIENTSITE
IOleContainer	IID_IOleContainer	LPOLECONTAINER
IOleInPlaceObject	IID_IOleInPlaceObject	LPOLEINPLACEOBJECT
IOleInPlaceSite	IID_IOleInPlaceSite	LPOLEINPLACESITE
IOleItemContainer	IID_IOleItemContainer	LPOLEITEMCONTAINER
IOleObject	IID_IOleObject	LPOLEOBJECT
IPersistFile	IID_IPersistFile	LPPERSISTFILE
IPersistStorage	IID_IPersistStorage	LPPERSISTSTORAGE
IPersistStream	IID_IPersistStream	LPPERSISTSTREAM
IStorage	IID_IStorage	LPSTORAGE
IStream	IID_IStream	LPSTREAM
IUnknown	IID_IUnknown	LPUNKNOWN
IViewObject	IID_IViewObject	LPVIEWOBJECT

The other two methods for IUnknown are AddRef() and Release(). These methods implement a reference-counting mechanism that allows the object to know if any consumers are currently using it.

Reference Counting

You use objects for every aspect of OLE; technically, even interfaces are objects. With so many types of objects floating around the system, we need a way to make sure they get cleaned up when they are no longer needed. The IUnknown methods AddRef() and Release() implement a reference-count mechanism that keeps track of the number of references to an object. When the reference count becomes 0, the object can be deleted. Whenever a new reference to an object is created, a call to AddRef() increments the reference count; when the reference is no longer needed, a call to Release() decrements the reference count. The Release() call automatically deletes the object when the reference count reaches 0. For any objects you write, you will create these methods for each interface. They are typically implemented as follows:

```
ULONG IMyInterface::AddRef()
{
    return ++m_RefCount ;
}
ULONG IMyInterace::Release()
{
    if( --m_RefCount == 0 ) {
        delete this ;
        return 0 ;
    }
    return m_RefCount ;
}
```

If you examine the preceding implementation of Release(), you will notice that IMyInterface calls the C++ delete operator when the m_RefCount member variable becomes 0. The other important piece to reference counting is to determine when the AddRef() and Release() methods should be called.

The Rules of Reference

As a rule, whenever a new copy of an interface pointer is created, the Add-Ref() method should be called for that interface, and users of an interface should call Release() when the interface is no longer needed. There are three specific scenarios for manipulating pointers when reference counting should be considered: input, output, and input/output.

Input   When an interface pointer is passed to a function as an input, the called function has no responsibility for calling `AddRef()` or `Release()` on the interface.

Here is an example:

```
HRESULT Function( LPUNKNOWN pInUnknown )
{
    return NOERROR ;
}
```

There is no need to call `AddRef()` or `Release()` when an interface is passed as an input parameter to a function unless we save a copy of the interface pointer for later. In our example, we need `pIUnknown` only for the duration of the function, so we don't need to call `AddRef()` or `Release()` at all. However, if we save a static or global copy of the pointer that will last outside the scope of this function, we must call `AddRef()` to make sure the object does not delete itself. Making a copy of the pointer falls under the general rule described at the beginning of this section.

Output   When an interface pointer is returned from a function as an output, usually the calling function passes the address of a pointer to be filled out. It is the called function's responsibility to call `AddRef()` on the interface before returning to the calling function. The calling function should release the interface when it is no longer needed.

Here is an example:

```
HRESULT Function( LPUNKNOWN *ppOutUnknown )
{
    // IMPORTANT: always NULL out all return
    // results in case of an error
    *ppOutUnknown = NULL ;

    // obtain the new unknown
    ...
    if( there was an error )
        return ResultFromScode( S_FAILED ) ;

    // Now assign the new unknown
    *ppOutUnknown = pNewUnknown ;
```

```
    // Addref it for the caller before returning
    (*ppOutUnknown )->AddRef() ;

    return NOERROR ;
}
```

Input/Output   The input/output case includes the situation in which an interface pointer is passed as an input to a function but may be changed by the function and returned as an output. This is a combination of the two preceding scenarios. The called function has no responsibility to call AddRef() or Release() on the interface unless it substitutes a new interface for the one passed as an argument. Then it must call Release() for the previous interface before storing the new interface pointer in the input/output parameter and call AddRef() for the new interface before returning to the caller.

Here is an example:

```
HRESULT Function( LPUNKNOWN *ppInOutUnknown )
{
    // some code goes here
    // pNewUnknown gets set here

    // Release the previous interface first
    (*ppInOutUnknown )->Release() ;

    // Now assign the new unknown
    *ppInOutUnknown = pNewUnknown ;

    // Addref it for the caller before returning
    (*ppInOutUnknown )->AddRef() ;

    return NOERROR ;
}
```

Using the reference-counting system properly is extremely important when implementing OLE-aware applications. If the calls to AddRef() and Release() become "out of sync" for an object, at best the object will never be destroyed; at worst, it will be destroyed prematurely, causing system errors.

Classes of Objects

The term *object class* is used to describe all objects that are created by a specific server and have the same behavior. An object class is identified by a unique identification number. (See the section "Globally Unique Identification Numbers" later in this chapter.) An object server can support one or more types of object classes. Each class of object must be registered in the registration database, and the server must provide a way to create an object of that class by providing a class factory.

Manufacturing Objects Using Class Factories

A *class factory* is an interface that the server registers with the system when it is loaded. The system can then use this interface to create objects for object consumers when needed.

Registering a class factory for a local server involves calling the routine `CoRegisterClassObject()`. In the server's initialization code, this routine is called once for each object class the server supports. The arguments to this routine are as follows:

```
HRESULT CoRegisterClassObject(    classID,
    pClassFactory,
    classContext,
    flags,
    pToken ) ;
```

The `classID` parameter is the class ID that the registered class factory will support. The `pClassFactory` parameter is a pointer to the class factory interface being registered. The `classContext` parameter defines the context in which the server is running. This can be any of the values listed in Table 2.3. The `flags` parameter can be set to either `REGCLS_SINGLEUSE` or `REGCLS_MULTIPLEUSE`. This determines whether the class factory can be used by more than one consumer at a time. `REGCLS_SINGLEUSE` causes the class factory to become unregistered while it is in use by a consumer. When the consumer is done with the class factory, it becomes available for use again by other consumers. `REGCLS_MULTIPLEUSE` allows any number of consumers to use the class factory at a time. And finally, the `pToken` parameter is passed back to the server to use when it is unregistering its class factory using the `CoRevokeClassObject()` routine.

TABLE 2.3: Class Context Constants

Context	Description
CLSCTX_INPROC_SERVER	Class context for requesting in-process objects (DLL)
CLSCTX_INPROC_HANDLER	Class context for requesting in-process object handlers
CLSCTX_LOCAL_SERVER	Used for requesting local servers (EXE)
CLSCTX_INPROC	Combination of CLSCTX_INPROC_SERVER and CLSCTX_INPROC_HANDLER
CLSCTX_SERVER	Combination of CLSCTX_INPROC_SERVER and CLSCTX_LOCAL_SERVER

In-process servers are handled in a slightly different fashion. Instead of registering its class objects on startup, the in-process server must have an exported routine called DllGetClassObject(). This routine is called in order to obtain a pointer to the class factory for specific object classes supported by the in-process server. After loading the server's DLL, the COM calls the exported function DllGetClassObject(). This routine is declared as follows:

```
HRESULT DllGetClassObject(    class_id,
        iid,
        pClassFactory ) ;
```

The first argument to this routine is a class ID that identifies the correct class factory to return. This allows a single server to support multiple classes of objects. The second argument specifies the interface ID that is initially desired. This argument is almost unneeded since it usually contains the IID_IClassFactory interface ID. The only other interface it would be valid to ask for is the IID_IUnknown. The third argument is an output variable, where the pointer to the class factory interface is returned.

There is one more routine that is exported by the server, called DllCanUnloadNow(). This routine just returns S_OK if the server can be unloaded or S_FALSE if there are any references to objects created by the server.

The IClassFactory Interface

The `IClassFactory` interface is one of the simplest interfaces in terms of methods (see Table 2.4). It has the `CreateInstance()` method, which creates objects for the class that was specified when the class factory was registered with the system, and the `LockServer()` method, which keeps the server from being unloaded.

TABLE 2.4: IClassFactory Methods

Method	Description
HRESULT LockServer(fLock)	Locks the server so it cannot be unloaded. fLock is either TRUE or FALSE, depending on whether it is a lock or an unlock operation
HRESULT CreateInstance(pOuterUnknown, iid, ppv Object)	Creates a new instance of the object created by this class factory. A pointer to the interface specified by iid is returned in ppvObject. pOuterUnknown is used when the object is being aggregated

Aggregating Objects

Aggregation is a slightly different object-oriented paradigm than inheritance. With inheritance all the behavior of a base class is automatically inherited by the new class. Object members must be explicitly overridden in order to modify the behavior of the new class. With aggregation, an object can encapsulate another object, explicitly exposing the desired behaviors. In short, an aggregate object is an object that contains other objects internally and exposes specific interfaces of those objects in order to supplement its own behavior.

In Figure 2.4, the editor object encapsulates the window object, exposing its IWindow interface. This model allows the editor object to provide all the functionality of the window object and expose this functionality to consumers through the IWindow interface.

Although aggregation is an important part of the COM, for the majority of the work you will do in OLE you will probably not implement an aggregatable object. All the same, it is important to understand the concepts.

FIGURE 2.4:

Aggregation model diagram

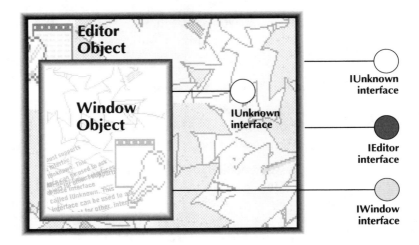

Consumers

The *consumer* is usually an executable program that creates and uses an object. For a consumer to use an object, the consumer must have knowledge of the interfaces supported by a particular object. After creating the object, the consumer asks the object for specific interfaces through which it can manipulate the object.

For example, let's assume we have an object class called CWindow (see Figure 2.5). After creating an object of the CWindow class, we obtain a pointer to the IWindow

FIGURE 2.5:

Example consumer program

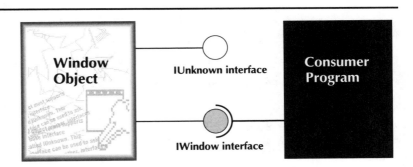

interface. This interface contains methods for performing actions such as opening, closing, resizing, and hiding or showing the window. It also contains methods for obtaining information about the window, such as its size and state.

Creating and Using Objects

In OLE, objects can be passed on the clipboard, dragged-and-dropped, and loaded from files. However, the COM provides only two basic ways to create objects. The object creation methods in OLE are layered on these two basic techniques.

The first method involves obtaining a pointer to the class factory and using it to create objects when needed. The other method uses `CoCreateInstance()`, which takes care of the class factory details and just returns a fully created object.

Using CoGetClassObject() to Create Objects

`CoGetClassObject()` allows an application to obtain a pointer to the class factory for an object. Once this is obtained, the programmer can call `IClassFactory::CreateInstance()` as many times as needed to create objects. The arguments to `CoGetClassObject()` are as follows:

```
HRESULT CoGetClassObject(    class_id,
                             class_context,
                             reserved,
                             initial_interface,
                             ppVoid ) ;
```

where the following is true:

- `class_id` is the class for which you would like to obtain the class factory.
- `class_context` is a bit mask that specifies the type of server that is acceptable for your use. (See Table 2.3 for class context settings.)
- `reserved` should always be `NULL`.
- `initial_interface` is the initial interface with which you would like to communicate to the object. This is usually `IID_IClassFactory`.
- `ppVoid` is the address of the interface pointer in which to return the object.

Following is an example of how the `CoGetClassObject()` routine can be used in conjunction with the `IClassFactory` interface to create an object of the class `CLSID_MyClass`:

```
HRESULT hErr ;
LPCLASSFACTORY pCF ;
LPUNKNOWN lpUnknown ;

hErr = CoGetClassObject( CLSID_MyClass,
                         CLSCTX_SERVER,
                         NULL,
                         IID_IClassFactory,
                         (LPVOID *)&pCF ) ;
if( SUCCEEDED( hErr ) ) {
    hErr = pCF->CreateInstance( NULL,
                         IID_IUnknown,
                         (LPVOID *)&lpUnknown ) ;
    if( SUCCEEDED( hErr ) ) {
        // now we have a pointer
        // to an object of CLSID_MyClass
        ...
        // Release the object when done
        lpUnknown->Release() ;
    }
    // Release the class factory
    pCF->Release() ;
}
```

The `IClassFactory::CreateInstance()` method must call `AddRef()` on the interface it passes back to our example code. This is why we only have to call `Release()` on the interface. The same goes for the class factory that we obtain from `CoGetClassObject()`.

The benefits of using this method mainly concern performance. When you are creating more than one object of the same class, you want to get the class factory only once. The `CoCreateInstance()` routine described in the next section, while simpler to use, would obtain a class factory every time you called it.

Using CoCreateInstance()

`CoCreateInstance()` allows you to save a few steps in the process of creating objects if you need to create only one or two objects for a specific class. `CoCreateInstance()`

takes care of obtaining the class factory for the object you want to create, calls the `CreateInstance()` method, and returns the specified interface for the object you requested. This routine is declared as follows:

```
HRESULT CoCreateInstance( class_id, pouter_unknown,
    class_context, interface_id, pvoid ) ;
```

where the following is true:

- `class_id` is the class ID for the object to be created.
- `pouter_unknown` is a pointer to the controlling unknown. This is used only for aggregation of objects.
- `class_context` is the class context.
- `interface_id` is the GUID of the interface to be returned.
- `pvoid` is the address of the variable to store the interface pointer.

Here is an example of how this routine is used:

```
HRESULT hErr ;
LPUNKNOWN lpUnknown ;
hErr = CoCreateInstance( CLSID_MyObject,
                         NULL,
                         CLSCTX_SERVER,
                         IID_IUnknown,
                         (LPVOID *)&lpUnknown ) ;
if( SUCCEEDED( hErr ) ) {
    // now we have a pointer
    // to an object of CLSID_MyClass
    ...
    // Release the object when done
    lpUnknown->Release() ;
}
```

The Registration Database

The *registration database* is a file named REG.DAT that exists in the WINDOWS directory on every system. This file contains a hierarchical collection of information about the installed system. It associates file extensions with their programs so that when you double-click a file in the Windows File Manager, the system knows which program to launch to allow access to the file. More important, the registration database is a key subsystem for the Component Object Model. Every object server that exists on a given system is registered in the registration database. Each object class has an entry associating it with its server. This association also determines the type of server.

When a client requests that an object be created, the client does not need to know whether the object is a local server or an in-process server. The COM simply looks up the object class in the registration database and determines which server to load to handle the object.

Memory Management

A common theme for all development efforts is memory allocation. OLE is no exception to this. In an environment where applications can mix and match objects, coordinating memory allocation becomes even more important. OLE specifies all the issues relating to memory allocation.

Each OLE-aware application has a memory allocator that is responsible for allocating all OLE memory. You can either use the default allocator that is provided by the COM or implement your own allocator and pass it to the `CoInitialize()` or `OleInitialize()` function at startup. The default allocator simply calls the Windows global memory routines to handle allocations. For most applications this should be sufficient; however, in cases where your application has sophisticated memory management requirements, you can provide the allocator you want the COM to use for memory management.

Whether you use the default or implement your own, the COM remembers the allocator you specified and can return a pointer to it at any time with a call to `CoGetMalloc()`. `CoGetMalloc()` takes two arguments: a memory allocation context (see Table 2.5) and, as is typical for COM routines, the address of the variable in which to store the interface pointer to the memory allocator. The memory context specifies whether you would like the allocator for shared memory or for task memory. The shared memory allocator is responsible for allocating memory that can be passed from one application to another. Since the COM takes care of the details of communicating with a remote process, your application will probably never need to call the shared memory allocator. The task allocator provides allocations for the current task. You will use this allocator often to free memory that was allocated by OLE functions and objects.

TABLE 2.5: Memory Context Constants

Context	Description
MEMCTX_TASK	Task memory allocator. This is specified in the call to CoInitialize( ) or OleInitialize( )
MEMCTX_SHARED	Shared memory allocator. The shared memory allocator is implemented in the OLE libraries

The IMalloc Interface

The IMalloc interface that is returned from CoGetMalloc( ) implements the methods listed in Table 2.6.

TABLE 2.6: IMalloc Methods

Method	Description
void *Alloc(cb)	Returns a block of memory that is cb bytes in size. Returns NULL if unsuccessful. It is valid to allocate a 0-length block of memory
void *Realloc(pv, cb)	Reallocates the memory in pv to size cb bytes. Returns the new block of memory. If pv is NULL, this method behaves just like Alloc( )
void Free(pv)	Frees the memory pointed to by pv
ULONG GetSize(pv)	Returns the size in bytes of pv
int DidAlloc(pv)	Returns TRUE if this allocator did allocate pv; otherwise it returns FALSE. If it returns −1, this indicates that it cannot determine whether it allocated the block of memory
void HeapMinimize()	Returns all unused memory back to the system heap

The majority of the methods are obvious. `Alloc()`, `Realloc()`, and `Free()` all work in a manner similar to the standard library routines. The `GetSize()` method returns the size of the allocated block in bytes. The `DidAlloc()` method returns `TRUE` or `FALSE` to indicate whether the allocator originally allocated the block of memory. It can also return −1 to indicate that it cannot determine whether it allocated the specified block of memory. If you implement your own memory allocator, it is acceptable to always return −1 from `DidAlloc()`. Finally, `HeapMinimize()` simply releases all unused memory back to the system heap.

Rules of Memory Allocation

Just as with reference counting, to get such a wide variety of software to cooperate requires rules regarding memory allocation. These rules specify which memory allocator, task or shared, can be used to allocate memory under different circumstances and who is responsible for freeing the memory that is passed between functions. The following table specifies the allocator and responsibility in most circumstances:

Parameter Type	Allocator	Responsibility
In	Task or shared	Allocated and freed by calling function
Out	Task only	Allocated by the called function and freed by the calling function
In/out	Task only	Allocated and freed by the calling function. If the called function changes the parameter, it must first free the input parameter

In case there is an error in the called function, the out parameters should be set so that they do not have to be freed by the calling function. In this situation the calling function is still responsible for all in parameters.

Globally Unique Identification Numbers

Objects are identified by a unique identification number called a *GUID*, or *globally unique ID*. You use GUIDs to identify object classes (CLSID), interfaces (IID), and other components in the OLE system. Since object classes are specified using GUIDs, the requirement that they be unique must be strictly enforced so end users will not encounter conflicts when using components developed by different software vendors.

A GUID is a hex number that is 16 bytes long. This number is usually represented as a hex string that looks like this:

```
{83769260-13A0-1069-BF6D-08001701F83E}
```

This is the standard string representation of the 16-byte structure the ID occupies.

Declaring and Using GUIDs

You declare GUIDs using the DEFINE_GUID() macro, which is defined as follows:

```
DEFINE_GUID(name,long,word,word,word,byte1,...byte8)
```

where name is the name of the ID. The naming convention for class IDs is CLSID_ClassName, and for interface IDs it is IID_InterfaceName.

The remaining parameters make up the actual ID number by passing hex constants for each specific field. A DEFINE_GUID() declaration for the ID we demonstrated above would look like this:

```
DEFINE_GUID(CLSID_SampleID,0x83769260,0x13A0,0x1069,0xBF6D,0x08,
0x00,0x17,0x01,0xF8,0x3E)
```

This macro is used to initialize GUIDs as well as declare them for reference throughout your application. To have this work properly, you must first create a header file for your GUIDs. This file should be included in your source code after the header COMPOBJ.H, which defines the GUID structure, functions, and macros. Using the DEFINE_GUID() macro declares the GUIDs for reference in your source code. To initialize them you must define the preprocessor constant INITGUID before including

COMPOBJ.H. This makes a change in the `DEFINE_GUID()` macro that causes it to initialize the GUID, as opposed to simply declaring it.

```
MYGUIDS.H
#ifdef _MYGUIDS_H_
#define _MYGUIDS_H_

DEFINE_GUID(CLSID_SampleID,0x83769260,0x13A0,0x1069,0xBF6D,0x08,
0x00,0x17,0x01,0xF8,0x3E)

#endif

MAIN.CPP
#define INITGUID        // cause GUIDs to be initialized
                        // NOTE: this should only be
                        //       done in one module
                        //       of the program
#include <COMPOBJ.H>
#include "MYGUIDS.H"

OTHER.CPP
#include <COMPOBJ.H>
#include "MYGUIDS.H"

// More code
```

Allocating GUIDs

When building your own objects, you will need to obtain GUIDs for all your object classes. You will also need to obtain GUIDs for each nonstandard interface your object supports. All the GUIDs used by the COM and OLE are defined in the OLE SDK.

Since these IDs must be unique, there are three ways to allocate a GUID: you can run a utility called UUIDGEN.EXE, you can call the API routine `CoCreateGUID()`, or you can call Microsoft and have a GUID or range of GUIDs assigned to you.

Using UUIDGEN.EXE

The UUIDGEN.EXE utility is a DOS program that takes advantage of the workstation IDs embedded in network cards. Network card manufacturers must make sure these IDs are unique for each network card so there will never be an ID conflict between two cards on the same network. UUIDGEN takes advantage of this fact to generate unique GUIDs whenever you need them. UUIDGEN uses the workstation ID combined with the current date and time to generate a new unique number.

TIP   Since UUIDGEN.EXE uses NETBIOS to access the workstation ID, you should load the NETBIOS emulator if your network does not support this interface intrinsically.

Calling CoCreateGUID()

The CoCreateGUID() routine was added to the API to generate GUIDs under program control. The routine is declared as follows:

```
HRESULT CoCreateGUID(GUID FAR *lpGuid)
```

When calling this routine, you should pass a pointer to a GUID, and if the routine is successful, it will return a GUID based on the unique characteristics of the machine.

Allocating GUIDs from Microsoft

The OLE SDK contains the number for Microsoft to use when allocating GUIDs. GUIDs that are obtained from Microsoft look like this:

```
{83769260-0000-0000-C000000000000046}
```

The first eight digits of the GUID change, but the rest of it remains the same. One benefit of obtaining your GUIDs from Microsoft is that the consistency can be used to validate arguments. In addition, it helps tremendously during development to be able to visually decipher an ID in the debugger.

Microsoft normally allocates 256 GUIDs at a time. (Contact Microsoft's Developer Services or refer to the OLE 2 SDK for more information on obtaining GUIDs.)

Error Handling

Most methods and API functions in OLE return an HRESULT. An HRESULT is defined in OLE as a result handle that can be used for determining the success or failure of a function. The HRESULT is a wrapper for a masked error value called an SCODE. The SCODE contains bit fields that describe the details of the error, including what it is, where it is, and how bad it is.

NOTE Although OLE 2 actually does return an error value, future versions of OLE will return a handle to a result stack that provides detailed information about error returns from multiple levels of detail. For example, when you call a routine called SaveObject() to save an object and it fails, you might examine the HRESULT to see that the routine failed because of an I/O error. The HRESULT also contains the failure code for the storage routine called by SaveObject(), so you can determine that it failed because the device was out of storage space. Handling errors in this fashion provides applications with the information needed to handle errors in a much more sophisticated manner than is typical in most applications.

How to Determine Success or Failure

The first thing you need to know after calling any function is, Did it work? The COM provides two macros that allow you to determine failure or success. These macros are FAILED(hErr) and SUCCEEDED(hErr).

These macros can be useful for simple error handling. If your application needs to determine the cause of the error, you will need to obtain a little more information from the HRESULT.

Status Codes

Before you can do anything other than determine success or failure from an HRESULT, you will need to obtain the SCODE by calling GetScode(hresult).

An SCODE is a 32-bit value containing bit-fields for the severity code, facility code, and result code (see Figure 2.6). The severity code is a simple true-or-false field for indicating success or failure. This is the how the FAILED( ) and SUCCEEDED( ) macros determine the severity of the error. The facility code allows you to determine which subsystem caused the error. The result code is probably the most important field since it contains the actual error code when the severity code indicates failure. There is also a field for a context code, although this field is not used in OLE 2.

FIGURE 2.6:

Layout of subfields in SCODE data type

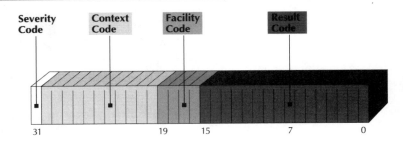

Severity Code   Context Code   Facility Code   Result Code

31   19   15   7   0

NOTE   Converting an HRESULT to an SCODE might seem like an unnecessary complication since an HRESULT is only a typecase SCODE. When you take into consideration that eventually HRESULTs will be a handle to an error stack on failure, this makes more sense.

Examining the Result

You can obtain the result code from an SCODE using the SCODE_CODE(SCODE) routine. When the severity code indicates failure, the result code contains the value that determines the cause of the failure. The following routine demonstrates how to examine an HRESULT for specific error codes:

```
HRESULT hErr ;
hErr = SomeFunctionReturningAnHRESULT() ;
if( FAILED( hErr ) ) {
    SCODE sc = GetScode( hErr ) ;
    switch( SCODE_CODE( sc ) ) {
    // FACILITY_NULL errors
    case E_OUTOFMEMORY:
        // Handle out of memory situation
        break ;
    case E_ACCESSDENIED:
        // Handle access denied error
        break ;
    default:
        // Handle other general errors
        break ;
    }
}
```

Where Did the Error Come from?

The *facility code* indicates where the error came from. OLE defines a facility code for each of the major subsystems in OLE. Use the SCODE_FACILITY(scode) macro to obtain the facility code from an SCODE. The facility codes are listed in Table 2.7.

TABLE 2.7: Facility Codes

Code	Description
FACILITY_NULL	General errors
FACILITY_RPC	Remote-procedure call errors
FACILITY_DISPATCH	Dispatch errors
FACILITY_STORAGE	Storage errors
FACILITY_ITF	Interface/API specific errors

The class of general errors is defined by OLE under the facility FACILITY_NULL. These errors are defined in Table 2.8.

TABLE 2.8: Error Codes for FACILITY_NULL

Error	Description
E_UNEXPECTED	Unexpected error
E_NOTIMPL	Function not implemented
E_OUTOFMEMORY	Out of memory
E_INVALIDARG	Invalid argument
E_NOINTERFACE	Interface not supported
E_POINTER	Invalid pointer
E_HANDLE	Invalid handle
E_ABORT	Operation aborted
E_FAIL	Operation failed for unspecified reason
E_ACCESSDENIED	General access denied

Propagation of HRESULTs

When HRESULTs need to propagated back from one function to another, the function must call PropagateResult() in order to properly set the context for the returned HRESULT:

```
HRESULT MyFunction()
{
    HRESULT hErr ;

    // call some function returning an HRESULT
    hErr = SomeFunction() ;
    if( FAILED( hErr ) ) {
        return PropagateResult( hErr,
                    MAKE_SCODE( SEVERITY_ERROR,
                    FACILITY_ITC,
                    0x200 )) ;
    }
}
```

The `PropagateResult()` macro takes the previous `HRESULT` as the first argument and the result `SCODE` as the second argument. The next section discusses some general rules regarding building your own result codes.

Defining Errors for Your Own Interfaces

Most OLE interfaces have a collection of result codes that are already defined. You should always use these when implementing an OLE-defined interface. The facility for these interfaces and all custom interfaces should always be `FACILITY_ITF`.

All the codes returned from OLE interfaces are in the range `0x0000` through `0x01ff`. Microsoft recommends that to remove any possible confusion, all custom interfaces use codes in the range `0x0200` through `0xffff`. This allows you to distinguish quickly between an OLE error code and one from a custom interface.

Summary

The COM provides an object-oriented design paradigm that allows software developers to build sophisticated software components and still have these components interact in a cooperative environment with other software components. It also provides object class registration and a lightweight remote-procedure call mechanism. It defines how object servers are built to provide services to consumers and defines how memory allocation and error handling are managed.

The Component Object Model is what enabled Microsoft to build a complicated system like OLE 2. The flexibility of the COM means that OLE will also be easily extensible and that end users and even developers will not have to rebuild their software for any but the most major of releases of OLE.

CHAPTER

THREE

Building a Component Object

- Implementation of a simple component object and object consumer

- Building an object as an in-process server

- Should you use C or C++?

- Initializing the Component Object Model

In the last chapter we discussed the concepts of the Component Object Model. In this chapter we will apply these concepts and actually implement a component object and a consumer to test our object. The techniques described in this chapter will be used throughout the rest of this book to build the sample programs.

Sample Object and Consumer (IBeep Sample)

For our sample object we will build a simple in-process server that supports two interfaces. The first is obviously the IUnknown interface. The second is a contrived interface that we will call IBeep. This interface will support a single method that does nothing but call the Windows MessageBeep() routine.

The consumer will create a beep object using the techniques described in the previous chapter and use the IUnknown interface to obtain the IBeep interface, as well as to release the object when it is no longer needed.

The IBeep Object

The object we must build consists of logical sections (see Figure 3.1). The support routines needed by the Component Object Model so it can use the server are DllGetClassObject() and DllCanUnloadNow(). DllGetClassObject() returns a pointer to the class factory for the object, and DllCanUnloadNow() tells the COM whether or not it can be unloaded. We must also implement the class factory to allow the system to create objects. This is the piece that will be passed to the COM by DllGetClassObject(). Finally, the object itself and the interfaces it supports must be implemented. Listing 3.1 contains the source code and the header file for the Beep Object Server.

FIGURE 3.1:

Logical structure of the beep object

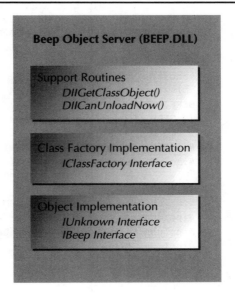

Listing 3.1

```
BEEP.H
#ifndef _beep_h_
#define _beep_h_

#undef  INTERFACE
#define INTERFACE    IBeep

DECLARE_INTERFACE_(IBeep,IUnknown) {
{
    // *** IUnknown methods ***
    STDMETHOD(QueryInterface)( THIS_ REFIID riid,
                             PVOID FAR* ppvObj) ;
    STDMETHOD_(ULONG,AddRef) ( THIS ) ;
    STDMETHOD_(ULONG,Release) ( THIS ) ;

    // *** IBeep methods ***
    STDMETHOD(DoBeep)( THIS_ UINT uAlert ) ;
};
typedef IBeep FAR* LPBEEP ;
```

```
DEFINE_GUID(CLSID_Beep,0x83769260,0x13A0,0x1069,0xBF,
            0x6D,0x08,0x00,0x17,0x01,0xF8,0x3E) ;
DEFINE_GUID(IID_IBeep,0x83769261,0x13A0,0x1069,0xBF,
            0x6D,0x08,0x00,0x17,0x01,0xF8,0x3E) ;

#endif
```

BEEP.CPP

```cpp
// BEEP.CPP: This file implements the IBeep object
//
#include <windows.h>      // Windows SDK of course
#include <string.h>        // This header is needed to
                           // include compobj.h
#define INITGUID
#include <compobj.h>      // COM Interfaces and Macros
#include <coguid.h>        // Initializes IID_IUnknown
#include <scode.h>         // Error handling include
#include "beep.h"


///////////////////////////////////////////////////////
// LibMain for BEEP.DLL
//
int CALLBACK LibMain( HINSTANCE hInst,
                      WORD wDataSeg,
                      WORD cbHeapSize,
                      LPSTR lpszCmdLine )
{
    if(cbHeapSize != 0)
        UnlockData(0);
    return TRUE ;
}


///////////////////////////////////////////////////////
// Beep Object Implementation
//
class BeepObject : public IBeep {
    ULONG refCount ;
public:
    BeepObject () ;
    ~BeepObject () ;

    // *** IUnknown methods ***
    STDMETHOD(QueryInterface)( THIS_ REFIID riid,
```

```
                                PVOID FAR* ppvObj) ;
    STDMETHOD_(ULONG,AddRef) ( THIS ) ;
    STDMETHOD_(ULONG,Release) ( THIS ) ;

    // *** IBeep methods ***
    STDMETHOD(DoBeep)( THIS_ UINT uAlert ) ;
} ;

BeepObject ::BeepObject ( )
{
    refCount = 0 ;
    numberBeepObjects++ ;
}

BeepObject ::~BeepObject ( )
{
    numberBeepObjects-- ;
}

STDMETHODIMP BeepObject ::QueryInterface( REFIID riid,
        LPVOID FAR *ppvObj )
{
    if( riid == IID_IUnknown || riid == IID_IBeep ) {
        *ppvObj = this ;
        AddRef( ) ;
        return NOERROR ;
    }

    // Null out the return argument
    *ppvObj = NULL ;

    // If the interface is not supported, then
    // the interface not supported error code
    return ResultFromScode(E_NOINTERFACE) ;
}

STDMETHODIMP_(ULONG) BeepObject ::AddRef( )
{
    return ++refCount ;
}

STDMETHODIMP_(ULONG) BeepObject ::Release( )
```

```
{
    if( --refCount == 0 ) {
        delete this ;
        return 0 ;
    }
    return refCount ;
}

STDMETHODIMP BeepObject ::DoBeep( UINT uAlert )
{
    MessageBeep( uAlert ) ;
    return NOERROR ;
}

////////////////////////////////////////////////////
// IBeepClassFactory
//
class BeepClassFactory : public IClassFactory {
public:
    ULONG refCount ;

    BeepClassFactory( ) { refCount = 0 ; }

    // *** IUnknown methods ***
    STDMETHOD(QueryInterface)( REFIID riid,
                             PVOID FAR* ppvObj) ;
    STDMETHOD_(ULONG,AddRef) ( ) ;
    STDMETHOD_(ULONG,Release) ( ) ;

    // *** IClassFactory methods ***
    STDMETHOD(CreateInstance)( LPUNKNOWN pUnkOuter,
                             REFIID riid,
                             LPVOID FAR* ppvObject) ;
    STDMETHOD(LockServer)(THIS_ BOOL fLock) ;
};

// Module globals include number of beep objects
static ULONG numberBeepObjects = 0 ;
static BeepClassFactory classFactory ;

STDMETHODIMP BeepClassFactory::QueryInterface(
        REFIID riid, LPVOID FAR *ppvObj )
```

```
{
    if( riid == IID_IUnknown ||
        riid == IID_IClassFactory ) {
        *ppvObj = this ;
        AddRef( ) ;
        return NOERROR ;
    }

    // Null out the return argument
    *ppvObj = NULL ;

    // If the interface is not supported,
    // then return this error code
    return ResultFromScode(E_NOINTERFACE) ;
}

STDMETHODIMP_(ULONG) BeepClassFactory::AddRef( )
{
    return ++refCount ;
}

STDMETHODIMP_(ULONG) BeepClassFactory::Release( )
{
    if( --refCount == 0 )
        return 0 ;

    return refCount ;
}

STDMETHODIMP BeepClassFactory::CreateInstance(
                LPUNKNOWN pUnkOuter,
                REFIID riid,
                LPVOID FAR* ppvObject)
{
    // Our object does not support aggregation
    if( pUnkOuter != NULL )
        return ResultFromScode(CLASS_E_NOAGGREGATION) ;

    // Allocate a new IBeep Object
    LPBEEP pBeep = new BeepObject ;
    if( pBeep == NULL )
        return ResultFromScode(E_OUTOFMEMORY) ;

    // Now return the requested interface
    HRESULT hErr = pBeep->QueryInterface( riid,
```

```
                                                 ppvObject ) ;
    if( FAILED( GetScode(hErr) ) ) {
        delete pBeep ;
        return hErr ;
    }

    return NOERROR ;
}

STDMETHODIMP BeepClassFactory::LockServer(
                        BOOL fLock )
{
    if( fLock )
        numberBeepObjects++ ;
    else
        numberBeepObjects-- ;

    return NOERROR ;
}

//////////////////////////////////////////////////
// Support Functions
// DllGetClassObject() and DllCanUnloadNow
//
STDAPI  DllGetClassObject(REFCLSID rclsid,
                        REFIID riid,
                        LPVOID FAR* ppv)
{
    *ppv = NULL ;

    if( rclsid != CLSID_IBeep )
        return ResultFromScode(E_FAIL) ;

    // Validate the interface request
    if(riid!=IID_IUnknown && riid!=IID_IClassFactory)
        return ResultFromScode(E_NOINTERFACE) ;

    // Return a pointer to our static class factory
    *ppv = &classFactory ;
    classFactory.AddRef( ) ;

    return NOERROR ;
}

STDAPI DllCanUnloadNow(void)
```

```
{
    if( numberBeepObjects == 0
        && classFactory.refCount == 0 )
        return ResultFromScode( S_OK ) ;

    return ResultFromScode( S_FALSE ) ;
}

BEEP.DEF
LIBRARY         BEEP
EXETYPE         WINDOWS
CODE            PRELOAD MOVEABLE DISCARDABLE
DATA            PRELOAD MOVEABLE SINGLE
HEAPSIZE        1024
EXPORTS
    WEP                     @1 RESIDENTNAME
    DllGetClassObject       @2
    DllCanUnloadNow         @3
```

The Header File

Since the object has an interface that is not defined in any of the OLE or COM headers, we place the interface definition for the IBeep interface in the BEEP.H header. We also use this header file to define the GUIDs for both the object class ID and the IBeep interface ID. The following lines define these variables for use in both our object implementation and the consumer program:

```
DEFINE_GUID(CLSID_Beep,0x83769260,0x13A0,0x1069,0xBF,
0x6D,0x08,0x00,0x17,0x01,0xF8,0x3E) ;
DEFINE_GUID(IID_IBeep,0x83769261,0x13A0,0x1069,0xBF,
0x6D,0x08,0x00,0x17,0x01,0xF8,0x3E) ;
```

At the beginning of the header file, the lines

```
#undef INTERFACE
#define INTERFACE IBeep

DECLARE_INTERFACE_(IBeep,IUnknown) {
```

begin the declaration of our new interface. The INTERFACE macro is redefined to the name of our interface, and the DECLARE_INTERFACE_() macro begins the declaration of our interface and specifies that it is derived from IUnknown. These lines are functionally equivalent to the following C++ code:

```
class IBeep : public IUnknown {
public:
```

These macros, used in the header file, allow the header to be included in either a C or C++ source file. This places fewer restrictions on the consumers that would use our object. The macros STDMETHOD( ) and STDMETHOD_( ) declare the methods for the interface. The STDMETHOD( ) macro takes the method name as its argument and declares the method to return the standard HRESULT error return. The STDMETHOD_( ) macro uses the underscore to indicate that there is more to come. You can use this macro to indicate a method that does not have an HRESULT as its return value. The line

```
STDMETHOD_(ULONG,AddRef)( THIS ) ;
```

declares the AddRef( ) method to return a ULONG result.

Should You Use C or C++?

What actually happens when an OLE or a COM header file is included is fairly detailed. First, the macros that are used throughout the interface definitions are defined differently, depending on whether they are compiled in C or C++. The C++ model is fairly straightforward since the entire COM is based on a C++-style object model. All methods on an interface are virtual so that when a pointer to an interface is obtained by a consumer, it can call the routines through the method pointers that are entered in the VTABLE for the object. This means that the program never has to link directly to the methods for an object. When an object server creates an object using the new operator (see the CreateInstance( ) implementation for the Beep-ClassFactory in Listing 3.1), the VPTR in the C++ object is initialized to point to the virtual table or VTABLE for the class (see Figure 3.2).

When using C, things get a little more complicated. Because the system must work exactly the same in both C and C++, the C++ model is duplicated in C. The macros used to define the interface and methods declare two structures. The first structure is the interface itself. It is declared to contain nothing more than a pointer to another structure. This duplicates the C++ implementation of the VPTR. The other structure that is automatically built is literally a VTABLE that contains a function pointer for each method in the interface. The only catch is that if the interface is implemented

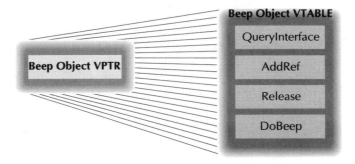

FIGURE 3.2:

Conceptual diagram of VPTR/VTABLE relationship for a beep object

in C, the VTABLE structure must be initialized in the startup code so that all the entries the VTABLE point to the appropriate method.

Also, C++ automatically passes a pointer—the this pointer—to each object as the first parameter to each method for the object. This pointer must also be duplicated for C by using the THIS and THIS_ macros. The THIS macro simply declares a pointer to an object of type INTERFACE. The THIS_ macro does the same thing but also appends a comma so that more arguments may follow.

All of this is why C++ is the language of choice for OLE. There is less work to do since the C++ compiler automatically initializes all the VTABLEs for your interfaces, as well as automatically initializing the VPTR for the newly created objects. C++ also automatically passes the this pointer to object methods, whereas in C you have to pass this value explicitly.

Regardless of which language you use, be careful to use the macros THIS and THIS_ in your headers if there is any chance that your objects or interfaces will be used in both C and C++.

The BeepClassFactory

In the source code we implement the class factory as a static object and return a pointer to this object in the DllGetClassObject() function. The IUnknown portion of the class factory is fairly standard except that we do not delete the object in the Release() method if the reference count becomes 0. This is because our class factory was not originally allocated with the new operator. In most cases you will use the new operator to allocate objects, but for the class factory it is a matter of preference since the class factory has little or no internal-state information to worry about. A class factory that creates more than one type of object would require a more sophisticated implementation.

The QueryInterface() method returns interfaces only for IUnknown and IClass-Factory and returns E_NOTIMPL for all other requests. The CreateInstance() method is the workhorse of this interface; it is responsible for creating all beep objects. First, the method checks to make sure that pUnkOuter is NULL. If this argument is not NULL, then another object is trying to aggregate our beep object. We decline this attempt by returning the result CLASS_E_NOAGGREGATION. Then we allocate a new BeepObject with the new operator. If there is not enough memory, we return the E_OUTOFMEMORY general result code. Otherwise, we call BeepObject::QueryInterface() so that we return a pointer to the interface requested in riid. It is important to realize that this call to QueryInterface() will call AddRef() on the object if it is successful. This is in accordance with the reference-counting rules for out arguments described in Chapter 2. Finally, we return NOERROR to indicate that a new BeepObject was created successfully.

The LockServer() method is required to keep the server in memory even if there are no outstanding references to any objects for the server. For our server it suffices to add a false object reference so the DllCanUnloadNow() will think there are outstanding references and will tell the COM that it cannot unload the DLL. It is a requirement that anyone using the LockServer() method always unlock the server when it is done by calling LockServer() with the fLock parameter set to FALSE.

Support Routines

The support routines include DllGetClassObject() and DllCanUnloadNow(). These are the routines that must be exported from the DLL when you write an in-process server. These routines should also have the specific ordinal values shown in BEEP.DEF.

The DllGetClassObject() routine is called by the COMPOBJ.DLL when it loads BEEP.DLL. It is passed a class ID for the object class and returns a pointer to the class factory object specified by the rclsid argument. If the server supported more than one class of object, the DllGetClassObject() routine would contain the logic to pass back a pointer to different class factories; or at least the class factories would be initialized differently to create the different object types. Since our server supports only one class of object, we simply verify that the rclsid is equal to

CLSID_IBeep. If it is not, an error is returned. This should not happen if the system is set up properly. However, if you have a synchronization problem with the registration file and the GUIDs that you initialized in your header, this situation might occur. We also validate the interface IDs that are requested. Since this routine is asking for a class factory, the only valid interfaces are IClassFactory and IUnknown. Finally, after validating all of the arguments, we return a pointer to our global class factory and call AddRef() to indicate that there is another live reference to the object.

The DllCanUnloadNow() routine is used by the system to ask the server if it is safe to unload the DLL. In our implementation of this routine, we check to see if there are any BeepObjects created by examining a global variable that is maintained by the constructor and destructor for the BeepObject class. We also check to see if the class factory reference count is equal to 0. If no BeepObjects exist and there are no references to the class factory, S_OK is returned; otherwise S_FALSE is returned to indicate that it is not yet safe to unload the DLL.

The BeepObject

The BeepObject class is the actual object itself. When the CreateInstance() routine is called in the class factory, it creates an object of this class type to return to the consumer. The declaration of the BeepObject class shows that it is derived from the IBeep interface, which in turn is derived from the IUnknown interface:

```
class BeepObject : public IBeep {
```

Since IBeep inherits the IUnknown methods, our simple two-interface object can support both interfaces with one pointer. Let's examine the implementation of BeepObject::QueryInterface():

```
STDMETHODIMP BeepObject ::QueryInterface( REFIID riid,
        LPVOID FAR *ppvObj )
{
    if( riid == IID_IUnknown || riid == IID_IBeep ) {
        *ppvObj = this ;
        AddRef() ;
        return NOERROR ;
    }

    // Null out the return argument
    *ppvObj = NULL ;
```

```
        // If the interface is not supported, then
        // the interface not supported error code
        return ResultFromScode(E_NOINTERFACE) ;
    }
```

The comparison of the `riid` parameter to the `IID_IBeep` and `IID_IUnknown` interface IDs determines whether the `QueryInterface()` is for an interface we support. If it is not, we always `NULL` out the return parameter and return `E_NOINTERFACE`. If it is one of the interfaces we support, we return the `this` pointer and call `AddRef()` to increment the reference count before returning `NOERROR` to indicate success. The `BeepObject` class implements only the `IBeep` interface. Since `IBeep` inherits the `IUnknown` methods, no one will ever know the difference if we return a pointer to an `IBeep` interface when an `IUnknown` is requested. This, in fact, is exactly what we do in our `QueryInterface()` implementation.

The remaining portions of the `BeepObject` class involve the constructor and destructor and our one custom `IBeep` method. The constructor and destructor simply maintain the global beep object count that is used by `DllCanUnloadNow()`. The custom `IBeep` method, called `DoBeep()`, is nothing more than a simple call to the Windows function `MessageBeep()`.

The Sample Client Program

Listing 3.2 demonstrates our sample consumer program for testing the Beep Object Server. This program demonstrates how OLE is initialized and shows the creation and usage of a simple object.

NOTE To limit the amount of code that was required for our consumer, we used the Microsoft Quickwin library to generate a Windows application using the C standard I/O library. Regardless of how the program is created, the steps required to initialize the COM and create and use the objects are the same.

Listing 3.2

```
BEEPTEST.CPP
#include <stdio.h>
#include <windows.h>            // Windows SDK of course
#include <string.h>                 // needed for compobj.h
#include <ole2ver.h>
#define INITGUID
#include <compobj.h>           // COM Interfaces and Macros
#include <coguid.h>                 // Initializes IID_IUnknown
#include <scode.h>                  // Error handling include
#include "beep.h"

BOOL InitCOM()
{
        // Check COM Build Version
        DWORD coVersion = CoBuildVersion() ;
        if(        HIWORD( coVersion ) != rmm ||
                LOWORD( coVersion ) < rup ) {
                printf( "Bad version of COM!\n" ) ;
                return FALSE ;
        }

        // Initialize COM
        HRESULT hErr = CoInitialize( NULL ) ;
        if( FAILED( GetScode( hErr ) ) ) {
                printf( "Failed to initialize OLE!\n" ) ;
                return FALSE ;
        }
        return TRUE ;
}

void DeinitCOM()
{
        CoUninitialize() ;
}

void main()
{
        HRESULT hErr ;
        LPBEEP pBeep ;
        LPUNKNOWN pUnk ;
        LPCLASSFACTORY pCf ;
```

```
        if(!InitCOM( )) return ;

        ///////////////////////////////////////////////
        // Method 1: Using CoGetClassObject()
        printf( "Method 1: Using CoGetClassObject() -" ) ;
        hErr = CoGetClassObject(         CLSID_IBeep,
                                         CLSCTX_INPROC,
                                         NULL,
                                         IID_IClassFactory,
                                         (LPVOID FAR *)&pCf ) ;

        if( FAILED( GetScode( hErr ) ) ) {
                printf( "failed!\n" ) ;
        }else{
                printf( "succeeded!\n" ) ;

                printf( "Creating the Beep object.-." ) ;
                hErr = pCf->CreateInstance(      NULL,
                                         IID_IBeep,
                                         (LPVOID FAR *)&pBeep ) ;

                // Release the class factory
                pCf->Release( ) ;

                if( FAILED( GetScode( hErr ) ) ) {
                        printf( "failed!\n" ) ;
                }else{
                        printf( "succeeded!\n" ) ;

                        // Now use the DoBeep method and
                        // release the object
                        pBeep->DoBeep( -1 ) ;
                        pBeep->Release( ) ;
                }
        }

        ///////////////////////////////////////////////
        // Method 2: Using CoCreateInstance()
        printf( "\nMethod 2: Using CoCreateInstance - " ) ;
        hErr = CoCreateInstance( CLSID_IBeep,
                                         NULL,
                                         CLSCTX_INPROC_SERVER,
                                         IID_IUnknown,
                                         (LPVOID FAR *)&pUnk ) ;
```

```
    if( FAILED( GetScode( hErr ) ) ) {
            printf( "failed!\n" ) ;
    }else{
            printf( "succeeded!\n" ) ;

            pUnk->QueryInterface( IID_IBeep,
                                        (LPVOID FAR *)&pBeep ) ;

            pUnk->Release( ) ;
            if( pBeep != NULL ) {
                    pBeep->DoBeep( -1 ) ;
                    pBeep->Release( ) ;
            }
    }

    // Shut down the COM
    DeinitCOM( ) ;
}
```

Initializing the Component Object Model

Before any program can call routines in the Component Object Model, it must initialize the COM using the `CoInitialize()` routine. In our test program the routine `InitCOM()` contains the necessary code to initialize the COM. To ensure compatibility with the version of the COM installed on a user's machine, it is always a good idea to call `CoBuildVersion()`. This routine returns the versions of the COM in a `DWORD` value that has the major version number encoded in the high word and the minor version in the low word. The header file OLE2VER.H contains constants that are used to check these versions. The following lines in our test consumer check the version number:

```
DWORD coVersion = CoBuildVersion() ;
if(HIWORD( coVersion ) != rmm ||
    LOWORD( coVersion ) < rup ) {
    printf( "Bad version of COM!\n" ) ;
    return FALSE ;
}
```

After all that, the call to initialize the COM is nothing more than

```
hErr = CoInitialize( NULL ) ;
```

Note that we passed NULL to CoInitialize(). As described in Chapter 2, this indicates that we want to use the default memory allocator. For almost all programs, the default allocator should be sufficient.

Creating Our Beep Object

BEEPTEST uses both of the techniques that were described in Chapter 2 to create a beep object. The first is to use CoGetClassObject() to obtain the class factory. The second technique is a simple call to CoCreateInstance().

The call to CoGetClassObject() obtains a pointer to the class factory and uses the IClassFactory::CreateInstance() method to create an object. After creating the object, the class factory is released. The pointer obtained by CreateInstance() can now be used to call our DoBeep() method. Notice that when we call Create-Instance(), we request a pointer to the IBeep interface with the IID_IBeep constant that is declared in the header BEEP.H.

The second method uses CoCreateInstance() to create the object. CoCreate-Instance() uses CoGetClassObject() to do the same thing we just did to create the first object. In this second case we request the IID_IUnknown interface to illustrate how QueryInterface() is used to obtain other interfaces for an object. CoCreateIn-stance() will return a pointer to the IUnknown interface if successful, and we then call QueryInterface() on this pointer to obtain our IBeep interface pointer. In the moment right after the call to QueryInterface(), we have two valid interface pointers to the same object. At this moment the reference count is 2. Then the IUnknown interface is released and the reference count goes down to 1. Finally, when the IBeep interface is released, the reference count goes to 0 and the object deletes itself.

The Registration File

The final piece in our object implementation is to register the object in the registration database. Without this part the calls to CoCreateInstance() and CoGetClass-Object() in our sample consumer program would fail with the error REGDB_E_CLASSNOTREG.

As mentioned in Chapter 2, the registration database is a hierarchical structure that contains key entries. Each key has a value and 0 or more subkeys. Each subkey can have both a value and possibly some subkeys of its own. Registering our object involves entering the object's class ID as a subkey under the CLSID key in the root of the database. Also, the IBeep interface must be registered as a subkey under the INTERFACE key.

Usually when your object is installed, part of your installation process is to register the object in the registration database. You do this by executing REGEDIT and passing the name of your registration file as the first argument. For example:

```
REGEDIT BEEP.REG
```

Following is the registration file for the Beep Object Server:

```
REGEDIT

HKEY_CLASSES_ROOT\CLSID\{83769260-13A0-1069-BF6D-08001701F83E} = Beep
    Object
HKEY_CLASSES_ROOT\CLSID\{83769260-13A0-1069-BF6D-
    08001701F83E}\InprocServer = BEEP.DLL
HKEY_CLASSES_ROOT\INTERFACE\{83769261-13A0-1069-BF6D-
    08001701F83E} = IBeep
```

The first line of the registration file is

```
REGEDIT
```

WARNING Because of printing limitations, the lines in the preceding code fragment have been broken to fit. However, the Registration Editor will not process these breaks properly. Refer to the file BEEP.REG on the companion disk for proper formatting.

This is an extra indicator to the system that this is a registration file. The remainder of the file contains the lines to register the object, the name of the object's in-process server, and the new interface that is supported by the object. The syntax of this file, as well as the structure of the registration database, is discussed in greater detail in Part IV and in Appendix B. However, you might take some time now to examine the registration database by running the REGEDIT program in advanced mode by using the /V switch when executing it (see Figure 3.3). The contents can provide a lot of insight into how OLE actually works since all of its object classes and interfaces are also defined here.

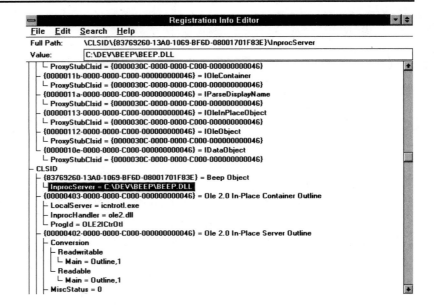

Summary

The sample programs introduced in this chapter were relatively simple for the purpose of illustrating the concepts introduced in Chapter 2. The concepts and implementation techniques you have learned in these first chapters will be used throughout the book as we build more complex programs. Indeed, you will find that OLE is nothing more than a collection of interfaces similar to the `IBeep` interface that we developed in this chapter. These interfaces all work together to provide the complicated feature set that makes up OLE 2.

PART II

Compound Files

The storage technology included with OLE is a sophisticated technology all by itself. It is built on the COM and provides developers with the ability to implement complex storage requirements easily and includes features such as multi-stage commit and revert and support for multiple users.

Chapter 4 provides a detailed introduction to the issues and techniques required to use compound files in your application.

Chapter 5 provides in-depth coverage of the IStorage and IStream interfaces.

Chapter 6 covers the technical and conceptual issues involved in using compound files in conjunction with databases. It also examines the issues involved in supporting and converting preexisting file formats when your upgraded application adds support for compound files. The chapter discusses the ILock-Bytes interface and its uses in nonstandard compound file implementations.

CHAPTER

FOUR

Using Compound Files in Your Application

- OLE Structured Storage Model and OLE compound files

- Multiple platform support

- Traditional model versus OLE Structured Storage Model

One of the major design issues in constructing any application is the storage format used for saving data. This problem is driven by the complexity of the application and the manner in which it must manipulate the data. If an application can load an entire file into memory for manipulation, the storage format is simplified. It is the case in which applications cannot load all the data at once because of memory limitations that has been the cause of some of the more interesting file formats. One class of file formats usually starts off with a header that contains byte offsets to the major sections of the file, while another class of file formats, driven by the need to add, delete, and sort data in a flexible manner, has developed into miniature database management systems. There are almost as many file formats as there are applications.

OLE has even more complex storage requirements than those of most applications. It must provide a mechanism for applications to save their native data formats in foreign applications' data files. In response to this requirement, the designers of OLE developed a structured storage mechanism called compound files.

What Are Compound Files?

Compound files are both a specification and an API. OLE defines a structured storage model that can be retrofitted to an existing application's storage format. Alternatively, the application can completely adopt the new storage model implemented by OLE. The first approach had to be provided to support existing applications with legacy storage formats that, for one reason or another, must be maintained. This is neither the recommended approach nor one that is easy to implement. However, converting an existing application to the OLE compound files can be a fairly easy task, and all new applications should definitely use compound files as a basis for their storage requirements. This will greatly reduce the work required to support object linking and embedding.

Compound files are essentially a file system in a file. The application can create a hierarchical file format using storage objects and stream objects that are similar to directories and files. At the top of this hierarchy is what is called the *root storage*. It is named by the file in which it is contained and is the mechanism by which all the elements of the compound file are referenced. The root storage can contain streams and storages (see Figure 4.1). A *stream* is very similar to the C run-time library concept of a stream, and *storages* are like folders that contain more streams and substorages.

Conceptual diagram of a
compound file

CMP FILE.DFL

Substorage 1   Stream A   Substorage 2   Stream B

Stream C   Stream D   Stream E

Compound files are similar in nature to most file system APIs. The Structured Storage APA is composed of several classes that allow the programmer to create, open, read, and write streams and storages. There is also a transaction mechanism that allows the developer to essentially implement a multilevel "undo." When a change is made to a stream or storage, the application programmer has the option to commit or revert the change. Committing a change causes that change to become permanent for the stream or storage. When a commit is finally executed on the root storage, all changes to the file are made permanent. Reverting a change causes the stream or storage to revert to its state before being opened.

Application Storage Models

The following sections describe three application storage models for implementing the standard File ➤ New, Open, Save, and Save As… functionality. The first two models represent typical storage scenarios that might be used in an application. The third model represents the Structured Storage Model introduced by OLE 2.

Model 1: Load the File into Memory

Model 1 relies on being able to load the entire file into memory. This is not possible with some applications either because of the complexity of the file format or because of the sheer size of the files that can be created.

Following are descriptions of how the standard File menu commands would be handled for this model:

Command	Description
File ➤ New	A new window is created and all new data entered is stored in memory that is associated with the window. The window is marked as dirty and as a new document
File ➤ Open	A new window is created and the selected file is loaded into memory that is associated with the window. The window is marked as clean
File ➤ Save	The changed data associated with the window is saved back to the file from which it was originally loaded. If it was a new window, then Save becomes the same as Save As…
File ➤ Save As…	The user selects a new file name, and all data associated with the window is written to this file

The user always has the option of not saving changes and can reload the original file at any time to revert the changes.

Model 2: Using Temporary Files

Model 2 uses temporary files to implement the standard file-manipulation features in cases in which the data is either too big or too complex to be conveniently loaded into memory. This model has the drawback of usually requiring two complete copies of the data on disk.

Following are descriptions of how the standard File menu commands would be handled for this model:

Command	Description
File ➤ New	A new window is created and all new data entered is stored in a temporary file associated with the window. The window is marked as dirty and as a new document
File ➤ Open	A new window is created and the data from the selected file is copied into a temporary file that is associated with the window. The window is marked as clean
File ➤ Save	Causes the contents of the temporary file to be written back to the original data file from which it was first copied. If it was a new window, Save becomes the same as Save As… in this model as well
File ➤ Save As…	The user selects a new file name, all data in the temporary file is copied into the new file, and the association with the original file is destroyed

The process of reverting to the original version of the file involves recopying the contents of the original file over the changes in the temporary file.

Model 3: The Structured Storage Model

Both of the preceding models for manipulating stored data are commonly used in many applications. The compound file technology provides an additional model that removes any memory limitations and mitigates the disk space requirements of the temporary file model.

Following are descriptions of how you would implement the storage model using OLE:

Command	Description
File ➤ New	A new window is created along with a temporary storage file. All new data is written directly into the storage file. The window is marked as a new document
File ➤ Open	A new window is created and the selected storage file is opened and associated with its window
File ➤ Save	Causes a commit on the associated storage file
File ➤ Save As...	The contents of the original storage file still must be copied to the new file name. However, with the compound file API this copy is handled entirely by the CopyTo method

The process of reverting to the original version of the file involves recopying the contents of the original file over the changes in the temporary file.

How OLE Uses Compound Files

Compound files provide a consistent storage medium for loading and unloading objects. The idea is simple: as long as an application provides a substorage to an object, it can save its data in any format it chooses.

Figure 4.2 shows a compound file that contains some native data as well as an embedded object named Object A. Object A also contains an embedded object named

FIGURE 4.2:
Embedded objects

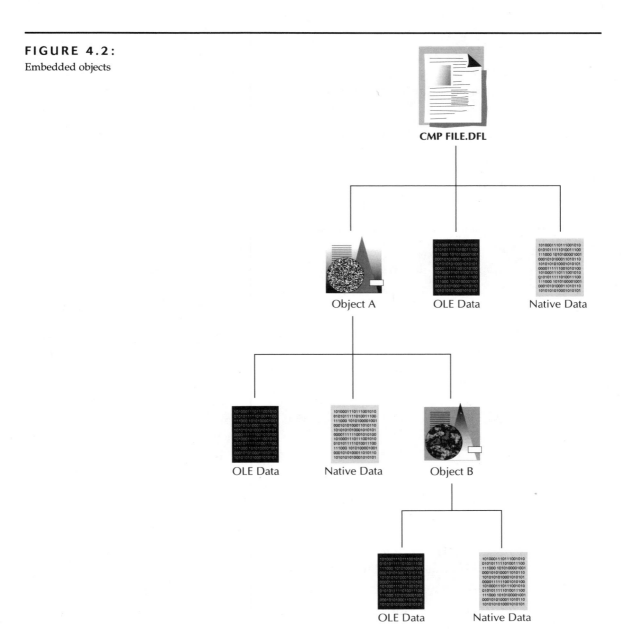

Object B. This diagram illustrates both the container's responsibility for providing a storage location for the object to store its data and the object's lack of restrictions in the manner in which it uses the provided storage. It is up to the container to name the storage that it creates for saving the object. This name is usually synthesized from a unique object ID that is generated by the container.

OLE also stores its own data with object information in specially named streams. The information stored in these streams includes information such as the CLSID and one or more cached representations of the object data. The object is responsible for saving its native data in the storage.

Properties in Compound Files

Properties are tagged values in specific formats that can provide useful general information to the operating system and browser applications. They are stored in specially named streams that are at the level of the compound file with which they are associated. Properties can be such things as thumbnail representations of documents, author's name, keywords, notes, document revision, security, and other useful information. Property stream names are prepended with \x05 to indicate that they are shared property sets. The only problem with property sets is that applications can choose to either support or ignore them. Partial support for properties by the applications on a given system will cripple the usefulness of this concept as far as the user is concerned. Because of this, it's best that if you use compound files, you support at least the SummaryInformation property set described in Appendix B.

Designing Your File Format

There are too many variations on file formats to take all possibilities into consideration here. However, this section discusses some issues to consider when building your file format, including performance in compound files and support for multiple platforms.

When designing file formats to support multiple platforms, there are many issues to be considered. OLE's compound file format is portable to Windows 4.1, Windows NT, and the Macintosh, but you will still have to make sure the contents of the streams are portable. If you are not using compound files, you must worry about the details of the file's structure, as well as the data it organizes.

Byte Swapping

Most programmers have heard of the Intel backwards byte-ordering system by now, the so-called Little Endian, Big Endian format. All this means is that in multiple-byte data types, bytes are ordered in reverse of what you would logically expect. For example, the hex value 0x1234 is stored in memory as 0x3412 on an Intel machine (all PC compatibles). This also means that when binary values are written to disk, they are written in this byte-backwards format. Other systems, such as Motorola-based systems, store bytes in logical order.

When these two storage formats are mixed, conversion has to take place. First, there must be some indicator, either explicit or implicit, to notify the reading application of the storage format being used. One of the easiest ways to do this is to always write files in one specific format, regardless of the system on which the file was created. This means that both Macintosh and Windows versions of your program would write out data in Intel format or Motorola format, regardless of the platform. This means that one system would always have to convert the data "on the fly."

The other alternative that some system designers like to use is to save a machine type indicator and store the file in the format for the system on which the file was created. The theory goes that if the file is created on a Macintosh, it will be used primarily on a Macintosh, and vice versa with Windows systems. Whichever format you use, you will still have to account for the format change if you want to support the various platforms.

Here is an example of some macros that swap 2-byte and 4-byte words between Motorola and Intel format:

```
#define swapword( word )(((word&0xff00)>>8) | \
                         ((word&0x00ff)<<8))
unsigned val ;
pStm->Read( &val, 2 ) ;
if( swapped ) val = swapword( val ) ;
```

Data Portability

There are a large number of hidden problems with supporting multiple platforms, things that may not be immediately obvious. For example, some applications save state information about the interface, such as window position, open files, and so on. Much of this information is system specific. Also, a lot of time can be spent in trying to determine a clean way of saving directory and file information inside a file format. This is complex because file and directory names can be different sizes, the reserved characters can be different on each system, and the separators between directories and volume specifiers are different. Since a lot of the details of this type of information are based on an application's specific needs, the most important thing is to make sure you are aware of these sorts of issues when setting out to define a multiplatform format.

Graphics and Other Display-Dependent Data

The final problem is almost as obvious as the byte-swapping problem. This is the issue of graphics storage formats. The good news is that OLE automatically converts the cached graphic representations of OLE objects for whatever platform you are running on. Other graphics-conversion problems include resolution and gamma correction of colors.

Handling Errors in the Storage System

Compound files are a part of the Structured Storage Model specification. All interfaces in this model return status codes using the FACILITY_STORAGE facility. For your reference the status codes are listed in Table 4.1.

TABLE 4.1: Storage System Status Codes

Status Code	Description
STG_E_ABNORMALAPIEXIT	Abnormal API exit
STG_E_ACCESSDENIED	Access to the file is not granted with the specified open mode
STG_E_DISKISWRITEPROTECTED	Disk is write protected
STG_E_FILEALREADYEXISTS	File or element already exists
STG_E_FILENOTFOUND	Specified file or element does not exist
STG_E_INSUFFICIENTMEMORY	Not enough memory for the operation
STG_E_INVALIDFLAG	Invalid flag passed to method
STG_E_INVALIDFUNCTION	This is returned if an unsupported mode flag is passed to a method
STG_E_INVALIDHANDLE	Invalid handle
STG_E_INVALIDHEADER	Invalid header for storage
STG_E_INVALIDNAME	Invalid name was specified
STG_E_INVALIDPARAMETER	Invalid parameter
STG_E_INVALIDPOINTER	Invalid pointer
STG_E_LOCKVIOLATION	Lock violation. Attempted to read or write region of locked stream or byte array (see the section "The ILockBytes Interface" in Chapter 6). This status code can also be returned if a lock cannot be granted because of other existing locks
STG_E_MEDIUMFULL	Storage medium is out of space
STG_E_NOMOREFILES	No more files can be created
STG_E_PATHNOTFOUND	Specified path does not exist
STG_E_READFAULT	General error reading data from storage medium
STG_E_SEEKERROR	Error seeking to specified position
STG_E_TOOMANYOPENFILES	Too many files are open. Try adjusting the FILES parameter in CONFIG.SYS or increase the open files settings for SHARE.EXE

TABLE 4.1: Storage System Status Codes (continued)

Status Code	Description
STG_E_UNIMPLEMENTEDFUNCTION	This is returned when unsupported mode flags are used. The current version of the IStorage and IStream interfaces will fail with this error if STGM_SHARE_EXCLUSIVE is not used
STG_E_UNKNOWN	Unknown error
STG_E_WRITEFAULT	General error writing data to storage medium
STG_E_CANTSAVE	Object cannot be saved at this time
STG_E_INUSE	Object is currently in use
STG_E_NOTCURRENT	Changes have been made by another user since the last commit operation. This code is returned from commit operations when used with the STGC_ONLYIFCURRENT commit mode
STG_E_OLDDLL	Older version of the STORAGE.DLL is being used for a newer file?
STG_E_OLDFORMAT	Older format of docfile?
STG_E_REVERTED	Unknown
STG_E_SHAREREQUIRED	Share must be loaded to perform this operation
STG_S_BUFFEROVERFLOW	Unknown
STG_S_CONVERTED	File was converted successfully and the contents are now saved in the element name CONTENTS
STG_S_TRYOVERWRITE	Unknown

Summary

This chapter has presented the OLE Structured Storage Model and how it compares to and differs from traditional storage techniques. The compound file technology that OLE introduces allows you to create files that are actually sophisticated storage systems. You can create streams that contain discrete chunks of data, as well as storages that can contain other streams and storages providing a hierarchical file system–like structure. By supporting standard property sets, files created by your application can become part of a sophisticated document management system that will allow users to locate and retrieve data more easily than ever before.

This chapter also discussed some of the considerations that must be dealt with when designing file formats that can be used on multiple platforms. Since the compound file technology is already available on several platforms, this will become a more important consideration for application designers than ever before.

The next chapter discusses the details of the `IStorage` and `IStream` interfaces, which make up the core of the Structured Storage Model implementation provided by OLE 2.

CHAPTER
FIVE

IStorages and IStreams

- The IStorage Interface

- The IStream Interface

- Using Transactions

- Limitations of OLE IStorage and IStream implementation

This chapter introduces you to the technical details of using compound files in your application. It includes discussions of the IStorage and IStream interfaces and how they are used. It also discusses some of the structures and techniques you can use when implementing support for compound files in your application.

The IStorage Class

Use the IStorage class to manipulate storages. This class provides functions for opening and creating substorages and streams, enumerating the contents of the storage, and obtaining and setting element information. A complete implementation of the IStorage class is provided with the OLE 2 SDK. Table 5.1 describes the methods available for the IStorage interface.

Creating and Using Storages

Several "helper" functions are provided to make it easy to create new storages and open existing storages.

The StgCreateDocFile() helper function creates a new storage, returning the IStorage interface if it is successful:

```
HRESULT StgCreateDocFile(file_name, mode_flags, reserved,
    root_storage)
```

where the following is true:

- file_name is the actual name of the storage file.
- mode_flags specifies how the file is to be opened and can be a combination of one or more of the predefined creation flags (see Table 5.2) and open mode flags (see Table 5.3).
- reserved should always be set to 0.
- root_storage is a pointer to an IStorage pointer and returns the IStorage pointer if the function is successful.

The return value for this function is an HRESULT and determines success or failure, as well as the type of error that occurred. (For more details on errors and return codes, see Chapter 2.)

TABLE 5.1: IStorage Methods

Method	Description
HRESULT CreateStream(name,mode,r1,r2,ppstm)	Creates a new stream name in the storage. The stream is returned in ppstm and is created using the modes specified in mode. (See Tables 5.2 and 5.3 for mode flags.) r1 and r2 are reserved and should be set to 0
HRESULT OpenStream(name,r1,mode,r2,ppstm)	Opens the stream name in the storage. The stream is returned in ppstm and is opened using the modes specified in mode. (See Table 5.3 for mode flags.) r1 and r2 are reserved and should be set to 0
HRESULT CreateStorage(name,mode,r1,r2,ppstg)	Creates a new storage name in the storage. The storage is returned in ppstg and is created using the modes specified in mode. (See Tables 5.2 and 5.3 for mode flags.) r1 and r2 are reserved and should be set to 0
HRESULT OpenStorage(name,pstgpriority,exclude,r1,ppstg)	Opens an existing substorage name and returns its interface in ppstg. If pstgpriority is used, this method converts the storage passed in this parameter to normal mode from priority mode

TABLE 5.1: IStorage Methods (continued)

Method	Description
HRESULT CopyTo(num_exclude,iid_exclude,exclude,pstgdest)	Copies the contents of the storage to the storage in pstgdest. The num_exclude parameter specifies the number of interfaces to be excluded. The interface IDs to be excluded are passed in iid_exclude. The exclude parameter contains a list of element names that should also be excluded from the copy. pStg->CopyTo(0,0,0,pStgDest) causes all elements to be copied to pStgDest
HRESULT MoveElementTo (name,pstgdest,new_name,move_flags)	Moves or copies the element name to the storage in pstgdest with the name new_name. The move_flags parameter can be STGMOVE_MOVE or STGMOVE_COPY
HRESULT Commit(commit_flags)	Commits all changes for this storage. This affects only storages open with the STGM_TRANSACTED mode (The commit_flags are described in Table 5.6.)
HRESULT Revert()	Reverts all changes back to the last commit or open. This method affects only storages open in STGM_TRANSACTED mode

TABLE 5.1: IStorage Methods (continued)

Method	Description
HRESULT EnumElements(r1,r2,r3,ppenum)	Returns a pointer to an IEnumSTATSTG interface in ppenum. r1, r2, and r3 are reserved and should be set to 0
HRESULT DestroyElement(name)	Removes the element name from the storage
HRESULT RenameElement(old_name,new_name)	Renames the element old_name to new_name
HRESULT SetElementTimes(name,ctime,atime,mtime)	Sets the creation (ctime), access (atime), and modification (mtime) times of the element name
HRESULT SetClass(clsid)	Sets the clsid as the class tag of the object stored in the storage
HRESULT SetStateBits(state_bits,mask)	Sets the state bits for a specific storage. No bits are currently defined for this version. All bits are reserved and should not be used
HRESULT Stat(pstatstg,stat_flag)	Returns statistics about the storage object in pstatstg. stat_flag can be either 0 or STATFLAG_NONAME, in which case the lpszName member of the STATSTG structure is returned as NULL and does not require the use of the current allocator to free it

TABLE 5.2: Creation Mode Flags

Flag	Description
STGM_CREATE	If the file exists, delete it before re-creating it
STGM_CONVERT	If the file exists, create a new file with the same name, saving the contents of the original file in a stream called CONTENTS
STGM_DELETEONRELEASE	Indicates that this file should be deleted on closing. The current implementation of OLE does not support this flag
STGM_FAILIFTHERE	If the file already exists, the function should fail

The following example demonstrates opening and creating a new storage file:

```
// Create and open root storage called "test.dfl"
// the file is created overwriting any existing file
// and is open in transacted mode for reading and
// writing
IStorage *pStg ;
HRESULT hErr = StgCreateDocFile("test.dfl",
    STGM_CREATE|STGM_TRANSACTED|
    STGM_READWRITE,
    0,
    &pStg ) ;

if( FAILED( hErr ) ) {
    // Handle failure
}
```

The StgOpenStorage() function opens an existing storage:

```
HRESULT StgOpenStorage(file_name, priority_storage, mode_flags,
    exclude, reserved, root_storage)
```

where the following is true:

- file_name is the actual name of the storage file.

- priority_storage should be NULL in most cases. This parameter converts a storage that was opened in STGM_PRIORITY to a normal operating mode.

- mode_flags specifies how the file is to be opened and can be one or more of the open mode flags in Table 5.3.

TABLE 5.3: Open Mode Flags

Open Mode Flag	Description
STGM_DIRECT	Opens the file in direct mode, where all changes to the file are permanent. This is the opposite of the transacted mode. It is also the default behavior if STGM_TRANSACTED or STGM_DIRECT is not specified
STGM_TRANSACTED	Opens the file in transacted mode so that all changes are buffered until a commit operation is performed. If a revert is performed on a transacted file, all changes made since the last commit operation will be discarded
STGM_READ	Opens the file for reading
STGM_WRITE	Opens the file for writing
STGM_READWRITE	Combination of STGM_READ and STGM_WRITE
STGM_PRIORITY	Opening a file in this mode restricts other openings of the same file from committing changes until the priority opening is released
STGM_SHARE_DENY_NONE	Allows other openings to read and write the same file. This is the default behavior if no other STGM_SHARE_ . . . flag is specified
STGM_SHARE_DENY_READ	Denies other openings read access to the file
STGM_SHARE_DENY_WRITE	Denies other openings write access to the file
STGM_SHARE_EXCLUSIVE	Denies all access to the file

- exclude is a pointer to an array of string pointers. It specifies a list of elements that should automatically be deleted upon opening the storage. This parameter may be set to NULL.

- reserved should be set to 0.

- root_storage is a pointer to an IStorage pointer and returns the IStorage pointer if the function is successful.

Priority Mode

Priority mode is a special mode that you use when the application needs to make a complete copy of the storage. The main feature of the STGM_PRIORITY mode is that it restricts other openings of the storage from performing a commit to preserve the integrity of the storage during the copy operation. For this reason you should restrict use of priority mode. Once an application is finished with priority mode, the storage can be either closed or converted to a normal mode operation by using the `priority_storage` argument of the `OpenStorage()` method.

Using the IStorage Class

The `IStorage` class provides a rich feature set for implementing complex file structures. A root storage file can be created or opened by calling the `StgCreate-DocFile()` and `StgOpenStorage()` routines. These routines both return a pointer to an `IStorage` instance. After obtaining an `IStorage` instance, an application can call the `IStorage` methods to manipulate the contents of the storage. To close the storage, an application need only call the `Release()` method to release the application's handle to the storage.

Since substorages and streams require the parent storage to be valid, releasing a storage invalidates all substorage and stream instances. In this situation the only valid method that can be executed for these nested instances is `Release()`.

Enumerating the Elements in a Storage

The elements in a given storage can be determined by calling `IStorage::Enum-Elements()`. This method returns an element enumerator. Enumerators are used extensively throughout OLE for iterating variable-length lists of items or elements. Different types of enumerators all function in exactly the same manner, varying only in the data they return.

An instance of an enumerator takes the form of a class called I Enum*XXXX*, where *XXXX* identifies the type of data. In this case the enumerator returns the STATSTG data structure (see Table 5.4) that contains the details for the elements of a storage. The `IEnumSTATSTG` (and all other enumerators) interface is listed in Table 5.5.

Most of the members of the STATSTG structure are self explanatory (see Table 5.4). A few of them, however, warrant more discussion.

TABLE 5.4: STATSTG Members

Field Name	Description
LPSTR lpszName	The name of the element. If this field is not NULL, it must be freed using the current task allocator (For more information about CoGetMalloc(), see the section "The IMalloc() Interface" in Chapter 2.)
DWORD type	Specifies the type of element described in the STATSTG. It can contain one of the following values: STGY_STORAGE, STGY_STREAM, or STGY_LOCKBYTES
ULARGE_INTEGER cbSize	The size of the element. This is a structure containing the members HighPart and LowPart to implement a 64-bit value. If the application will never use files that can grow to this size, it is acceptable to just use LowPart
FILETIME mtime	Modification time
FILETIME ctime	Creation time
FILETIME atime	Last access time. Note that this value is an approximation
DWORD grfMode	This member is valid only when returned from Stat() methods. This is the mode that was used to open the element
DWORD grfLocks Supported	Bit flags indicating which lock types are supported. This uses the lock type flags (see Table 6.2)
CLSID clsid	The class ID that is associated with the storage. This is valid only if the type is STGTY_STORAGE and is set to CLSID_NULL when the storage is originally created
DWORD grfStateBits	Last value set with SetStateBits(). Since all the bits are currently undefined, this value is not currently used
DWORDreserved	Reserved

The mtime, ctime, and atime members are various stored time values relevant to the element. These values are of type FILETIME, which is a 64-bit value representing the number of 100-nanosecond intervals since January 1, 1601. Several aspects of these time values need to be discussed in detail:

- Comparison of FILETIME structures
- Conversion to usable date/time information
- The point at which the values are set for a specific element

TABLE 5.5: IEnumSTATSTG Methods

Method	Description
HRESULT Next(num_elem, statstg_buffer, elems_returned)	Fills the elem_buffer with the number of STATSTG elements specified in num_elem. The total number of elements returned is specified in elems_returned. If this parameter is not used, num_elem must be 1
HRESULT Skip(num_elem)	Forces the enumerator to skip num_elem elements
HRESULT Reset()	Resets the enumerator to the beginning
HRESULT Clone(ppenum)	Returns an exact clone of the current enumerator in ppenum. The state includes the current position

Since the FILETIME data type is larger than the largest primitive data type that most compilers can handle, it is defined as a structure of two DWORDs, as follows:

```
typedef struct FARSTRUCT tagFILETIME {
    DWORD dwLowDateTime;
    DWORD dwHighDateTime;
} FILETIME;
```

The function CompareFILETIME() demonstrates how to compare two FILETIME structures, returning a −1 if fTime1 is less than fTime2, a 0 if the times are the same, and 1 if fTime2 is greater than fTime1:

```
int CompareFILETIME( const FILETIME& fTime1,
    const FILETIME& fTime2 )
{
    int cmp ;
    if( fTime1->dwHighDateTime > fTime2->dwHighDateTime )
        cmp = 1 ;
    else if( fTime1->dwHighDateTime < fTime2->dwHighDateTime )
cmp = -1 ;
    else{
        if( fTime1->dwLowDateTime > fTime2->dwLowDateTime )
            cmp = 1 ;
        else if( fTime1->dwLowDateTime <
            fTime2->dwLowDateTime ) cmp = -1 ;
        else cmp = 0 ;
    }
```

```
        return cmp ;
    }
```

To extract actual date and time information, the routines CoDosDateTimeToFileTime()
and CoFileTimeToDosDateTime() are provided to convert between DOS date and time
values and FILETIME structures.

When elements are opened in transacted mode, the modification time, mtime, is the
time of the last commit that was invoked for the element. For elements opened in
direct mode, the modification time is the greater of the time of the last commit or
the time of the last release.

```
LPMALLOC pMalloc ;
LPSTORAGE pStg ;
LPENUMSTATSTG pEnum ;
STATSTG statStg ;
HRESULT hErr ;

// Obtain the enumerator
hErr = pStg->EnumElements(0,NULL,0,&pEnum) ;
if( FAILED( hErr ) ) {
    Message( "IStorage::EnumElements() failed!" ) ;
    pStg->Release() ;
    return FALSE ;
}

// Get the IMalloc interface
CoGetMalloc(MEMCTX_TASK,&pMalloc) ;

// Now enumerate the elements
(hErr) = S_OK);
while( GetScode(hErr) = S_OK ) ;
    hErr = pEnum->Next(1,&statStg,NULL) ;
    if( GetScode(hErr) == S_FALSE ) break ;
    if( statStg.pwcsName != NULL ) {
        Message( statStg.pwcsName ) ;
        pMalloc->Free( statStg.pwcsName ) ;
    }
}
// Release everthing
pMalloc->Release() ;
pEnum->Release() ;
pStg->Release() ;
```

Using the Next( ) method returns the next count data elements, setting the current element to be the element immediately after the last element returned. If count is set to 1, the count_returned argument can be NULL. The Next( ) method will fail if count_returned is NULL and count is greater than 1. This method returns S_OK if successful and S_FALSE if not. It is also important to note that when a data structure contains a pointer, the enumerator is responsible for allocating the memory, but the caller is responsible for freeing the memory. This is done using the memory allocator. (See Chapter 2 for more information on memory allocation.)

Naming Conventions for Elements

Element names are much less restricted than with the normal DOS file-naming convention, even though the name of the compound file itself must adhere to the restrictions of the file system. All other elements in the compound file can have names up to 32 characters long. These names can include all ASCII characters greater than ASCII 32, with the exception of the following characters:

. \ / : !

Element names that start with characters below ASCII 32 are reserved and have special meaning to OLE, as well as to containers and objects.

Transactions in Storages

Since transactions are a major feature of compound files, it is worthwhile to discuss them in a little more depth. As described earlier, transactions cause all changes to a storage to be buffered until either a commit or a release is performed. What does that mean in terms of what the storage looks like to the current opening? To other openings?

When changes are made to a storage that is opened in STGM_TRANSACTED mode, all changes made to that storage are visible to that instance of the storage but not to other instances.

Committing Changes to a Storage

There are several types of commit operations (see Table 5.6). The STGC_DEFAULT commit mode should be used for most cases, with the application trying other commit modes when the default mode fails. The STGC_DEFAULT mode may fail because of lack of space on the current drive. If this happens, the STGC_OVERWRITE mode may be used to try to save the changes. If the STGC_OVERWRITE mode does not have enough disk space, it will leave the old data intact. The drawback in using the STGC_OVERWRITE mode as a default mode is that if some other failure occurs while committing the changes, there is no guarantee that either the old data or the new data will remain uncorrupted.

TABLE 5.6: Commit Flags

Flag	Description
STGC_DEFAULT	The default commit mode, this is the most robust mode available. If any sort of failure occurs before the commit is complete, the uncommited version of the data will still be intact
STGC_OVERWRITE	Commits the changes as compactly as possible and should be used when disk space is a concern
STGC_ONLYIFCURRENT	Detects situations in which the storage has been changed by another user since the last commit. The error STG_E_NOTCURRENT is returned if this situation occurs, and the program can then decide how to handle the situation and, if desired, perform the commit anyway, using one of the other commit modes
STGC_DANGEROUSLYCOMMITMERELYTODISKCACHE	A trade-off between performance and robustness, this flag causes the system to not flush the disk drive cache to disk. Because of this, in case of a crash, there is no guarantee that the data will actually make it to the disk

It is also important to note that the Commit() method does not consume any additional memory when saving the changes. This allows compound files to be saved properly even in emergency low-memory situations.

> **TIP**
>
> If the application does not call `IStorage::Revert()` or `IStorage::Commit()` explicitly, then when the storage is released through the `IStorage::Release()` method, a revert happens implicitly.

The IRootStorage Interface

The `IRootStorage` interface is implemented by the root `IStorage`. At this point there may be some confusion since a root `IStorage` is obtained when initially opening the compound file. Since the `IStorage` interface obtained is a component object, it also supports the `AddRef()`, `Release()`, and `QueryInterface()` methods. The root `IStorage` supports another interface that can be obtained to perform actions that pertain only to the root storage. This is the `IRootStorage` interface. A pointer to this interface can be obtained for a specific compound file in the following manner:

```
IRootStorage *pRootStorage ;

HRESULT hErr = pStg->QueryInterface( IID_IRootStorage,
    &RootStorage ) ;
if( FAILED( hErr ) ) {
}
```

The only method supported by the `IRootStorage` interface is `IRootStorage::SwitchToFile()` (see Table 5.7). This method allows the application to create a copy of a compound file. All uncommitted changes that had been made to the original are now associated with the new file and are still uncommitted (see Figure 5.1). A commit to the new file is needed to make these changes permanent.

TABLE 5.7: IRootStorage Methods

Method	Description
SwitchToFile(lpszFileName)	Copies the current storage to a new file specified by `lpszFileName`. All uncommitted changes are transferred to the new base file and remain uncommitted

FIGURE 5.1:

Effects of the
IRootStorage::SwitchToFile() method

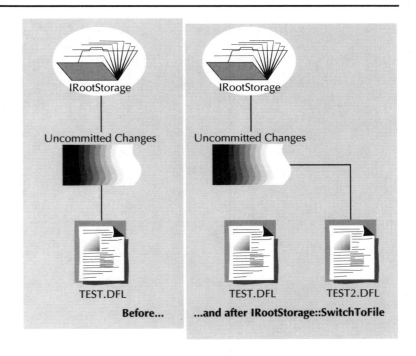

The IStream Class

The IStream class provides similar functionality to the standard I/O library in the C language. Methods are provided for reading, writing, seeking, locking, copying, and getting or setting statistics information for a stream (see Table 5.8). An instance of an IStream is usually obtained from the IStorage::OpenStream() or IStorage::CreateStream() method of the parent storage.

Using the IStream Class   In most cases the application must have an instance of an IStorage to obtain an IStream. Calling the IStorage methods CreateStream() and OpenStream() returns a pointer to a new IStream instance if successful.

TABLE 5.8: IStream Methods

Method	Description
HRESULT Read(buffer, bytes, bytes_read)	Reads bytes' worth of data into buffer. The total number of bytes read is returned in bytes_read
HRESULT Write(buffer, bytes, bytes_written)	Writes out bytes' worth of data from buffer. The total amount written is returned in bytes_written
HRESULT Seek(seek_offset, seek_mode, new_pos)	Seeks to seek_offset relative to the position specified by seek_mode. seek_mode can be STREAM_SEEK_SET (from the beginning of the stream), STREAM_SEEK_CUR (from the current position), or STREAM_SEEK_END (from the end of the stream). The new position is returned in new_pos
HRESULT SetSize(new_size)	Sets the size of the stream to new_size bytes. If this is larger than the current stream size, the new portion of the stream should be considered uninitialized. If new_size is smaller, the stream is truncated
HRESULT Clone(ppstm)	Makes a clone of the current stream, maintaining all state information. The new stream pointer is returned in ppstm
HRESULT CopyTo(pstm, bytes, bytes_read, bytes_written)	Copies bytes' worth of data from current stream to pstm. The total number of bytes read and bytes written is returned in the bytes_read and bytes_written parameters, respectively

TABLE 5.8: IStream Methods (continued)

Method	Description
HRESULT Commit(commit_flags)	Commits all changes to the stream to its parent storage. commit_flags should be one of the flags listed in Table 5.6. The current implementation of IStream supports only STGM_DIRECT mode, so this operation is effectively a NULL operation
HRESULT Revert()	Reverts all changes to the file to the last commit. For the current implementation of IStream, this is a NULL function
HRESULT LockRegion(offset, bytes, lock_flag)	Locks the region starting at offset for bytes' worth of data. lock_flag specifies the lock type. Region locking is not supported in the current implementation of IStream
HRESULT UnlockRegion(offset, bytes, lock_type)	Unlocks the region specified by offset and bytes. This is not supported in the current implementation of IStream
HRESULT Stat(pstatstg, stat_flag)	Returns the stream status in the STATSTG structure passed in pstatstg. stat_flag is 0 if the lpszName field should be returned. If stat_flag is set to STATFLAG_NONAME, this field is returned as NULL

Limitations of the IStream Class   The OLE implementation of the IStream interface does not support the locking mechanisms, transactions, or nonexclusive open modes.

Transactions in Streams   Since the OLE 2 IStream implementation supports only the direct and exclusive open modes, passing STGM_TRANSACTED or any share mode other than STGM_SHARE_EXLUSIVE will fail with an error return of STG_E_INVALIDFLAG. Even though transactions are not supported directly, all changes to an IStream are subject to a transaction that is in progress by the parent IStorage, but the IStream itself cannot be committed or reverted. The IStream::Commit() and IStream::Revert() methods are no-op functions. This should not be a major limitation since transactions are fully supported by the IStorage class. Be aware that a commit or a revert to an IStream's parent IStorage class will affect all other elements in the storage.

Summary

This chapter has covered a lot of the specifics of implementing and using the compound file technology through the IStorage and IStream interfaces. You can create or open a compound file by calling the StgCreateDocFile() or StgOpenStorage() (no, I don't know why the naming convention is different here) and use the IStorage interface that these methods return to create and manipulate streams and storages in your compound file. By opening the storage using the STGM_TRANSACTED mode, you can create a sophisticated multi-level transaction that will allow you to commit or revert your changes at any level. The current implementation of compound files only supports transactions at the level of the compound files.

The next chapter discusses techniques for using the Structured Storage Model to access existing file formats and databases. It also introduces the ILockBytes interface and how it is used.

CHAPTER

SIX

Accessing Databases and Existing File Formats

- The ILockBytes interface

- Supporting databases in the Structured Storage Model

- Supporting existing file formats with the Structured Storage Model

- Converting existing file formats to compound files

OLE requires that all OLE-aware applications support the Structured Storage Model. As you will see in more detail later in this chapter, what this means is that when your application manipulates an OLE object, you are required to provide a pointer to an IStorage interface for that object's exclusive use. Chapter 5 described how you create compound files that support the Structured Storage Model implicitly. This chapter discusses the situations in which you cannot implement compound files for storing objects. These situations usually occur where an application has to support an existing file format or where the natural storage medium for the application is a database.

The ILockBytes Interface

The compound file implementation of the IStorage and IStream interfaces comprises a simple-to-use mechanism for reading and writing complex file formats. At some level the operating system's file I/O services will be used to write the data to a file even for routines such as read(), write(), and seek(). Under OLE there is a layer called ILockBytes that emulates the operating system's file I/O services. The whole purpose of this interface is to separate the operating system from the storage mechanism (see Figure 6.1).

FIGURE 6.1:

How ILockBytes is used by the Structured Storage Model

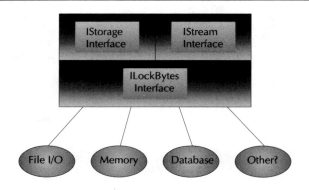

Since the interface for ILockBytes is relatively simple to implement, the method for providing storages on other types of media is obvious. Simply provide an ILockBytes interface that supports reading and writing data to that medium. The ILockBytes interface implements the concept of a byte array with the methods listed in Table 6.1.

TABLE 6.1: ILockBytes Interface Methods

Method	Description
HRESULT ReadAt (ULARGE_INTEGER ulOffset, VOID HUGEP *pv, ULONG cb, ULONG *pcbRead)	Reads cb bytes of memory into the buffer pv beginning at the offset ulOffset. If pcbRead is non-NULL, the number of bytes actually read will be stored in the ULONG to which it points
HRESULT WriteAt (ULARGE_INTEGER ulOffset, VOID const HUGEP *pv, ULONG cb, ULONG *pcbWritten)	Writes cb bytes of memory into the buffer pv beginning at the offset ulOffset. If pcbWritten is non-NULL, the number of bytes actually read will be stored in the ULONG to which it points
HRESULT Flush()	Flushes any cached data to the storage medium
HRESULT SetSize (ULARGE_INTEGER cb)	Sets the size of the file to cb bytes. If this value is smaller than the current file size, the file is truncated. If it is larger, the file is expanded and the contents of the new portion of the file are undefined
HRESULT LockRegion (ULARGE_INTEGERlibOffset, ULARGE_INTEGER cb, DWORD dwLock-Type)	Locks the region of the file at libOffset for cb bytes. Use the lock type specified by dwLockType
HRESULT UnlockRegion (ULARGE_INTEGERlibOffset, ULARGE_INTEGER cb, DWORD dwLock-Type)	Unlocks the region of the file at libOffset for cb bytes. Use the lock type specified by dwLockType. There must be a matching unlock for every call to LockRegion()
HRESULT Stat(STATSTG *pstatstg, DWORD grfStatFlag)	Returns the status for the ILockBytes interface in the STATSTG structure pointed to by pstatstg. (For more details of this structure see Table 5.4.) The grfStatFlag value can be STATFLAG_DEFAULT (0) or STATFLAG_NONAME (1) to determine whether the lpszName field is filled out

Implementations of ILockBytes are not required to have a concept of the current position. The I/O methods ReadAt() and WriteAt() must be passed the specific location from which to access the data. One of the important things to notice about OLE is that the designers are already thinking about the shape of things to come. The offset into the byte array that is passed as an argument to these methods is a 64-bit unsigned integer of type ULARGE_INTEGER. This type is declared in the OLE header files as follows:

```
typedef struct _ULARGE_INTEGER {
    DWORD LowPart;
    DWORD HighPart;
} ULARGE_INTEGER, *PULARGE_INTEGER;
```

To manipulate this number, OLE provides macros to set the values for these numbers, up to the 32-bit limit:

```
ULARGE_INTEGER largeNum ;
// Set the large integer to the max 32-bit value
ULISet32( largeNum, ULONG_MAX ) ;
```

NOTE   Even though the types are defined to manipulate numbers larger than 32 bits, you must write your own handler code or wait until compilers support data types this large. OLE also has a signed 64-bit integer called LARGE_INTEGER, along with the corresponding macro LISet32(largeint, val32).

The other arguments to ReadAt() and WriteAt() are more obvious, including a huge pointer to the data buffer for the operation, a ULONG for the number of bytes to be read or written, and a pointer to a ULONG to return the number of bytes actually processed.

The Flush() method forces any buffered data to be written to the storage medium. Of course, this may be a no-op for some implementations of ILockBytes. Other methods include SetSize(), which can be used to either truncate the size of the byte array or increase it. If the new size is larger, the byte array values for the new portion are undefined. If the operation fails because of lack of space on the storage medium, the method returns STG_E_MEDIUMFULL.

ILockBytes also supports region locking, but this is not required as part of the standard implementation. If a particular implementation of ILockBytes does not implement locking, it returns STG_E_INVALIDFUNCTION. The lock methods function similarly to most operating system locking mechanisms: you specify the range, in this case with an offset and a byte count, along with a lock type. The lock types that are supported are listed in Table 6.2. To release a lock, UnlockRegion() must be called with the same parameters with which LockRegion() was called.

TABLE 6.2: Lock Type Constants

Constant	Description
LOCK_WRITE	A write-only lock that excludes all other write access to the locked region
LOCK_EXCLUSIVE	An exclusive lock that excludes all other access to the region
LOCK_ONLYONCE	Unknown at this time

The OLE libraries already provide two implementations of ILockBytes—one for file I/O and another for accessing memory as a byte array. The file I/O interface is not directly available to the programmer. Whenever a compound file is created or opened, this is the ILockBytes that is used. There is also an ILockBytes implementation for global memory. This version implements all of the ILockBytes methods, except locking, on a global memory handle, or HGLOBAL.

Supporting Existing File Formats

There are at least two ways to add OLE 2 support and still be backward-compatible with existing file formats. The first is extending the existing file format to include the ability to insert OLE object data into the data stream of the format. The second method is based around the concept of supporting the old file format by automatically converting it to a compound file. Ideally, an OLE application should support the compound files as its native storage method. However, because of the nature of software development, this choice will be based upon the requirements of each specific product.

Adding OLE Objects to an Existing File Format

The most important aspect of supporting objects in an existing file format is allowing arbitrarily sized data objects to be added to the document format. After this requirement is met, the remaining work is relatively simple.

The trick is to create OLE objects in memory by creating an `IStorage` on a global memory handle using the methods described later in this chapter. When the user selects Save, obtain the memory handle and serialize the data to your file format. Loading the object involves allocating the memory, reading the data from your file format, and creating the storage using the `CreateILockBytesOnHGlobal()` and `StgOpenStorageOnILockBytes()` functions.

The drawback of this technique is that objects are forced to be completely resident in memory, which is not the case when using compound files.

There is a more complex implementation of this method that an avid developer may pursue if existing file formats must be supported. This involves implementing the `ILockBytes` interface on top of specific regions of the existing file format. This action would solve the memory issues, but after going to this much effort, one might ask whether it would have been easier to convert to compound files.

Automatic Conversion of Existing File Formats

The automatic conversion of existing file formats is the method that provides the best of all worlds. That is, it allows you to keep your existing file format and convert to compound files at the same time. Too good to be true? Well, there is some work involved. The first step is to be able to determine which type of file you are looking at when the file is opened. For the old file format, this will be completely up to you. For compound files, the developer simply has to call the `StgIsStorageFile( fileName )`, passing the storage file name as the sole parameter. This function returns `S_FALSE` if the file is not a compound file and returns `S_OK` if it is. After determining the file type, you must then open the files in two different ways.

If it is in an old file format, open the file using `StgOpenStorage()` with the `STGM_CONVERT` mode specified in the open mode flags. This causes a compound file to be created, with the contents of the existing file saved in a stream called CONTENTS. The rest is easy. Compound files are opened with the standard open mode flags for your application. When you save the files, you should follow the standard techniques for committing compound files. (See Chapters 3 and 4 for more details.) Also note that if an old format file is opened using the `STGM_TRANSACTED` mode and is never committed, the conversion is not permanent. The following code demonstrates how you can determine whether a file is not a storage and automatically convert it.

```
extern char fullFileName[] ;
if( StgIsStorageFile( fullFileName ) ){
    hErr = StgOpenStorage( fullFileName,
                           NULL,
                           STGM_TRANSACTED |
                           STGM_READWRITE |
                           STGM_SHARE_DENY_NONE|
                           STGM_CONVERT,
                           NULL,
                           0L,
                           &pStg ) ;
}else{
    hErr = StgCreateDocfile( fullFileName,
                           STGM_TRANSACTED |
                           STGM_READWRITE |
                           STGM_SHARE_DENY_NONE |
                           STGM_CONVERT,
                           0,
                           &pStg ) ;
}
if( FAILED( hErr ) ) {

}
```

This method requires that the new file format use the CONTENTS stream in the root of the storage as the location for storing the primary data but allows the application to convert to compound files at a controlled pace. The format will then store references to substorages in the compound file for each object reference.

In Figure 6.2 the file OLDDOC.DAT is in a legacy file format, and the file NEW-DOC.DAT is the converted version of this file, where the old data is now in a stream called CONTENTS.

FIGURE 6.2:

Old file format and new file format

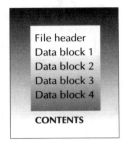

OLDDOC.DAT   NEWDOC.DAT

Using Structured Storages on Memory Handles

As pointed out earlier in this chapter, there are times when it is helpful to create a structured storage on a block of memory. The most important example is when an application has an existing file format that it cannot change but still needs to call the OLE routines that require a pointer to an `IStorage`. The application can simply create a storage in memory and then write the block of memory to the disk under the existing file format.

Creating a storage in memory requires several steps:

1. Call `CreateILockBytesOnHGlobal()` to create an `ILockBytes` on a block of memory.

2. Use `StgCreateDocfileOnILockBytes()` to initialize the compound file and obtain a pointer to the new storage.

These are the steps you take the first time you create the storage. To use an existing object that has been saved in a data file, use the following steps:

1. Load the block of data associated with the storage into a block of shared global memory.

2. Call `CreateILockBytesOnHGlobal()` to obtain an `ILockBytes` interface on the allocated memory.

3. Call the `StgOpenStorageOnILockBytes()` to open the storage.

The `CreateILockBytesOnHGlobal()` routine is declared as follows:

```
HRESULT CreateILockBytesOnHGlobal(HGLOBAL hMem,
    BOOL fDeleteOnRelease,
    LPLOCKBYTES FAR *ppLckBytes ) ;
```

The hMem argument is a handle to global memory that should be allocated as moveable, nondiscardable memory. It should also be shared if the memory block is ever to be used by more than one application. If the hMem argument is NULL, a new shared memory block is automatically allocated. If you do pass a memory handle in hMem, the contents of the memory block will be undisturbed during the creation of the ILockBytes instance.

The fDeleteOnRelease flag indicates whether you want the memory block to be automatically deleted when the ILockBytes instance is released. Set this flag to TRUE if you want the memory handle released and to FALSE if you want to manage the memory handle yourself.

Finally, the ppLckBytes parameter is a pointer to an LPLOCKBYTES in which the pointer to the new ILockBytes is stored as a return argument if the routine is successful.

The following sample code demonstrates how to create an IStorage on a memory handle:

```
#include <stdio.h>
#include <windows.h>       // Windows SDK of course
#include <string.h>        // needed for compobj.h
#include <ole2ver.h>
#include <ole2.h>

BOOL InitCOM()
{
    // Check COM Build Version
    DWORD coVersion = CoBuildVersion() ;
    if( HIWORD( coVersion ) != rmm ||
        LOWORD( coVersion ) < rup) {
        printf( "Bad version of COM!\n" ) ;
        return FALSE ;
    }
```

```
    // Initialize COM
    HRESULT hErr = CoInitialize( NULL ) ;
    if( FAILED( GetScode( hErr ) ) ) {
        printf( "Failed to initialize OLE!\n" )

        return FALSE ;
    }
    return TRUE ;
}

void DeinitCOM()
{
    CoUninitialize() ;
}

void main()
{
    HRESULT hErr ;
    LPVOID memPtr ;
    HGLOBAL hMem ;
    LPSTORAGE pStg ;
    LPLOCKBYTES pLckBytes ;

    if(!InitCOM()) return ;

    // First create the new ILockBytes instance
    // on an HGLOBAL
     hErr=CreateILockBytesOnHGlobal(NULL,
                            TRUE,
                            &pLckBytes) ;
    if( SUCCEEDED( hErr ) ) {

        // Now create the Storage on the
        // ILockBytes
        hErr = StgCreateDocfileOnILockBytes(
                    pLckBytes,
                    STGM_CREATE |
                    STGM_DIRECT |
                    STGM_READWRITE |
                    STGM_SHARE_EXCLUSIVE,
                    NULL,
```

```
                    &pStg ) ;
if( SUCCEEDED( hErr ) ) {

    // Use the storage here

    // done with storage
    pStg->Release() ;

}
// Now do something with the memory
GetHGlobalFromILockBytes( pLckBytes,
                    &hMem ) ;
memPtr = GlobalLock( hMem ) ;

// save the memory to some storage

GlobalUnlock( hMem ) ;

// Now release the iLockBytes
pLckBytes->Release() ;

// Now create a new iLockBytes
hErr=CreateILockBytesOnHGlobal( hMem,
                    FALSE,
                    &pLckBytes ) ;

if( SUCCEEDED( hErr ) {
    hErr = StgOpenStorageOnILockBytes(
            pLckBytes,
            NULL,
            STGM_DIRECT |
            STGM_READWRITE |
            STGM_SHARE_EXCLUSIVE,
            NULL,
            OL,
            &pStg ) ;
    if( SUCCEEDED( hErr ) ) {
        // do something with pStg
```

```
                    // release the storage
                    pStg->Release() ;
                }

                pLckBytes->Release() ;

                // Since we set the fDelOnRelease
                //flag to false, we must free the
                // memory
                GlobalFree( hMem ) ;
            }
        }


        // Shut down the COM
        DeinitCOM() ;
    }
```

The first time we call CreateILockBytesOnHGlobal( ), we pass NULL for the hMem parameter. This causes the memory to be allocated for us. A call to the routine StgCreateStorageOnILockBytes( ) creates a new storage on our ILockBytes instance. After this we are free to do whatever we want with the storage (realizing that instead of disk space limitations, we now have to worry about memory limitations). Instead of complicating the example, we simply release the storage and use the GetHGlobalFromILockBytes( ) routine to obtain the memory handle that was allocated for by CreateILockBytesOnHGlobal( ). The calls to GlobalLock( ) and GlobalUnlock( ) illustrate the fact that we are free to manipulate this memory in any way we want. This memory would most probably be written to a disk or a database record. Then we release the ILockBytes instance.

The second call to CreateILockBytesOnHGlobal( ) passes the original memory handle as the hMem parameter to reuse the storage that we already created. This illustrates how to use StgOpenStorageOnILockBytes( ) to open an existing storage on a memory handle. Finally, after releasing the second ILockBytes instance, we call GlobalFree( ) since we set the fDeleteOnRelease parameter to FALSE in both calls to CreateILockBytesOnHGlobal( ). This means we are responsible for the memory handle.

Using ILockBytes to Access a Database

Now we get to the issue of storage objects in a database. By now you know that you must have some sort of compound file, whether you fake it (using storages in memory, as discussed earlier in this chapter) or you actually have a compound file as the native storage medium for your data. Even if the storage system you are using is a database, you must have a pointer to an `IStorage` interface for the server to be able to store its data.

There are several ways to do this with a database. First, it helps if the database supports some sort of variable-length record. This could be a special case of the memo field in an Xbase system or some other implementation. In this case the simplest way to add support for OLE objects is to create a storage in memory and then write the contents of the memory block out to the database record (see Figure 6.3).

FIGURE 6.3:
Memory-based database support for OLE objects

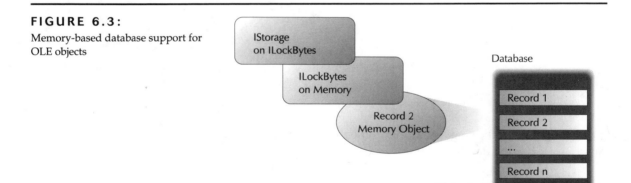

If the variable-length record support is not sufficient, you will have to implement some method of extending the database, perhaps by storing a reference to a file that would contain the object. You either have one file per object per record (see Figure 6.4) or one file with all the objects and an object reference in the record (see Figure 6.5).

FIGURE 6.4:

File/record-based database support for OLE objects

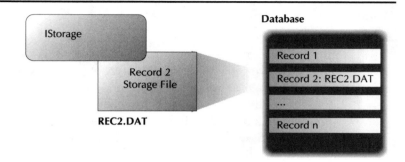

FIGURE 6.5:

Single file-based database support for OLE objects

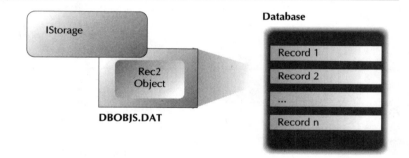

In the single compound file implementation, a single file contains all the objects in the database. First, you create a compound file (called DBOBJS.DAT in Figure 6.5) and create a substorage for each object stored in the database. You would have to determine some naming convention and perhaps save a reference to each record's object storage in the record itself. (Because these issues are application specific, they are not discussed here in depth.)

Performance Issues with Compound Files

In two of the scenarios discussed in the preceding section, there was the potential to have a large number of objects. (Presumably, a database is being used to maintain a relatively large number of records for convenient access.) It must be mentioned that the potential for performance problems exists.

In the example that uses a different compound file to store the object(s) for each record, a noticeable performance problem will develop when the number of files becomes large. Since the DOS file system directory structure requires a linear search through the directory entries to find a file, the average time to open an object will grow as the number of objects affects the number of files in the directory.

This problem would seem to be eliminated by using a single file to store all the objects. Surprise! The compound file implementation also uses a linear search to find the substorage entry. The same problem will develop in trying to open the substorage for objects inside the main storage file.

There is no quick solution to these problems. It is best simply to be aware that these situations can occur. That way when you design a system, you can take these limitations into account ahead of time.

Summary

Not all applications will be able to support the Structured Storage Model, because of a need to support an existing file format or because the application requires a database. This is why the designers of OLE layered the storage model so it could easily accommodate other storage media. The ILockBytes interface is the layer that will be replaced when you need to support another storage format. This layer contains methods for reading and writing streams of bytes to some storage medium. OLE provides default implementations of this layer for storages and for global memory.

You can use two techniques to add support for OLE to existing storage formats. The first is to extend the format to accommodate arbitrarily sized blocks of data in which to store OLE objects, and the second is to create a conversion process to convert old storage formats to OLE compound files. To add support for OLE objects into existing files, you will have to provide an IStorage to the OLE object. Since the existing format is not a compound file, you will have to either create an IStorage on global memory and read and write the memory contents to your storage or develop an ILockBytes interface that directly accesses your file format or database. The first technique is easier to implement, but it will place exacting memory requirements on your application that may or may not be tolerable. Implementing the second technique is, of course, more time consuming.

OLE provides some support for converting existing file formats to compound files, using the STGM_CONVERT switch. If the file is not a compound file, the file is automatically converted to a compound file, with the orginal data placed in a stream called CONTENTS.

Now that we have covered the basics of the structured storage model, we are ready to apply these techniques to building full OLE containers and object servers.

PART III

Containers

This section covers the interface specifications for building basic containers, linking containers, and in-place containers. It also includes a sample container called OLE Publisher that implements all the concepts explained in this section.

Chapter 7 covers the basic container and the IOLEClientSite and IAdviseSink interfaces. It also explains the OLE user interface requirements for a basic container and how to use the OLE 2 User-Interface Library to add these interface components to your application.

Chapter 8 explains how to add support for linking to your application and all the related user-interface components. It covers the details of adding and registering an IClassFactory, as well as for implementing the IOleItemContainer and IPersistFile interfaces.

Chapter 9 describes how to add support for in-place editing to your basic container. It covers the IOleInPlaceFrame, IOleInPlaceUIWindow, and IOleInPlaceSite interfaces.

Chapter 10 presents the details of adding support for drag-and-drop to your application. It covers the IDropSource and IDropTarget interfaces.

CHAPTER

SEVEN

Building a Simple Container

- Building the OLE Publisher container

- Implementing the basic container interfaces

- Using OLE with the clipboard

- Drawing OLE objects

- Activating OLE objects

This chapter discusses the types of containers and walks you through the process of building a simple OLE container. The discussion covers the various OLE interfaces involved in building a container, as well as the techniques required to insert new objects and paste objects from the clipboard into a container.

What Are Compound Documents?

While using an application that is an OLE container, the user can create documents composed of many types of objects. This type of document is called a *compound document*. (This is a different concept from the compound file technology discussed in Part II.)

On Windows systems today the user can create rich documents using data from many different sources (see Figure 7.1). This is much different from the days when sharing data meant understanding all the arcane secrets of obscure (but supposedly standard) file formats with puzzling three- and four-letter acronyms. Today, sharing data is as simple as cut-and-paste or drag-and-drop. If you want to create a spreadsheet in the middle of your word processor document, you simply select Insert ➤ Object, select your spreadsheet program, and voila! This is the essence of the compound document concept.

FIGURE 7.1:

Compound document

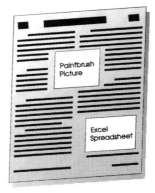

COMPOUND.DOC

Types of Containers

There are two basic types of containers: the embedding container and the linking container.

The embedding container simply allows embedded objects to be inserted into its documents. Objects are either pasted from the clipboard or created from scratch (see Figure 7.2).

FIGURE 7.2:
Conceptual diagram of an embedding container

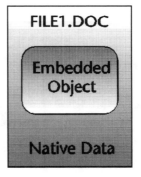

Linking containers perform all the functions of embedding containers, but a linking container also allows links to data and allows other containers to link to any embedded objects. This ability allows you to handle situations in which the user selects an embedded object within a container and tries to paste a link to the object into another container.

Figure 7.3 shows the difference between containers linking to an external object and a container linking to an object embedded in another container. In diagram A there are two compound documents, each with a link to an object that is stored externally. Diagram B illustrates a situation in which FILE2.DOC contains a link to the embedded object in FILE1.DOC. In diagram A the link to the external object is maintained and serviced by the object's server and OLE. No other software is needed to handle this situation. However, in diagram B, before FILE2.DOC can obtain access to the embedded object, the container for FILE1.DOC must provide access to the embedded object since it owns the compound file.

FIGURE 7.3:

Conceptual diagram of linking containers

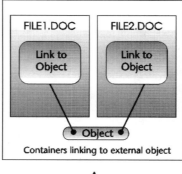
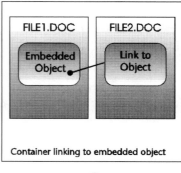

A   B

How Containers Work

To understand how containers work, let's try to design an application with functionality similar to an OLE container. We need to design an application that can support and manipulate a large number of data types.

Let's start by identifying the common ways in which we will need to work with the various data types. We will

- Transfer the data on the clipboard for your application and others to use

- Render a representation of the data on the screen

- Edit the data in its native format

- Save the data to a file that contains a heterogeneous collection of various data types

This is a simple requirement list that requires a sophisticated solution. If we had not thought the problem through, we might have designed the application to handle just one data type and then added "kludges" to support each new required type. This is the sort of application design technique (if you can call it a design) responsible for the spaghetti code we are all so familiar with. Let's be proactive with our design and account for the fact that we may be adding any number of new data types at any time. This means that the majority of the application should deal with each new data type in exactly the same manner.

A Fictional Design Model

For our design we will develop a generic way of talking to the data that allows us to write our application to a simple common API (see Figure 7.4) to deal with all objects. We will call this the GenericObject API. For convenience we will now categorize the methods in the GenericObject API into *interfaces* (collections of related methods). These interfaces are illustrated in Figure 7.4 and are described in the following table.

Interface	Description
Persistent Storage interface	Methods used to save and load the persistent state of an object
Object interface	Manipulates the object directly, including editing
View interface	Renders a visual representation of an object on a device

FIGURE 7.4:

Conceptual architecture of our GenericObject API

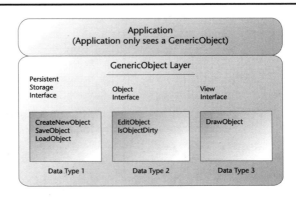

Now let's look at the steps required to demonstrate how our design might be used in an application.

1. Creating a new object:

```
type = PresentObjectTypeListToUser()
pObject = CreateNewObject( type )
pObject->DrawObject()
pObject->EditObject()
```

2. Pasting an object from the clipboard:

```
if valid object on the clipboard then
    pObject = CreateNewObject( typeOnClipboard )
    pObject->LoadObject( pClipboardStorageDataStructure )
    end if
```

3. Copying an object to the clipboard:

```
pSelectedObject->SaveObject(
    pClipboardStorageDataStructure )
```

4. Saving and loading the objects from the file:

```
pObject->CreateNewObject( typeInStorage )
pObject->LoadObject( pStorageDataStructure )

// code to change object here...user editing perhaps

pObject->SaveObject( pStorageDataStructure )
```

5. Editing the selected object:

```
pSelectedObject->EditObject()
```

Notice that the preceding pseudocode requires the programmer to know the data type of the object before the object can be created. This is a requirement in OLE as well, where the proper object server must be asked to create an object of that specific type. The LoadObject() and SaveObject() methods for loading and saving our objects to a storage medium require a reference to a data structure that defines the medium from which the object should be loaded and stored. Since there are similar requirements for supporting the clipboard, if we make the clipboard look like just another place to store and load objects, we can reuse a lot of the code we have already created. Of course, it isn't really that simple in OLE, but the concepts are the same.

The OLE Interfaces

The GenericObject API just presented is a simplified presentation of exactly how OLE is structured. The interfaces we defined have analogs in OLE that perform similar functions. The major difference is that for the operations just discussed in terms of our fictitious API, OLE defines a collection of helper functions that take care of the details.

The interfaces we will use in this chapter make up the foundation for the embedded and linkable object. Some of the interfaces must be implemented by the container, and others must be implemented by the server. Even though we will not implement them in this chapter, we will discuss several interfaces that are implemented in the server simply because we will use them extensively to build our container.

Figure 7.5 illustrates the major OLE interfaces that are either implemented or used by your basic container.

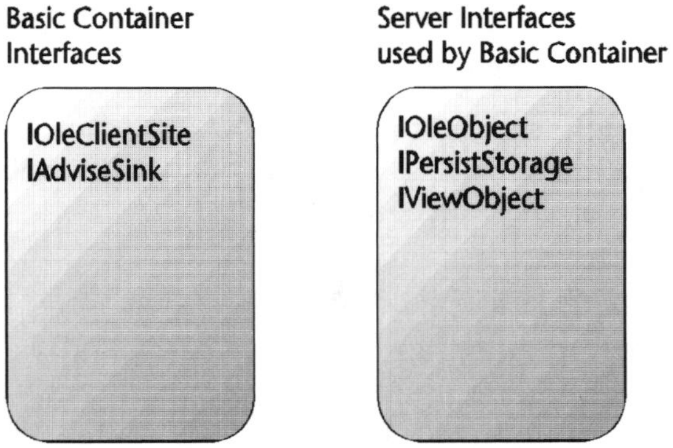

FIGURE 7.5:

OLE interfaces used in the basic container

Basic Container Interfaces

IOleClientSite
IAdviseSink

Server Interfaces used by Basic Container

IOleObject
IPersistStorage
IViewObject

The interfaces implemented on the server side may be implemented by the server itself or by the default object handler that OLE provides. Part IV discusses this subject in detail.

The IDataObject Interface

If you recall from our GenericObject API, we said that if we made the clipboard look like a place to store and load objects, we could leverage the code in the Persistent Storage interface to implement the clipboard. Well, that is exactly what the IDataObject interface does for OLE. (Of course, it does quite a bit more than this and is used in situations that have nothing to do with the clipboard, but when you deal with the clipboard in OLE, you use this interface.) When you want to examine the contents of the clipboard, you must call the OleGetClipboard() routine, which returns a pointer to an IDataObject interface (or LPDATAOBJECT). You can then use the methods in this interface to query which data types are available and request a copy of the data for your own use.

The IOleObject Interface

The `IOleObject` interface is implemented by the object server and is similar to the Object interface for our GenericObject API. We use this interface to get and set various pieces of information about an object, as well as to execute the verbs for an object. An object's *verbs* are the object-defined actions your container is responsible for providing to the user for the currently selected object. Whenever a user double-clicks an object, the standard reaction for any container should be to automatically execute the primary verb. This verb is usually Edit, but for objects such as sound files, it can be Play or whatever else is significant for the object.

The IPersistStorage Interface

The `IPersistStorage` interface is also implemented by the server, and it is the interface used for all storage requirements for an object. This interface contains the methods for saving, loading, and initializing new objects.

The IViewObject Interface

The `IViewObject` interface renders the object in the container's window. This interface is supplied by OLE, although there are some special cases of servers that actually implement this interface themselves (see Part IV for details).

The IOleClientSite Interface

The `IOleClientSite` interface is implemented by the container application. It provides the object with a way of communicating with the container to request such actions as saving the object.

The IAdviseSink Interface

Since an object that resides in your container can be changed in the server application while the container is open, there must be some way of notifying the container when some aspect of the object changes. This is exactly what the `IAdviseSink` interface provides. This interface is implemented by the container and provided to the object so it can notify the container when some aspect of the object changes.

The State of the Object

As our discussion of OLE objects and how they are used in containers continues, we will be talking about the objects in various states of execution. You need to be familiar with these states before continuing (see Figure 7.6).

FIGURE 7.6:
Object states

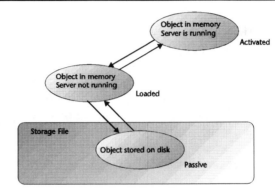

Initially, an object that resides in a container is in the passive state. The object is in this state when it resides on disk in the container's data file and has no in-memory representation. When the container opens this data file, the object is usually brought into the loaded state (but not always).

In the loaded state, the object is represented in memory by the typical object interfaces that we have discussed, and OLE is handling all the details of the object's interaction with the container. The object's server is not running (or if it is, it is not aware of our object).

In the active state, the object's server is launched on the object's behalf to perform some service, such as editing the object. There are two variations on this state: OLE may occasionally launch the server invisibly to request some service from it, and the object may be activated by the user in order to edit, play, or execute other verbs the object might support.

Using the Clipboard

Working with the clipboard in OLE is very similar to using the clipboard with the Windows SDK. In pre-OLE Windows applications you had to obtain ownership of the clipboard before you could use it. This was done through the `OpenClipboard()` function. When you were done with the clipboard you would call the Windows `CloseClipboard()` function. To support OLE, you will probably replace your existing clipboard code with the OLE code since it completely supports all the previous functionality of the clipboard (and trying to mix and match the two models would be a nightmare). In OLE you call the `OleGetClipboard()` function to obtain ownership of the clipboard. After obtaining ownership of the clipboard, things start looking a little different. You are returned a pointer to an `IDataObject` interface that is essentially an object model of the old clipboard concept. This interface provides access to a collection of data types that you can manipulate in much the same way that you use the clipboard in Windows. For example, if you wanted to determine whether a particular data type were on the clipboard, you would use the `IDataObject` interface to ask whether the desired format was available, just as you would use the `IsClipboardFormatAvailable()` function in Windows. When you are done with the clipboard, instead of using `CloseClipboard()`, all you have to do is release the data object. Table 7.1 shows the correlations between the Windows clipboard-handling functions and the OLE 2 functions and methods.

TABLE 7.1: Windows versus OLE 2.0 Clipboard Handling

Windows	OLE
`OpenClipboard()`	`OleGetClipboard()`
`CloseClipboard()`	`pDataObject->Release()`
`IsClipboardFormatAvailable()`	`pDataObject->QueryGetData()`
`GetClipboardData()`	`pDataObject->GetData()`
`EnumClipboardFormats()`	`pDataObject->EnumFormatEtc()`
`SetClipboardData()`	`OleSetClipboard()`
`RegisterClipboardFormat()`	You will still use this function!

Notice in Table 7.1 that the `RegisterClipboardFormat()` routine has no analog in OLE. This routine is still needed, but there is quite a bit more to it than there used to be. Previously, in a non-OLE application, you would have used the `RegisterClipboardFormat()` routine to create a unique token that represented your clipboard format, or you would have used one of the predefined clipboard formats with the naming convention CF_ *formatname*. After determining that a clipboard format you could use existed on the clipboard, you would have called `GetClipboardData()` to obtain a handle to the global memory in which the data resided. Of course, since this data was owned by the clipboard, you would have had to make a copy of it before you could do anything with it.

In that respect, nothing has changed; you still must obtain a reference to the data and make a copy using the `IDataObject` interface. However, there are two significant differences. The first is that the data is not only differentiated by the CF_*types*, but also by the display aspect and the target device it is displayed on. The second major difference is that the data can now be stored in a variety of storage media, not just in a global memory handle.

The FORMATETC Structure

The `GetClipboardData()` method required you to specify the clipboard format you wanted a reference to. To accommodate the richer data transfer requirements for OLE 2, you must now specify the data you want to manipulate by using a FORMATETC structure:

```
typedef struct tagFORMATETC {
    CLIPFORMAT cfFormat ;
    DVTARGETDEVICE FAR *ptd ;
    DWORD dwAspect ;
    LONG lindex ;
    DWORD tymed ;
} FORMATETC ;
```

The fields of this structure specify the various aspects of the data you would like to obtain from the `IDataObject::GetData()` method. The `cfFormat` member is exactly the same as the clipboard format identifiers that you used with the Windows clipboard code.

The `ptd` member is a pointer to a description of a target device in case you want to obtain a format that is customized for a specific device. After you have gotten into the details of building OLE into your application, you will know when you need to use this member. For our purposes we can set it to NULL, which means we don't care whether the data is specific to the device we want to render it on.

The `dwAspect` member specifies the display aspect for which you want to obtain the data. The `lindex` member is interpreted differently, depending on the value of `dwAspect`. The `dwAspect` member requests different versions of the same data. For example, you can obtain a metafile representation of the data by setting `dwAspect` to the DVASPECT_CONTENT constant. Similarly, you can obtain a thumbnail metafile representation by using the DVASPECT_THUMBNAIL constant. The values of dwAspect and the interpretation of lindex are listed in Table 7.2.

TABLE 7.2: Aspect Constants

Constant	Description
DVASPECT_CONTENT	Normal content representation of the data. The lindex member should always be set to −1
DVASPECT_THUMBNAIL	Thumbnail representation; lindex is ignored
DVASPECT_ICON	Iconic representation; lindex is ignored
DVASPECT_DOCPRINT	Obtains a representation suitable for printing; lindex specifies the desired page number. A value of −1 indicates that all pages are desired. The page numbering starts at 1

Finally, the tymed member of this structure specifies the storage medium. In Windows the only place to store clipboard data was in global memory. Now you can store data in global memory, files, streams, storages, GDI objects, or metafiles. The values used to specify the different media are listed in Table 7.3; we will discuss more of the details as they relate to the STGMEDIUM structure.

TABLE 7.3: Storage Medium Types

Type	Description
TYMED_HGLOBAL	Data is stored in global memory block
TYMED_FILE	Data is stored in a file on disk
TYMED_ISTREAM	Data is stored in an IStream
TYMED_ISTORAGE	Data is stored in an IStorage
TYMED_GDI	Data is stored as a GDI object
TYMED_MFPICT	Data is stored as a metafile picture
TYMED_NULL	Indicates that no data is available

The STGMEDIUM Structure

The STGMEDIUM structure is required for managing all the various medium types that OLE supports on the clipboard. This structure is defined as follows:

```
typedef struct tagSTGMEDIUM {
    DWORD tymed ;
    union {
        HANDLE hGlobal ;
        LPSTR lpszFileName ;
        LPSTREAM pstm ;
        LPSTORAGE pstg ;
    } ;
    LPUNKNOWN punkForRelease ;
} STGMEDIUM ;
```

It should be clear how this structure works. After successfully requesting a data format using a FORMATETC structure and calling the IDataObject::GetData() method, you are returned a filled-out STDMEDIUM structure. The tymed member will contain the medium type constant for the medium you requested, and one of the members of the union will be filled, depending on the value of tymed. For example, if you request an IStorage-based format, tymed will be set to the TYMED_ISTORAGE constant and the pstg member of the union will contain a pointer to a valid IStorage interface. The punkForRelease member is used to make sure the proper cleanup is performed for the storage medium. You will never use this member directly since OLE provides the ReleaseStgMedium() function, which properly cleans up the storage medium when you are finished with it.

OLE Objects on the Clipboard

OLE objects are stored on the clipboard using several clipboard formats to represent embedded objects and linked objects, as described in Table 7.4. The CF_OBJECTDESCRIPTOR format contains the object's native data. There are also the standard visual representations of the data, such as bitmaps, metafiles, or text. When you transfer objects on the clipboard, all of these formats can contribute to the creation of your copy of the object. The mechanics of the operations will become clear when we implement these features in the section "Pasting Static Objects from the Clipboard" later in this chapter.

TABLE 7.4: OLE Clipboard Formats

Format	Format String	Description
CF_OBJECTDESCRIPTOR	"Object Descriptor"	Contains a description of the embedded object being transferred. Includes information such as the size and the aspect of the object
CF_EMBEDSOURCE	"Embed Source"	Represents a new embedded object for a server
CF_EMBEDDEDOBJECT	"Embedded Object"	Represents an embedded object that already exists in a container
CF_LINKSOURCE	"Link Source"	Represents a new link to an object for a specific server
CF_LINKSRCDESCRIPTOR	"Link Source Descriptor"	Description of the link that is on the clipboard; similar to the CF_OBJECTDESCRIPTOR
CF_CUSTOMLINKSOURCE	"Custom Link Source"	Represents a custom link source. This format is offered when the server implements its own link interfaces

NOTE   The clipboard formats listed in Table 7.4 are not preregistered formats. This means that to use them, you need to call the `RegisterClipboard-Format()` routine to obtain the token value.

Guidelines for Using the Clipboard

It may seem to you that things are becoming hopelessly complicated, but don't worry. There are some rules and guidelines that make it all easier to deal with.

First of all, when you request a format from the clipboard, don't request a data type for a storage medium that doesn't make sense. For example, you would never ask for any of the predefined Windows formats on anything other than a `TYMED_HGLOBAL`. This somewhat reduces the complexity. Also, OLE does provide routines to take care of many of the details of dealing with the clipboard. You will learn about these routines when we discuss the implementation of the IDataObject interface in the section "Copying Objects to the Clipboard" later in this chapter.

Saving and Loading OLE Objects

From the moment you create an OLE object or paste one from the clipboard, you need to provide it with an IStorage where it can save its data. The easiest way to do this is to support compound files directly in your application, but there are other ways to obtain an IStorage pointer, even if your application does not support compound files (see Chapter 6). The IPersistStorage interface mentioned earlier in this chapter is responsible for loading and saving the state of an OLE object. Each server provides an implementation of the IPersistStorage that you can obtain by using IUnknown::QueryInterface() on the object. This interface contains methods for saving and loading the object. For examples of different storage models that can be implemented in an application, see Chapter 4.

Drawing the Object

Use the IViewObject interface to draw the object. You obtain this interface by calling QueryInterface() on any other interface pointer on an OLE object. Since a container needs to be able to draw an object that is not currently active (whose server is not running), the IViewObject interface is implemented by OLE and uses the cached representation of the object.

Activating the Object

Activating an object involves loading the object's server and having the server provide the editing interface for the object. This is what happens when you double-click a bitmap and it appears in Paintbrush, ready to be modified. This type of activation is sometimes referred to as *open activation*, or *OLE 1–style activation*.

NOTE Chapter 9 discusses another type of activation, when the object is edited inside the container. This is called *in-place activation*. The server negotiates with the container to obtain space for menus, toolbars, and the other adornments needed to provide an editing interface for the user.

The OLE Publisher Application

For this chapter we will build a simple (well, at least compared to what we will cover later) embedding-only container with all the user-interface trappings.

The container application we will build is called OLE Publisher (see Figure 7.7). We will use this application as our sample throughout this part of the book to demonstrate the techniques required to build the various flavors of containers.

FIGURE 7.7:

Screen snapshot for OLE Publisher

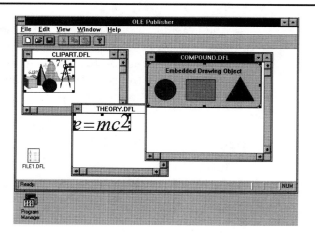

Structure of the OLE Publisher Application

The OLE Publisher application is written in simple C++. For the same reason that OLE Publisher does nothing more than support OLE 2 features, it does not use any complicated syntax or try to get tricky with the inheritance and member access protection that C++ provides. This keeps the code clear and easy to read. (After all, this is a book on OLE, not C++.) However, OLE Publisher does use C++'s ability to define and create objects with associated methods. It's a good idea to use at least this much C++ for any application that supports OLE. (All the techniques and details described here also apply to C, but it is more arduous to support OLE with C since you must handle initialization of the VTBLs and unique naming of your OLE interface methods.)

The source code for the application is included on the companion disk included with the book. The source files are named according to the class and methods for the application. The class architecture for the application is illustrated in Figure 7.8.

FIGURE 7.8:

Class architecture for OLE Publisher with supported interfaces

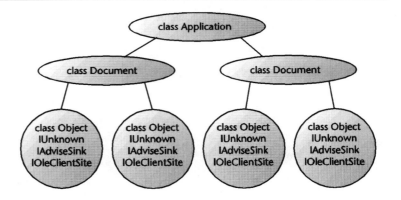

This class architecture also supports various OLE interfaces at the different levels. As you add more support for the different OLE features in your application, you will be adding more and more OLE interfaces. Because of this it is probably a good idea to go ahead and add the code to create an IUnknown for each level of your application. Since the OLE Publisher application is structured so that the Application class, the Document class, and the Object class are all based on IUnknown, it is a simple matter to add new interfaces to each one of these classes. The code for the main IUnknown for each of the classes is contained in the source files AP-PUNK.CPP, DOCUNK.CPP, and OBJUNK.CPP, respectively.

One of the main benefits of having a sample application that demonstrates anything is being able to use it as a reference. For all but the simplest applications, this usually is not a trivial process. To help you navigate through the source, the header files for OLE Publisher are APPL.H, DOC.H, and OBJ.H. These header files contain the class definitions for the three main classes in OLE Publisher's source code. Each class definition lists the methods that are defined, as well as which source file these methods are located in.

MDI or SDI

OLE Publisher is an MDI application for the simple reason that this is a more complicated application model to support. However, in a well-structured MDI application (for our purposes, *well-structured* means having a clear distinction among your frame window, your documents, and the objects contained within your documents), there should be no major difficulty in adding OLE support.

An SDI application is not very different, in terms of the effort expended to support OLE. The major differences arise when you are adding support for in-place activation (see Chapter 9).

The Application Class

Our `Application` class, defined in APPL.H, handles all the application-level features, such as startup, shutdown, the frame window, the message loop, and application-level commands, such as File ➤ New and File ➤ Open. Since this class does handle the frame window, it also handles the details of dealing with our toolbar and status bar.

It is important to realize that all command messages not handled by the frame window are passed to the active document window. Both the `Application` class and the `Document` class use some simple techniques to attach a C++ class to a Windows `HWND`. Also, all global variables in the application are stored in the single instance of the application class called `theApp`.

Last but not least, the `Application` class also supports what is probably the very first major feature developed for any application: the About box.

What about WinMain?

The `WinMain()` procedure is in the file WINMAIN.CPP and is relatively simple. Since we do not allow multiple instances of our application, there is no instance-level initialization. `WinMain()` is presented in Listing 7.1.

Listing 7.1

```
//////////////////////////////////////////////////////////////////////
// Main Entry Point for the entire application
//
#define INITGUID
#include "appl.h"

Application theApp ;

int PASCAL WinMain( HINSTANCE hinstCurrent,
        HINSTANCE hinstPrevious,
        LPSTR lpszCmdLine,
        int nCmdShow)
{
    if( hinstPrevious != NULL ) {
        MessageBox( NULL, "This application is already running!",
                    "",
                    MB_OK|MB_ICONINFORMATION ) ;
        return FALSE ;
    }

    // Initialize the application globals
    theApp.m_hInst = hinstCurrent ;
    theApp.m_hInstPrev = hinstPrevious ;
    theApp.m_nCmdShow = nCmdShow ;
    theApp.m_lpszCmdLine = lpszCmdLine ;

    // Perform initializations
    if( !theApp.Initialize())
        return FALSE ;

    // Execute the message loop for the application
    int status = theApp.Run( ) ;

    // Deinit Application
    theApp.Deinitialize( ) ;

    return status ;     // return value of PostQuitMessage
}
```

The only significant point to note about this listing is the #define INITGUID at the top of the file WINMAIN.CPP. This causes all GUIDs that are declared using the macro DE-FINE_GUID( ) to be initialized. If you don't do this, you won't get past the compile stage of development.

The Document Class

The Document class is defined in the header file DOC.H and takes care of the details of managing the document windows. These include the document-level commands, such as Save and all the Edit menu commands.

To handle the objects that can be inserted into our document, the Document class maintains a linked list of objects and is also responsible for assigning a unique ID to each object, which is generated from a seed value the document saves in its data file.

Note also that the document is an arbitrarily fixed size that is contained in m_docRect, which is set in the document's constructor in the file DOC.CPP. Although you will probably not do this in your application, it removes a lot of the complexity from the scrolling code and makes it easier to read.

The Object Class

The Object class encapsulates the objects themselves. It maintains a backward pointer to the document it belongs to and contains all the code for saving the object it contains to an IStorage provided by the document class. All coordinates handled at the object level are in the virtual coordinates of the document (see Figure 7.9). Most coordinates will be translated by the document before they are passed to the object.

FIGURE 7.9:
Virtual coordinate space for documents

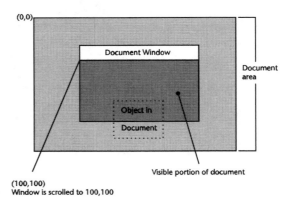

The Storage Model

The document class has an associated IStorage that is saved in the m_pStg member variable. When a new document is created, a temporary storage is created that the document uses to save any objects that are created. This is necessary since we have to provide storage for any objects that are created. When the file is finally saved, the storage is transferred to a new storage file using the IRootStorage interface. If the file is not a new file, when the document receives a File ➤ Save message it runs through each of the objects, asking them to save themselves. Then, after writing out a simple file format to track the information associated with the objects that are stored in the file, it executes an IStorage::Commit().

The File Format for OLE Publisher

The file format for OLE Publisher is very simple. At the root level of the storage files it creates, it writes out a native format stream called CONTENTS, in which we store all the information needed to rebuild our object list (see Figure 7.10).

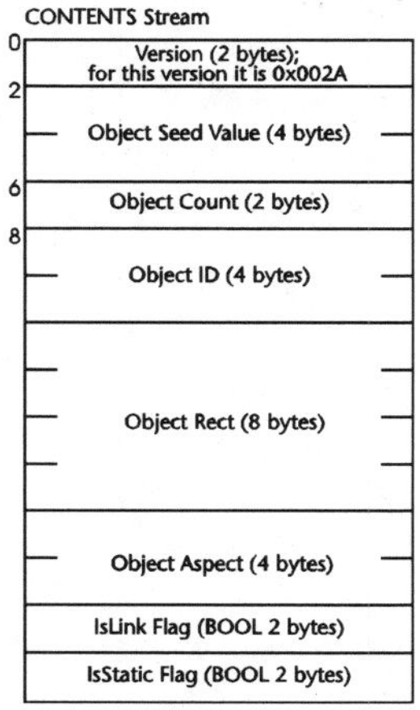

FIGURE 7.10:
Format of the CONTENTS stream for OLE Publisher

Other than this root-level stream we create, the rest of our data file is populated by the child storages created for the purpose of storing the object's data. You can use the DFVIEW.EXE utility application that is shipped with the OLE 2 SDK to look at a compound file. Figure 7.11 demonstrates how to use this application to view one of OLE Publisher's data files.

FIGURE 7.11:
DFVIEW.EXE viewing an OLE
Publisher file

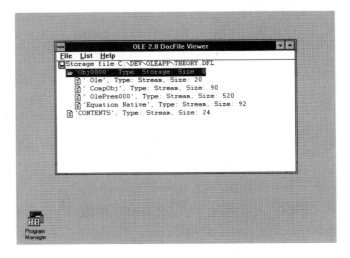

The OLE User-Interface Library

Due to the sophisticated interface requirements, a user-interface library called OLE2UI is provided with the OLE 2 SDK. Actually, it is much more than a user-interface library; it provides a large collection of helper functions, as well as debugging routines. Because this library does not support concurrent use by multiple applications, you must either link it into your application or build the OLE2UI.DLL with a different name. The details of how to build this are included with the library on the OLE 2 SDK. Regardless of this drawback, this library is difficult to live without. Throughout the remainder of this book, we will be using functions and macros provided by the OLE2UI.DLL. You will see how to do so, and in specific cases you will see what these functions actually do for you.

> **TIP**
>
> Take some time to become familiar with the OLE2UI library, and even spend some time just browsing the header files OLE2UI.H and OLESTD.H. It may save you some time later.

Implementing the IOleClientSite and IAdviseSink Interfaces

The IOleClientSite and IAdviseSink interfaces are the primary interfaces you will need to implement to support embedded objects in your container. As illustrated in Figure 7.8, both of these interfaces are implemented at the object level. This means you will need a separate instance of both interfaces for every object that is in your container.

Listing 7.2 contains a partial definition of the Object class, followed by the implementations of the IAdviseSink and IOleClientSite interfaces.

Listing 7.2

```
OBJ.H (partial listing)
class Object : public IUnknown {
public:

    /////////////////////////////////////////////////////
    // Constructor/Destructor : OBJ.CPP
    //
    Object() ;
    ~Object() ;

    /////////////////////////////////////////////////////
    // IUnknown methods    : OBJUNK.CPP
    //
    STDMETHOD(QueryInterface)(REFIID,LPVOID FAR *) ;
    STDMETHOD_(ULONG,AddRef)() ;
    STDMETHOD_(ULONG,Release)() ;

    //
    // Declarations Omitted here!
    //

    /////////////////////////////////////////////////////
    // IOleClientSite interface : OBJCSITE.CPP
    //
    class ObjClientSite : public IOleClientSite {
    public:
        Object *m_pObj ;
```

```
        ObjClientSite( Object *pObj ) ;

        STDMETHOD(QueryInterface)(REFIID,LPVOID FAR *) ;
        STDMETHOD_(ULONG,AddRef)() ;
        STDMETHOD_(ULONG,Release)() ;
        STDMETHOD(SaveObject)() ;
        STDMETHOD(GetMoniker)(DWORD, DWORD,
                    LPMONIKER FAR* ppmk) ;
        STDMETHOD(GetContainer)(LPOLECONTAINER FAR*) ;
        STDMETHOD(ShowObject)() ;
        STDMETHOD(OnShowWindow)(BOOL) ;
        STDMETHOD(RequestNewObjectLayout)() ;
    } ;
    ObjClientSite m_clientSite ;

    ///////////////////////////////////////////////////
    // IAdviseSink interface    : OBJASINK.CPP
    //
    class ObjAdviseSink : public IAdviseSink2 {
    public:
        Object *m_pObj ;
        ObjAdviseSink( Object *m_pObj ) ;

        STDMETHOD(QueryInterface)(REFIID,LPVOID FAR *) ;
        STDMETHOD_(ULONG,AddRef)() ;
        STDMETHOD_(ULONG,Release)() ;
        STDMETHOD_(void,OnDataChange)(FORMATETC FAR *,
                STGMEDIUM FAR *) ;
        STDMETHOD_(void,OnViewChange)(DWORD,LONG) ;
        STDMETHOD_(void,OnRename)(LPMONIKER) ;
        STDMETHOD_(void,OnSave)() ;
        STDMETHOD_(void,OnClose)() ;
    } ;
    ObjAdviseSink m_adviseSink ;

    //
    // More code omitted here!
    //
} ;

OBJASINK.CPP
Object::ObjAdviseSink::ObjAdviseSink( Object *pObj )
{
    m_pObj = pObj ;
    m_refCount = 0
```

```
}

STDMETHODIMP Object::ObjAdviseSink::QueryInterface( REFIID riid,
                    LPVOID FAR *lpVoid )
{
    return m_pObj->QueryInterface(riid,lpVoid) ;
}

STDMETHODIMP_(ULONG) Object::ObjAdviseSink::AddRef()
{
    return m_pObj->AddRef() ;
}

STDMETHODIMP_(ULONG) Object::ObjAdviseSink::Release()
{
    return m_pObj->Release() ;
}

STDMETHODIMP_(void) Object::ObjAdviseSink::OnDataChange(
        FORMATETC FAR* pFormatetc,
        STGMEDIUM FAR* pStgmed)
{
}

STDMETHODIMP_(void) Object::ObjAdviseSink::OnViewChange(
            DWORD dwAspect, LONG lindex)
{
    m_pObj->UpdateObjectSize() ;
    m_pObj->Invalidate() ;
    m_pObj->m_pDoc->SetModified( TRUE ) ;
}

STDMETHODIMP_(void) Object::ObjAdviseSink::OnRename(
    LPMONIKER pmk)
{
}

STDMETHODIMP_(void) Object::ObjAdviseSink::OnSave()
{
}

STDMETHODIMP_(void) Object::ObjAdviseSink::OnClose()
{
}
OBJCSITE.CPP
```

```
Object::ObjClientSite::ObjClientSite(Object *pObj)
{
    m_pObj = pObj ;
}

STDMETHODIMP Object::ObjClientSite::QueryInterface( REFIID riid,
            LPVOID FAR *lpVoid )
{
    return m_pObj->QueryInterface(riid,lpVoid) ;
}

STDMETHODIMP_(ULONG) Object::ObjClientSite::AddRef()
{
    return m_pObj->AddRef() ;
}

STDMETHODIMP_(ULONG) Object::ObjClientSite::Release()
{
    return m_pObj->Release() ;
}

STDMETHODIMP Object::ObjClientSite::SaveObject()
{
    return m_pObj->Save( m_pObj->m_pStg, TRUE ) ;
}

STDMETHODIMP Object::ObjClientSite::GetMoniker( DWORD dwAssign,
        DWORD dwWhichMoniker,
        LPMONIKER FAR *ppmk )
{
    *ppmk = NULL ;
    return ResultFromScode( E_FAIL ) ;
}

STDMETHODIMP Object::ObjClientSite::GetContainer(
        LPOLECONTAINER FAR* ppContainer )
{
    ppContainer = NULL ;
    return ResultFromScode(E_NOTIMPL) ;
}

STDMETHODIMP Object::ObjClientSite::ShowObject()
{
    m_pObj->m_pDoc->MakeRectVisible( &m_pObj->m_objRect ) ;
    return NOERROR ;
```

```
    }

    STDMETHODIMP Object::ObjClientSite::OnShowWindow( BOOL fShow )
    {
        m_pObj->m_objWinOpen = fShow ;
        if( !fShow ) {
            BringWindowToTop( m_pObj->m_pDoc->m_hWnd ) ;
            SetFocus( m_pObj->m_pDoc->m_hWnd ) ;
        }else
            // We add our own call to ShowObject here for
            // aesthetic reasons
            ShowObject() ;
        m_pObj->Invalidate() ;
        return NOERROR ;
    }

    STDMETHODIMP Object::ObjClientSite::RequestNewObjectLayout()
    {
        return NOERROR ;
    }
```

The first thing you will notice is that the majority of the methods are not implemented. These methods are not required for our basic container. The IOleClientSite::On-ShowWindow() and IOleClientSite::ShowObject() methods are the only two significant methods in our client-site interface. In the IAdviseSink interface, we have implemented the OnViewChange() method. The details of what these methods do and how they are used will become clear in the section "Handling Notifications" later in this chapter.

Clipboard Operations

The clipboard operations are the heart of supporting OLE. This section discusses the basics of implementing the File ➤ Paste and File ➤ Copy operations.

Implementing the Paste Function

Conceptually, the Paste operation involves obtaining a reference to the object on the clipboard, making a copy of it, and storing it locally in your application's storage (see Figure 7.12).

FIGURE 7.12:

Conceptual diagram of the Paste operation

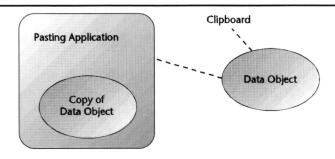

The Paste operation always starts when some application puts a data object on the clipboard. (Later in this chapter you will learn what it means to put a data object on the clipboard.) It is then up to your application to enable/disable the Paste menu item based on the presence of an appropriate data object and also to handle the actual Paste operation.

Enabling the Paste Menu Item

Enabling the Paste menu item is an important part of any application and should be handled carefully. For our purposes we will enable the Paste menu item whenever any data object is present. Examine the following code:

```
...
theApp.EnableMenu( IDM_FILE_SAVE,
    ((m_dirty)?MF_ENABLED:MF_GRAYED)) ;
...
BOOL Document::CanPaste()
{

    BOOL canPaste = FALSE ;
    LPDATAOBJECT pDataObject ;

    m_pasteStatic = FALSE ;

    HRESULT hErr = OleGetClipboard( &pDataObject ) ;
    if( SUCCEEDED( hErr ) ) {
        HRESULT hErr = OleQueryCreateFromData(
                pDataObject ) ;
        if( GetScode( hErr ) == S_OK ) {
```

```
            canPaste = TRUE ;
        }else if( GetScode( hErr ) == OLE_S_STATIC ) {
            canPaste = TRUE ;
            m_pasteStatic = TRUE ;
        }
        pDataObject->Release() ;
    }

    return canPaste ;
}
```

This code supports enabling and disabling the Paste menu item whenever a document window becomes active or the application is made active. This is important since the state of the clipboard can change when your application is not active. The first line of this code uses our single instance of the application class theApp to call the Application::EnableMenu() method. The reason we have a method like this is to support setting the state of the menu, as well as the appropriate toolbar button. When we set the state for the Paste button, we use the Document::CanPaste() method to determine whether or not we can enable the Paste menu item. Although this method will become more complex later on in the book, all it must do now is obtain access to the data object on the clipboard by calling OleGetClipboard() and then asking OLE whether it can create an embedded object from this data object on the clipboard by calling OleQueryCreateFromData(). This routine will return S_OK if you can create an embedded object from the data object. It could also possibly return an OLE_S_STATIC success result, but we will discuss this in the section on pasting static objects a little later, in the section "Pasting Static Objects from the Clipboard."

Once we are done with the data object, we must release it. Notice that just obtaining a data object from the clipboard does not mean you can create an OLE object. If anything at all exists on the clipboard, you will obtain a data object. A *data object* is an object that supports the IDataObject interface. This interface supports a collection of methods that allow you to access and manipulate the contents of the clipboard, but we will discuss this interface in more detail later, in the section "Copying Objects to the Clipboard."

Pasting Objects from the Clipboard

The process of pasting an object from the clipboard starts off by obtaining access to the clipboard as well. Take a look at the following code:

```
void Document::OnEditPaste()
{

    // paste object from the clipboard
    LPDATAOBJECT pDataObject ;
    HRESULT hErr = OleGetClipboard( &pDataObject ) ;
    if( SUCCEEDED(GetScode(hErr)) ) {

    POINT pt = { 0, 0 } ;
    CreateFromDataObject( pDataObject, pt ) ;

    // Release the data object
    pDataObject->Release( ) ;

    SetModified( TRUE ) ;
    }
}
```

This code starts out by obtaining the data object using `OleGetClipboard()` as well. The difference is that now we will actually use the data object to create a copy of the object. The routine `CreateFromDataObject()` in our application takes care of the details of creating the embedded object.

The `CreateFromDataObject()` routine gets a little complex, so let's take it one step at a time. This routine starts by creating an instance of our `Object` class. It also does some initialization of this class by setting a pointer back to the new `Objects` document class and assigning an object ID. This will become important in a minute, when we assign the storage for the object.

After initializing our new `Object`, we call the routine `OpenStorageForObject()`. As you may remember from Part II of this book, there are a number of different ways to handle this. The important thing to note is that no matter what you do, you *must* have a storage of some sort to pass off to the object when you create it. We could just as easily have created a storage on a memory handle and used that. Instead, we create a child storage directly in the OLE Publishers data file, using the object ID to give the object a distinct name. This also means that when we save the document, we must store the last-used object ID as a seed so that we don't reuse object IDs in the document.

After creating the storage, we call the `Object::CreateFromDataObject()` method to allow it to perform the rest of the steps necessary to create an embedded object. (I have layered the steps for performing the creation to give you a sense of the level at which the steps are taking place.) The document is responsible for assigning a storage location in the document and providing a place on the screen for it to display itself. After these steps, the object can take care of itself.

The `Object::CreateFromDataObject()` method now takes care of the remaining details of creating the object. The actual creation of the new object is handled by an OLE routine called `OleCreateFromData()`. However, to use this routine we must provide some initial information—at a minimum, a storage for the new object and a pointer to our client-site interface.

NOTE It is not actually necessary to pass this information to the `OleCreate-FromData()` routine, but even if you do not, you must use one of the object's methods to set the storage and client site for the object before the object can be used effectively.

The following code is responsible for almost all new objects that get created in our container:

```
BOOL Object::CreateFromDataObject( POINT pt,
            LPDATAOBJECT pDataObject,
            HGLOBAL hMetaPict )
{
    // Create the client site
    HRESULT hErr ;
    LPOLECLIENTSITE pClientSite ;
    QueryInterface( IID_IOleClientSite,
        (LPVOID *)&pClientSite ) ;

    if( !m_isStatic ) {
        // Create from data object
        hErr = OleCreateFromData( pDataObject,
            IID_IOleObject,
            OLERENDER_DRAW,
            NULL,
```

```
            pClientSite,
            m_pStg,
            (LPVOID *)&m_pOleObj ) ;

    }else{
        // Create static from data object
        hErr = OleCreateStaticFromData( pDataObject,
            IID_IOleObject,
            OLERENDER_DRAW,
            NULL,
            pClientSite,
            m_pStg,
            (LPVOID *)&m_pOleObj ) ;
    }

    if( FAILED( GetScode( hErr ) ) ) {
        Error( "Failed to create object!" ) ;
        return FALSE ;
    }

    // Set the aspect
    HGLOBAL hMem ;
    STGMEDIUM stgMedium ;

    if( hMem = OleStdGetData( pDataObject,
        RegisterClipboardFormat( CF_OBJECTDESCRIPTOR ),
        NULL,
        DVASPECT_CONTENT,
        &stgMedium ) ) {

        LPOBJECTDESCRIPTOR pObjDesc ;
        pObjDesc = (LPOBJECTDESCRIPTOR)GlobalLock(
            hMem ) ;

        if( hMetaPict == NULL &&
            pObjDesc->dwDrawAspect == DVASPECT_ICON )
            m_dvAspect = DVASPECT_ICON ;

        GlobalUnlock( hMem ) ;
        ReleaseStgMedium( &stgMedium ) ;

        if( hMetaPict == NULL ) {
            // Now get the metafile pict
            if( m_dvAspect == DVASPECT_ICON ) {
                hMetaPict = OleStdGetData(
```

```
                        pDataObject,
                        CF_METAFILEPICT,
                        NULL,
                        DVASPECT_ICON,
                        &stgMedium ) ;
                if( hMetaPict == NULL )
                        m_dvAspect = DVASPECT_CONTENT ;
            }
        }else{
            stgMedium.tymed = TYMED_MFPICT ;
            stgMedium.hGlobal = hMetaPict ;
            stgMedium.pUnkForRelease = NULL ;
            m_dvAspect = DVASPECT_ICON ;
        }
    }

    // If iconic aspect, then change display aspect
    if( m_dvAspect == DVASPECT_ICON ) {

        DWORD dw = DVASPECT_CONTENT ;
        BOOL fMustUpdate ;
        OleStdSwitchDisplayAspect( m_pOleObj,
                &dw,
                DVASPECT_ICON,
                hMetaPict,
                TRUE,
                FALSE,
                NULL,
                &fMustUpdate ) ;

        if( hMetaPict != NULL )
            ReleaseStgMedium( &stgMedium ) ;
    }

    // Create view and persist interfaces
    m_pView = (LPVIEWOBJECT)OleStdQueryInterface(
        (LPUNKNOWN)m_pOleObj, IID_IViewObject ) ;
    m_pPs =   (LPPERSISTSTORAGE)OleStdQueryInterface(
        (LPUNKNOWN)m_pOleObj, IID_IPersistStorage ) ;

    // Setup advise
    SetHostNames( ) ;

    // Recalculate rects
    SIZEL sizel ;
```

```
m_pOleObj->GetExtent( m_dvAspect, &sizel ) ;
HDC hDC = GetDC( m_pDoc->m_hWnd ) ;
Move( pt.x, pt.y,
    MAP_LOGHIM_TO_PIX(sizel.cx,
    GetDeviceCaps(hDC,LOGPIXELSX)),
    MAP_LOGHIM_TO_PIX(sizel.cy,
    GetDeviceCaps(hDC,LOGPIXELSY))) ;
ReleaseDC( m_pDoc->m_hWnd, hDC ) ;

return TRUE ;
}
```

NOTE   This routine is slightly different on the companion disk because we will be adding more features in later chapters, but you can still see how this routine functions. This also happens to be one of the more complicated routines in the program because it is responsible for creating data objects in a variety of ways from several sources.

If you examine the `Object::CreateFromDataObject()` routine, you will notice that immediately after it calls the `OleCreateFromData()` routine there is a section of code that examines the data object and finally calls `OleStdSwitchDisplay-Aspect()`. This code supports the ability to display objects as icons. What this means is that when an object is created, we either decide, through a user-interface dialog such as the Insert Object dialog or by examining the `CF_OBJECTDESCRIPTOR` format, that the object wants to be displayed as an icon. Either way, we must then obtain the metafile that represents the icon (note that it is not an HICON because it must also include a label) and then make sure the object's cache contains the iconic representation. The first trick is to determine whether it should be displayed as an icon. There are two situations in which it should:

- When the routine is passed a pointer to a metafile, it should be displayed as an iconic format.

- If the `CF_OBJECTDESCRIPTOR` structure has its `dwDrawAspect` member set to `DVASPECT_ICON`, it must be displayed as an icon.

If we did not receive a pointer to a metafile, we must obtain one by calling the `OleStdGetData()` routine. This routine is in the OLE 2 User-Interface Library, and we could have just called `pDataObject->GetData()`, but the helper routines clean up after themselves, making the code easier to read. After determining that it should be displayed as an icon and obtaining the metafile, you need only call another OLE 2 User-Interface Library routine, called `OleStdSwitchDisplay-Aspect()`. This routine mainly replaces the current cached representation of the object with the iconic representation. The routine uses the `IOleCache` interface from the object to switch the display aspect. (The details of this interface are left as a research project for the reader.)

Pasting Static Objects from the Clipboard

In the code that was presented to enable the Edit ➤ Paste menu item, there was a case we did not discuss—where `OleQueryCreateFromData()` returned a result of `OLE_S_STATIC`. This happens when the formats required to create a full OLE embedded object are not present, but a metafile, bitmap, or device-independent bitmap is present on the clipboard. When this occurs, we set a flag, `m_pasteStatic`, for convenience and use the routine `OleCreateStaticFromData()` exactly the way we used the `OleCreateFromData()` routine discussed earlier in this chapter. This creates an object that can display itself but that cannot be activated. Because it cannot be activated, we save the routine.

Copying Objects to the Clipboard

Copying objects back to the clipboard is a little more complicated than a Paste operation. When we pasted an object from the clipboard, we first had to obtain an `IDataObject` using `OleGetClipboard()`. And that's where we need to start with the Copy operation, but first, let's look at some subtleties of the operation.

The first thing to realize is that all OLE objects must implement the `IDataObject` interface. This means we can call `IUnknown::QueryInterface()` on an object, specifying the `IID_IDataObject` interface. Earlier in this chapter we discussed the GenericObject API Copy operation, when we made a complete copy of the object on a storage data structure that represented the clipboard. Because we do not want to put a live copy of the object on the clipboard, we must make a copy of it first and then place the copy on the clipboard (see Figure 7.13).

FIGURE 7.13:

Conceptual diagram of a Copy operation

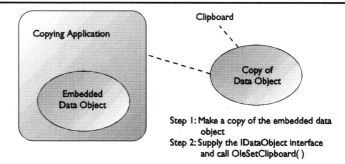

Step 1: Make a copy of the embedded data object

Step 2: Supply the IDataObject interface and call OleSetClipboard( )

All that needs to go on the clipboard is an `IDataObject` that supports the following methods:

```
IDataObject::GetData()
IDataObject::QueryGetData()
IDataObject::GetDataHere()
IDataObject::EnumFormatEtc()
```

Of course, the `IDataObject::EnumFormatEtc()` method must return an interface pointer to an `IEnumFORMATETC` interface, but in our case that is an extremely easy interface to implement. Here is the code for our data object:

```
IDATAOBJ.H
///////////////////////////////////////////////////
// IDataObject Class Header: IDATAOBJ.H
//
#ifndef _idataobj_h_
#define _idataobj_h_

// This header file includes our data object source
// as well as the corresponding
// implementation of EnumFORMATETC
// All source for these classes
// is contained within IDATAOBJ.CPP
//
class GenericDataObject : public IDataObject {
public:

    ULONG m_refCount ;
    LPFORMATETC m_pFmtEtc ;
    LPSTGMEDIUM m_pStgMedium ;
```

```
        UINT m_count ;

        // Internal methods
        int FindMatchingFormat( LPFORMATETC pformatetcIn ) ;

        // Constructor destructor
        GenericDataObject( LPFORMATETC pFmtEtc,
            LPSTGMEDIUM pStgMedium,
        UINT count ) ;
        ~GenericDataObject( ) ;

        // IUnknown methods
        STDMETHOD(QueryInterface)( REFIID riid,
            LPVOID FAR *ppvObj ) ;
        STDMETHOD_(ULONG,AddRef)() ;
        STDMETHOD_(ULONG,Release)() ;

        // IDataObject methods
        STDMETHOD(GetData)( LPFORMATETC pformatetcIn,
            LPSTGMEDIUM pmedium ) ;
        STDMETHOD(GetDataHere)( LPFORMATETC pformatetc,
            LPSTGMEDIUM pmedium ) ;
        STDMETHOD(QueryGetData)( LPFORMATETC pformatetc ) ;
        STDMETHOD(GetCanonicalFormatEtc)(
            LPFORMATETC pformatetc,
            LPFORMATETC pformatetcOut) ;
        STDMETHOD(SetData)( LPFORMATETC pformatetc,
            STGMEDIUM FAR * pmedium,
            BOOL fRelease) ;
        STDMETHOD(EnumFormatEtc)( DWORD dwDirection,
            LPENUMFORMATETC FAR* ppenumFormatEtc) ;

        STDMETHOD(DAdvise)( FORMATETC FAR* pFormatetc,
            DWORD advf,
            LPADVISESINK pAdvSink,
            DWORD FAR* pdwConnection) ;
        STDMETHOD(DUnadvise)( DWORD dwConnection) ;
        STDMETHOD(EnumDAdvise)( LPENUMSTATDATA FAR* ppenumAdvise) ;
} ;

class GenericEnumFormatETC : public IEnumFORMATETC {
public:

    int m_index ;
    ULONG m_refCount ;
```

```
    GenericDataObject *m_pDataObject ;

    // Constructor destructors
    GenericEnumFormatETC(
        GenericDataObject *pDataObject ) ;
    ~GenericEnumFormatETC( ) ;

    // IUnknown methods
    STDMETHOD(QueryInterface)( REFIID riid,
        LPVOID FAR *ppvObj ) ;
    STDMETHOD_(ULONG,AddRef)() ;
    STDMETHOD_(ULONG,Release)() ;

    // IEnumFORMATETC methods
    STDMETHOD(Next)( ULONG celt,
        FORMATETC FAR *rgelt,
        ULONG FAR *pceltFetched ) ;
    STDMETHOD(Skip)( ULONG celt ) ;
    STDMETHOD(Reset)( ) ;
    STDMETHOD(Clone)(IEnumFORMATETC FAR * FAR *ppenum) ;
} ;

IDATAOBJ.CPP
///////////////////////////////////////////////////
// IDataObject Class Source: IDATAOBJ.CPP
//
#include "appl.h"
#include "idataobj.h"

// Constructor/Destructor
GenericDataObject::GenericDataObject( LPFORMATETC pFmtEtc,
            LPSTGMEDIUM pStgMedium,
            UINT count )
{
    m_refCount = 0 ;
    m_pFmtEtc = pFmtEtc ;
    m_pStgMedium = pStgMedium ;
    m_count = count ;
}

GenericDataObject::~GenericDataObject( )
{
    // release all storage media
    for(int i=0;i<m_count;i++)
        ReleaseStgMedium(&m_pStgMedium[i]) ;
```

```
    // Free the allocated memory
    LPMALLOC pMalloc ;
    CoGetMalloc( MEMCTX_TASK,&pMalloc ) ;
    pMalloc->Free( m_pStgMedium ) ;
    pMalloc->Free( m_pFmtEtc ) ;
    pMalloc->Release() ;
}

// IUnknown methods
STDMETHODIMP GenericDataObject::QueryInterface(
        REFIID riid, LPVOID FAR *ppvObj )
{
    if( riid == IID_IDataObject ||
        riid == IID_IUnknown ) {
        *ppvObj = this ;
        AddRef() ;
        return NOERROR ;
    }
    *ppvObj = NULL ;
    return ResultFromScode(E_NOINTERFACE) ;
}

STDMETHODIMP_(ULONG) GenericDataObject::AddRef()
{
    return ++m_refCount ;
}

STDMETHODIMP_(ULONG) GenericDataObject::Release()
{
    if(--m_refCount == 0 ) {
        delete this ;
        return 0 ;
    }
    return m_refCount ;
}

// IDataObject methods
STDMETHODIMP GenericDataObject::GetData(
        LPFORMATETC pformatetcIn,
        LPSTGMEDIUM pmedium )
{
    int match = FindMatchingFormat( pformatetcIn ) ;
    if( match < 0 )
        return ResultFromScode( DATA_E_FORMATETC ) ;
```

149

```
        AddRef() ;
        *pmedium = m_pStgMedium[match] ;
        pmedium->pUnkForRelease = this ;

        return NOERROR ;
}

STDMETHODIMP GenericDataObject::GetDataHere(
        LPFORMATETC pformatetcIn,
        LPSTGMEDIUM pmedium )
{
    if( pformatetcIn->tymed != TYMED_ISTORAGE )
        return ResultFromScode( DATA_E_FORMATETC ) ;

    int match = FindMatchingFormat( pformatetcIn ) ;
    if( match < 0 )
        return ResultFromScode( DATA_E_FORMATETC ) ;

        return m_pStgMedium[match].pstg->
            CopyTo(0,0,0,pmedium->pstg ) ;
}

STDMETHODIMP GenericDataObject::QueryGetData(
        LPFORMATETC pformatetcIn )
{
    int match = FindMatchingFormat( pformatetcIn ) ;
    if( match < 0 )
        return ResultFromScode( S_FALSE ) ;

        return NOERROR ;
}

STDMETHODIMP GenericDataObject::GetCanonicalFormatEtc(
        LPFORMATETC pformatetc,
        LPFORMATETC pformatetcOut)
{
    return ResultFromScode(DATA_S_SAMEFORMATETC) ;
}

STDMETHODIMP GenericDataObject::SetData(
        LPFORMATETC pformatetc,
        STGMEDIUM FAR * pmedium,
        BOOL fRelease)
{
```

```
        return ResultFromScode(E_FAIL) ;
}

STDMETHODIMP GenericDataObject::EnumFormatEtc(
        DWORD dwDirection,
        LPENUMFORMATETC FAR* ppenumFormatEtc)
{
    if( dwDirection == DATADIR_SET )
        return ResultFromScode(S_FALSE) ;
    *ppenumFormatEtc = new GenericEnumFormatETC( this ) ;
    (*ppenumFormatEtc)->AddRef() ;
    return NOERROR ;
}

int GenericDataObject::FindMatchingFormat(
    LPFORMATETC pformatetcIn )
{
    for(int i=0;i<m_count;i++)
        if( pformatetcIn->cfFormat ==
            m_pFmtEtc[i].cfFormat &&
            pformatetcIn->tymed & m_pFmtEtc[i].tymed &&
            pformatetcIn->dwAspect ==
            m_pFmtEtc[i].dwAspect )
            return i ;
    return -1 ;
}

STDMETHODIMP GenericDataObject::DAdvise(
        FORMATETC FAR* pFormatetc,
        DWORD advf,
        LPADVISESINK pAdvSink,
        DWORD FAR* pdwConnection)
{
    return ResultFromScode(OLE_E_ADVISENOTSUPPORTED) ;
}

STDMETHODIMP GenericDataObject::DUnadvise(
        DWORD dwConnection)
{
    return ResultFromScode(OLE_E_NOCONNECTION) ;
}

STDMETHODIMP GenericDataObject::EnumDAdvise(
        LPENUMSTATDATA FAR* ppenumAdvise)
{
```

```
        return ResultFromScode(OLE_E_ADVISENOTSUPPORTED) ;
}

// Constructor destructor
GenericEnumFormatETC::GenericEnumFormatETC(
    GenericDataObject *pDataObject )
{
    m_refCount = 0 ;
    m_index = 0 ;
    m_pDataObject = pDataObject ;
}

GenericEnumFormatETC::~GenericEnumFormatETC()
{
}

// IUnknown methods
HRESULT GenericEnumFormatETC::QueryInterface(
        REFIID riid, LPVOID FAR *ppvObj )
{
    if( riid == IID_IEnumFORMATETC ||
        riid == IID_IUnknown ) {
        *ppvObj = this ;
        AddRef( ) ;
        return NOERROR ;
    }
    *ppvObj = NULL ;
    return ResultFromScode(E_NOINTERFACE) ;
}

ULONG GenericEnumFormatETC::AddRef()
{
    return ++m_refCount ;
}

ULONG GenericEnumFormatETC::Release()
{
    if(--m_refCount == 0 ) {
        delete this ;
        return 0 ;
    }
    return m_refCount ;
}

// IEnumFORMATETC methods
```

```
HRESULT GenericEnumFormatETC::Next( ULONG celt,
        FORMATETC FAR *rgelt,
        ULONG FAR *pceltFetched )
{
    if( m_index >= m_pDataObject->m_count )
        return ResultFromScode( S_FALSE ) ;

    if( celt != 1 && pceltFetched == NULL )
        return ResultFromScode( E_UNEXPECTED ) ;

    UINT numFmts = m_pDataObject->m_count - m_index ;

    numFmts = (numFmts<celt)? numFmts : celt ;
    for(int i=0;i<numFmts;i++,m_index++)
        rgelt[i] = m_pDataObject->m_pFmtEtc[m_index] ;

    if( pceltFetched != NULL ) *pceltFetched = numFmts ;

    return ResultFromScode( S_OK ) ;
}

HRESULT GenericEnumFormatETC::Skip( ULONG celt )
{
    UINT numFmts = m_pDataObject->m_count - m_index ;
    numFmts = (numFmts<celt)? numFmts : celt ;
    if( celt != numFmts ) ResultFromScode( S_FALSE ) ;

    return NOERROR ;
}

HRESULT GenericEnumFormatETC::Reset()
{
    m_index = 0 ;
    return NOERROR ;
}

HRESULT GenericEnumFormatETC::Clone(
        IEnumFORMATETC FAR * FAR *ppenum )
{
    GenericEnumFormatETC *pEnum =
        new GenericEnumFormatETC( m_pDataObject ) ;
    pEnum->m_index = m_index ;
    pEnum->AddRef( ) ;
    *ppenum = pEnum ;
    return NOERROR ;
```

```
    }

    #endif
```

After the `IDataObject` interface is implemented, it is a small matter to copy one of our embedded objects to the clipboard. The following code does exactly that by making a copy of one of our objects and storing the data in our `IDataObject`:

```
LPDATAOBJECT Object::CreateTransferDataObject( POINT pt )
{
    POINTL pointl ;
    pointl.x = pt.x ;
    pointl.y = pt.y ;

#define NUMFORMATS3

    LPFORMATETC pformats = NULL ;
    LPSTGMEDIUM pmediums = NULL ;
    LPMALLOC pmalloc = NULL ;
    LPSTORAGE pStg ;

    HRESULT hErr = StgCreateDocfile( NULL,
                    STGM_DFALL |
                    STGM_CREATE |
                    STGM_DELETEONRELEASE,
                    0, &pStg ) ;
    if( FAILED( hErr ) ) return NULL ;

    // Now save the entire contents of
    // the object to the new temp storage
    Save( pStg, FALSE ) ;

    CoGetMalloc(MEMCTX_TASK,&pmalloc) ;
    pformats =
    (LPFORMATETC)pmalloc->
        Alloc(sizeof(FORMATETC)*NUMFORMATS) ;
    pmediums = (LPSTGMEDIUM)pmalloc->
        Alloc(sizeof(STGMEDIUM)*NUMFORMATS) ;
    if( pformats == NULL || pmediums == NULL )
        return NULL ;

    int fmtidx = 0 ;

    // Set the CF_EMBEDDEDOBJECT
    pformats[fmtidx].cfFormat = RegisterClipboardFormat(
```

```
        CF_EMBEDDEDOBJECT ) ;
pformats[fmtidx].dwAspect = m_dvAspect ;
pformats[fmtidx].ptd = NULL ;
pformats[fmtidx].lindex = -1 ;
pmediums[fmtidx].tymed = TYMED_ISTORAGE ;
pmediums[fmtidx].pstg = pStg ;
pmediums[fmtidx].pUnkForRelease = NULL ;
fmtidx++ ;

// Set the CF_OBJECTDESCRIPTOR
pformats[fmtidx].cfFormat = RegisterClipboardFormat(
    CF_OBJECTDESCRIPTOR ) ;
pformats[fmtidx].ptd = NULL ;
pformats[fmtidx].dwAspect = m_dvAspect ;
pformats[fmtidx].lindex = -1 ;
pformats[fmtidx].tymed = TYMED_HGLOBAL ;
XformSizeInPixelsToHimetric( NULL,
    (LPSIZEL)&pointl, (LPSIZEL)&pointl ) ;
pmediums[fmtidx].hGlobal =
    OleStdGetObjectDescriptorDataFromOleObject(
        m_pOleObj,
        m_pDoc->m_windowTitle,
        m_dvAspect,
        pointl,
        NULL ) ;
pmediums[fmtidx].tymed = TYMED_HGLOBAL ;
pmediums[fmtidx].pUnkForRelease = NULL ;
fmtidx++ ;

// Set the cached representation
pformats[fmtidx].cfFormat = CF_METAFILEPICT ;
pformats[fmtidx].ptd = NULL ;
pformats[fmtidx].dwAspect = m_dvAspect ;
pformats[fmtidx].lindex = -1 ;
pformats[fmtidx].tymed = TYMED_MFPICT ;
LPDATAOBJECT pObjData =
    (LPDATAOBJECT)OleStdQueryInterface(
        (LPUNKNOWN)m_pOleObj, IID_IDataObject ) ;
pObjData->GetData( &pformats[fmtidx],
    &pmediums[fmtidx] ) ;
pObjData->Release() ;
fmtidx++ ;

// Create a new data object
LPDATAOBJECT pDataObject =
```

```
        new GenericDataObject(
                pformats,
                pmediums,
                NUMFORMATS ) ;
    if( pDataObject == NULL ) return NULL ;
    AddRef() ;

    return pDataObject ;
    }
```

This code takes an object and creates an IDataObject out of it. It builds up an array of FORMATETC and STGMEDIUM to both describe and store the actual data that represents the object before placing both on the clipboard. The formats stored are CF_OB-JECTDESCRIPTOR, CF_EMBEDDEDOBJECT, and the CF_METAFILEPICT format used to represent the object visually. The CF_OBJECTDESCRIPTOR is created by calling the OLE2UI routine OleStdGetObjectDescriptorFromData(), which will create a global memory handle with all the object descriptor data for you, using the pointer to the object that you pass as an argument, as well as some other information. The CF_EM-BEDDEDOBJECT format is relatively easy; the only catch is that you have to create a new temporary storage for the object. It is simply a copy of the object's data. To accomplish this, we can simply ask the object to save itself to the temporary storage.

Drawing Objects

You can draw objects directly using the IViewObject::Draw() method, or you can call the OleDraw() routine provided by OLE. We cache a copy of the IViewObject interface for the object in the member variable m_pView in the Object class. The following code is relatively straightforward in the way it calls the IViewObject::Draw() method. One interesting point, however, is the way OLE makes extensive use of very large data structures (presumably to account for future systems) such as the RECTL structure, which the IViewObject interface takes as an argument. This requires us to convert the standard RECT that we use to save the object's position in the document before drawing the object:

```
void Object::Draw( HDC hDC, BOOL fSelected )
{
    // First check to see if the item is in the clip region
    if( !RectVisible( hDC, &m_objRect ) ) return ;
```

```
// Draw the item
RECTL rectl ;
rectl.top = m_objRect.top ;
rectl.bottom = m_objRect.bottom ;
rectl.left = m_objRect.left ;
rectl.right = m_objRect.right ;
m_pView->Draw( m_dvAspect,
               -1,
               NULL,
               NULL,
               NULL,
               hDC,
               &rectl,
               NULL,
               NULL,
               0L ) ;

// If the object was selected, then draw the handles
if( fSelected )
    OleUIDrawHandles( &m_objRect, hDC,
            OLEUI_HANDLES_INSIDE,
            6, TRUE ) ;

// If the object is currently being shown
// then draw the show object effect
if( m_objWinOpen )
    OleUIDrawShading( &m_objRect, hDC,
        OLEUI_SHADE_FULLRECT, 1 ) ;

// Update the clipping region
ExcludeClipRect( hDC, m_objRect.left,
                      m_objRect.top,
                      m_objRect.right,
                      m_objRect.bottom ) ;
}
```

The m_objWinOpen flag is set by our IAdviseSink interface and forces us to shade the object appropriately when the object is active. We do this using the OleUIDraw-Shading() method, which takes care of the details of making sure the object's state is indicated.

Also, we draw the resize handles on the object by using yet another OLE 2 UI Library routine, called OleUIDrawHandles(). We do this only if the object is selected, and in our case we always have at least one object selected.

When drawing the object on any device other than the screen, you should pass as much information as you can to the IViewObject::Draw() method. It has parameters for a target device descriptor, as well as an information context to be passed. These parameters may help the object render its image more appropriately when printing.

Handling Advise Notifications

The IAdviseSink interface that we implemented for our Object class handles notifications from the server, such as when the visible representation of the object changes. When this happens our object will receive an OnViewChange() notification. Our implementation is then responsible for updating any portion of the object that is visible to the user to reflect the changes that have taken place. Listing 7.2 contains the code for the IAdviseSink::OnViewChange() notification. This code calls the Object::UpdateObjectSize() method to update the size of the object using the IOleObject::GetExtent() method. The code for Object::UpdateObjectSize() follows:

```
void Object::UpdateObjectSize()
{
    // Update the size of the object
    SIZEL sizel ;
    HDC hDC = GetDC( m_pDoc->m_hWnd ) ;

    m_pOleObj->GetExtent( m_dvAspect, &sizel ) ;

    Move( m_objRect.left, m_objRect.top,
        MAP_LOGHIM_TO_PIX(sizel.cx,
        GetDeviceCaps(hDC,LOGPIXELSX)),
        MAP_LOGHIM_TO_PIX(sizel.cy,
        GetDeviceCaps(hDC,LOGPIXELSY))) ;

    ReleaseDC( m_pDoc->m_hWnd, hDC ) ;
}
```

The macro MAP_LOGHIM_TO_PIX() converts the extents that are received from the IOleObject::GetExtents() method from HIMETRIC to pixels. This macro is provided by the OLE 2 User-Interface Library in the OLESTD.H header.

Zooming the Object

A lot of applications support a zoom feature (OLE Publisher does not) that allows the user to scale objects up or down in size. This is accomplished by simply scaling the RECTL structure that is passed to the IViewObject::Draw() method. If you need to actually resize the object permanently, you should use the IOleObject::SetExtents() method. This method allows the object to optimize itself for the new display size.

Activating Objects on Double-Clicks

The OLE interface guidelines specify two ways for an object to be activated. The first is by double-clicking the object. The guidelines specify that this action should activate the object by executing the primary verb for the object. The second method is to activate the object by selecting one of its verbs from a special menu created just for that purpose. We will discuss the first method here. The second is covered later in this chapter, in the section "Object Verb Menu."

Calling IOleObject::DoVerb()

The IOleObject::DoVerb() method activates the object. When you call this method, it takes as its only argument a constant value that specifies which verb or action you want the object to execute. Table 7.5 lists the constants that can be passed to this routine.

The following code is used by OLE Publisher to activate the object. (This code can be found in OBJACTIV.CPP).

```
void Object::Activate( DWORD verb )
{
    // Cannot activate static objects
    if( m_isStatic ) return ;

    // Convert the rect for the item
    // from the logical coordinate
    // space to the local coordinate space
    RECT cvtRect = m_objRect ;
    m_pDoc->VirtualToClientRect( &cvtRect ) ;
```

TABLE 7.5: DoVerb Constants

Constant	Description
OLEIVERB_PRIMARY	Indicates that the object should execute its main verb
OLEIVERB_SHOW	Causes the object to be displayed for editing. It is used for both in-place and open editing (editing in a separate window)
OLEIVERB_OPEN	Causes the object to be open edited, regardless of whether or not it can be edited in place
OLEIVERB_HIDE	Causes the object to be hidden but remain in a running state
OLEIVERB_UNACTIVATE	Causes an object to be in-place activated and displays any menus, tools, or other user-interface adornments
OLEIVERB_INPLACEACTIVATE	Causes an object to display its window in place and not display any other user-interface adornments
OLEIVERB_DISCARDUNDOSTATE	Requests the object to discard any undo state it might be maintaining

```
        // Obtain another pointer to the client site
        LPOLECLIENTSITE pClientSite ;
        QueryInterface( IID_IOleClientSite,
                (LPVOID *)&pClientSite ) ;

        theApp.HourGlassOn() ;

        HRESULT hErr = m_pOleObj->DoVerb( verb,
                NULL,
                pClientSite,
                0,
                m_pDoc->m_hWnd,
                &cvtRect ) ;
        pClientSite->Release() ;
        theApp.HourGlassOff() ;

        if( FAILED( GetScode( hErr ) ) )
            Error( "Failed to activate item!" ) ;
    }
```

Notice that we check the `m_isStatic` flag to avoid activating an object that is static. The verb passed to the `Object::Activate()` method is usually `OLEIVERB_SHOW`, which is what the system recommends for double-clicks.

> **NOTE** The details of hit-testing the objects are fairly trivial. If you're interested, examine the code in the `Document::OnLButton-DblClk()` method in the file DOCMOUSE.CPP.

User Interface Support for a Basic Container

The OLE 2 User-Interface Library provides all the dialogs needed to support the standard OLE application. This Library contains a collection of dialog routines that work very similarly to the common dialogs provided with the SDK. That is, most of the dialog routines take a structure that is filled out by the programmer and passed to a routine that executes the dialog.

Insert New Object

The Insert New Object dialog is probably the single most useful interface feature of OLE 2. This dialog provides the user with the ability to create a new object from any of the OLE servers that are registered in the database, using a simple interface in which the user selects the object type and perhaps the visual aspect of the object to be displayed.

Implementing this dialog requires you to call the `OleUIInsertObject()` routine in the OLE 2 User Interface Library. This routine takes a single argument, which is a pointer to an `OLEUIINSERTOBJECT` structure. The implementation of this routine leaves you with a lot of choices, including whether you want it to create the object for you, whether you want to support linking (more in Chapter 8 on linking), and whether you want to validate the existence of the object servers that will be placed in the list. Since this dialog uses the registration database, it is possible that servers that no longer exist could be registered. Therefore, this dialog, at the expense of creation time, can optionally validate whether or not the server is there. The code for creating and loading this dialog is in the file OBJDATA.CPP. For simplicity of implementation, we allow this dialog to create the objects for us.

Object Verb Menu

The Object verb menu is the portion of the interface that changes, depending on which object is selected. This is usually a submenu of the Edit menu that contains entries for all the verbs an object supports. The OLE 2 User-Interface Library also takes care of this requirement by supplying a routine called `OleUIAddVerbMenu()`, which automatically creates this menu for you based on a currently selected object. All you have to do is call this routine in your `WM_INITMENUPOPUP` processing. If an object is not selected, call this same routine, and it will supply the default disabled menu entry as well. The code for calling this routine is in the source file DOCMENU.CPP.

Paste Special

The Paste Special dialog is handled by the OLE 2 User Interface Library routine `OleUIPasteSpecial()`. This routine takes care of all the details of displaying the dialog and returning the information required to perform the specified Paste operation. The Paste ➤ Special dialog requires you to set up an `OLEUIPASTESPECIAL` structure, specifying the details of which formats your container can handle. Most of this structure is pretty straightforward, but it does require you to define an array of format entries that define the details of the specific clipboard formats you want listed in the dialog. Take a look at this code:

```
BOOL Object::PasteSpecial( POINT pt,
        LPDATAOBJECT pDataObject )
{
    // Initialize the paste array
    OLEUIPASTEENTRY pasteEntries[5] ;

    SETDEFAULTFORMATETC(pasteEntries[0].fmtetc,
            CF_METAFILEPICT, TYMED_MFPICT ) ;
    pasteEntries[0].lpstrFormatName="%s Object" ;
    pasteEntries[0].lpstrResultText="%s Object" ;
    pasteEntries[0].dwFlags = OLEUIPASTE_PASTE |
                OLEUIPASTE_ENABLEICON ;

    SETDEFAULTFORMATETC(pasteEntries[1].fmtetc,
```

```
            CF_METAFILEPICT, TYMED_MFPICT ) ;
    pasteEntries[1].lpstrFormatName="Metafile" ;
    pasteEntries[1].lpstrResultText="as Metafile" ;
    pasteEntries[1].dwFlags = OLEUIPASTE_PASTEONLY ;

    SETDEFAULTFORMATETC(pasteEntries[2].fmtetc,
        CF_DIB, TYMED_HGLOBAL ) ;
    pasteEntries[2].lpstrFormatName=
        "Device-Independant Bitmap" ;
    pasteEntries[2].lpstrResultText=
        "as Device-Independent Bitmap" ;
    pasteEntries[2].dwFlags = OLEUIPASTE_PASTEONLY ;

    SETDEFAULTFORMATETC(pasteEntries[3].fmtetc,
            CF_BITMAP, TYMED_GDI ) ;
    pasteEntries[3].lpstrFormatName="Bitmap" ;
    pasteEntries[3].lpstrResultText="as Bitmap" ;
    pasteEntries[3].dwFlags = OLEUIPASTE_PASTEONLY ;

    OLEUIPASTESPECIAL ps ;

    memset( &ps, O, sizeof(ps) ) ;
    ps.cbStruct = sizeof(ps) ;
    ps.hWndOwner = theApp.m_hWnd ;
    ps.dwFlags = PSF_SELECTPASTE ;
    ps.arrPasteEntries = pasteEntries ;
    ps.cPasteEntries =
        sizeof(pasteEntries)/
        sizeof(pasteEntries[0]) ;
    ps.lpSrcDataObj = pDataObject ;

    // Execute the dialog
    if( OleUIPasteSpecial(&ps) ) {

        m_isStatic = (ps.nSelectedIndex!=0) ;

        return CreateFromDataObject( ps.fLink,
                        pt, ps.lpSrcDataObj,
                        ps.hMetaPict ) ;
    }
    return FALSE ;
}
```

The OLEUIPASTEENTRY array contains the list of formats that OLE Publisher will support. Each entry includes a format name, as well as a string that is used in the dialog to describe the format the user has selected. The dwFlags member specifies the details of how that entry is to be treated. For all the non-OLE formats, you will usually specify that the entry is OLEUIPASTE_PASTEONLY. The first entry in this array accounts for the embedded object data formats. The format we request for this entry is the CF_METAFILEPICT format. For this format we set the flag's parameter to OLEUIPASTE_PASTE | OLEUIPASTE_ENABLEICON. This allows the user to specify that the embedded object should be pasted with an iconic display aspect.

What We've Learned So Far

All basic containers must implement the IOleClientSite and IAdviseSink interfaces. The IOleClientSite interface is called by the object to request services from the container. These services include saving the object using the IOleClientSite::SaveObject() method, making the object visible using IOleClientSite::ShowObject(), and indicating that the object is being edited through the IOleClientSite::OnShowWindow() method. When the object's window is being shown, it is up to the container to repaint the object so that it is shaded according to the OLE 2 User-Interface guidelines. The IAdviseSink method is a container-implemented interface that the object calls to inform the container of changes to various aspects of the object's state. For a basic container, the only method of major concern is IAdviseSink::OnViewChange(). A call to this method indicates that the visual aspect of the object has changed.

The object-implemented interfaces used by a basic container include the IOleObject, IPersistStorage, and IViewObject interfaces. The IOleObject interface gets and sets various aspects of the object's state, such as the extents. The IPersistStorage interface is used by the container when saving and loading the object. This interface is sometimes used directly, as in the case of calling the IPersistStorage::SaveCompleted() method, and it is sometimes used indirectly, by the OleSave() and OleLoad() helper functions. The IViewObject interface simply draws the object.

For a container to transfer objects by means of the clipboard, the container must use the IDataObject interface and the helper functions OleGetClipboard() and OleSetClipboard(). When the user requests to paste the contents of the clipboard, you obtain a pointer to an IDataObject and call OleCreateFromData() or OleCreateStaticFromData() to actually create the object. Which one of these routines you call depends on the return result from the `OleQueryCreateFromData()` routine, which indicates whether a static object or a fully embeddable object is on the clipboard. For a Copy operation, things are a little more complex. First, you must implement your own `IDataObject` interface in order to place an object on the clipboard. You must also supply the formats needed to represent an embedded object and be able to respond to the requests by other containers to obtain specified formats from the clipboard using `IDataObject::GetData()`.

The only thing left to do at this point is some basic user-interface support, obtained by calling the appropriate routines in the OLE 2 User-Interface Library. These routines include Edit ➤ Paste Special… and Edit ➤ Insert Object….

Summary

This chapter has covered the theory and practice of implementing a basic container. We started with a simple design model in which we used a fictional API called GenericObject, designed to parallel the OLE 2 object API, and from a practical approach, we looked at the code that provides basic container support in OLE Publisher.

We have covered the embedding aspect of object linking and embedding, and the next chapter will walk you through the details of adding both functional and user-interface support for linking to objects.

CHAPTER
EIGHT

Link Containers

- Supporting linked objects in your container

- Using the OLE User Interface Library for the Update Links dialog

- Pasting links to objects from the clipboard

- Adding the user interface for updating links

Adding support to containers for linking is the next step after using embedded objects. Embedded objects are the easy part of OLE. All of the object's native data resides locally in the container's storage. Things become dramatically more complicated when you decide to add the ability to store only a reference to data that is stored elsewhere. This sort of behavior is desirable when you want to have many references to a single source data that are updated whenever the source is changed. This is useful in workgroup situations in which several users are working on different aspects of a compound document—for example, a proposal that includes a requirements analysis, supporting illustrations, and a spreadsheet detailing the financial aspects. Using links, the three separate pieces of this document could be developed independently, with the requirements analysis document using links to the illustrations and the spreadsheet.

In several areas, supporting links causes an impact on the container's interface. These areas include the process of loading documents, of making certain additions and modifications to the Edit menu, and of adding some new dialogs. When loading documents, the container must now run through all the objects in the compound document and update any automatic links. An *automatic link* is one that should be updated whenever the data on the link changes. A *manual link* should be updated only when the user requests it. The process of updating a link involves comparing the link to the actual data to make sure the link has the most up-to-date representation of the data. If it doesn't, it is updated. In the Edit menu, the addition of the Paste Link menu item allows the user to explicitly request that a link be made instead of a new embedded object. Also, the Insert Object dialog and Paste Special dialogs should be set up to allow links. The Update Links dialog needs to be added to allow the user to maintain and manage any links in the document. And finally, the Show Objects command should provide the visual feedback required by the OLE user interface guidelines by drawing a dotted line around all linked objects.

How Do Links Work?

When you store a link to an object in a document, you are not storing the object's data. What you are actually storing in your container is a fully qualified path name to the document itself. The path name includes the class ID of the object's server, the path to the file containing the data, and a description of the data itself. Figure 8.1 illustrates a link to a range of spreadsheet cells in the spreadsheet file ROI_DATA.WKS.

Conceptual illustration of a link to a
range of cells in a spreadsheet

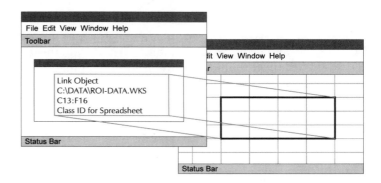

Notice that the link contains the full file name, as well as the top left and bottom
right of the spreadsheet cells. This is a simplistic view of links, but it serves to illustrate the concept.

Using Monikers to Represent Objects

If we were going to develop support for links, we would probably want to make the
links work as much like embedded objects as possible. That way we would have to add
only a small amount of code to support links into an embedding container. And that is
exactly how links are implemented. A new type of object, called a moniker, is introduced with links. *A moniker* is an object that tries to act as much as possible like an embedded object, standing in for an object that actually resides somewhere else. For
example, a moniker tries to act like an embedded object when the software activates
the object as the result of a double-click or selection of one of the object's verbs from the
Object menu. What actually happens is that the container calls the IOleObject::DoVerb() method on the moniker that represents the linked object. The
moniker is responsible for loading the server and resolving the data required to
specify the linked object. This process of resolving the different pieces of the data
reference is called *binding*.

Although the IMoniker interface in most cases is not actually used directly by a container, it is important to understand that there are different types of monikers. In fact,
there are even monikers that are composed of other monikers. Some monikers represent files (*file monikers*), and some monikers represent items in a document

(*item monikers*). These two types of monikers are very heavily used in linking, but it is not enough to use just one or the other. In most cases the system combines the two types, using a file moniker to represent the file in which a range of data is saved and using an item moniker to represent the portion of the data that is actually being linked to. This way, the process of binding a link involves asking the file moniker to load the file it represents. Then the item moniker is used to link to the actual data. You can see that each moniker type is needed to supplement the other. Without the file moniker, the item moniker would not know which file the data was in, and without an item moniker, we would always have to link to the entire file.

Finally, to keep all of these moniker types manageable, there is another type of moniker, called a *composite moniker*. This moniker class is responsible for handling just those situations that involve two or more monikers. When a process binds to a composite moniker, it in turn binds to each of the monikers it contains.

Automatic or Manual

Links can be either automatically or manually updated. This has to do with the way the cached representations of the links are updated. An automatic link has its cached representation updated when the document is loaded. The container is responsible for iterating through all the links and calling `IOleLink::Update()` to force the system to update the cache when the document is loaded. You can use the `IOleLink::GetUpdateOptions()` method to determine which update option is set for a specific link. This method allows you to change the link status. The constants that these routines support for determining the update status are `OLEUPDATE_ON-CALL` (manual) and `OLEUPDATE_ALWAYS` (automatic). The Edit Links dialog provides the user with an interface directly to this aspect of a link that allows the user to control the link updates.

The Running Object Table

Now that we have added links to the picture, we have the potential for two or more applications to be linked at once to the same data. What happens when the user tries to activate both of these links at the same time—total confusion? No. When links are used, the server must do a couple of extra things. The first link that is activated causes the server to be loaded and the linked data to be presented for editing. In the process of loading the data, the server is required to register the object with the system in the *running object table*. It is the running object table's job to make sure that two or more activated links to the same object end up using the same running version of the object. The first link that is activated causes the object that is being linked to be registered in the running object table; but when the second link is activated, the system checks the running object table and finds that the object is already loaded. At this point the second link is connected to the object that is already running.

Monikers for the Container

Although you will probably never have to call the `IMoniker` interface directly, there are several cases in which you will have to create monikers both for your documents and for the items contained in the documents. There are two main reasons to use these monikers: to inform linked objects of their location so they can attempt better link tracking when files are moved, and to support links to embedded objects in the container.

When you first load a document in your container application, you create a file moniker using the `CreateFileMoniker()` routine. A file moniker is a component object that represents a link to a document or file. After creating your file moniker, you must register the moniker with the running object table so that other applications will have access to this document while it is running.

Next, you must create an item moniker for each of the items that are loaded by calling `CreateItemMoniker()` with a name that the `IOleItemContainer` interface can use to determine exactly which object is being referenced. In this case you will not have to register the moniker with the system, but you will have to add some code to your client site to handle the `IOleClientSite::GetMoniker()` method properly. This method is called whenever the object needs information about the container in which it is residing.

Registering the Container

When supporting links to embeddings, the system must be able to load the container and obtain access to the documents it creates. This requires that we register the container with the system using techniques similar to those discussed in Chapter 3, when we created a component object. It also means we will have to support an IClassFactory interface on our container as well. The class factory will be responsible for creating new document objects that support the IPersistFile interface.

Link-Related Interfaces

In our example, we will come into contact with three link-related interfaces: IOleLink, IOleItemContainer, and IPersistFile. The IOleLink interface is provided by OLE on the object's behalf, and the IOleItemContainer interface must be provided by the container.

The IOleLink Interface

The IOleLink interface is responsible for handling most of the details of a linked object's behavior. It contains methods that allow you to determine whether a moniker is an automatic (OLEUPDATE_ALWAYS) or a manual (OLEUPDATE_ONCALL) link, methods to get and set the link source, and methods that support binding the object. You should not need to call the binding methods on this interface.

The IOleItemContainer Interface

The IOleItemContainer interface provides the information needed to support links to objects that are embedded within the container. To do this, the container has to participate by supplying this interface and supplying monikers for the container's file. The main purpose of this interface is to provide the ability for the system to retrieve a specific object by name (moniker) after the document is loaded.

The IPersistFile Interface

The IPersistFile interface is not directly involved with links but is required to support links to embedded objects. Use this interface to request that the container load a specific file containing an object that is being linked to. When a link to an embedded object in your container is activated, the system loads your application using the class ID of your container, obtains a pointer to your document object through your class factory, and uses the IPersistFile::Load() method to load the file in which the object is stored. You use this method in conjunction with the IOleItemContainer interface just described.

Adding Support for Links to OLE Publisher

Adding support for links to OLE Publisher is relatively simple. The features required to support links are the ability to

- Create links from the clipboard by calling `OleQueryCreateLinkFromData()` and `OleCreateLinkFromData()` and supporting the Edit ➤ Paste Link command

- Implement the `IOleUILinkContainer` interface defined by the OLE 2 UI Library

- Add the code to display the Edit Links dialog box

- Add the code to update the links and display the Update Links progress indicator

- Enable linking in the Insert Object dialog box

Figure 8.2 illustrates the architecture required in OLE Publisher to support links.

FIGURE 8.2:

Class architecture for OLE Publisher as a linking container

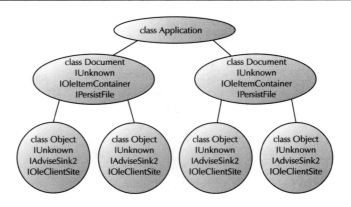

Creating Links from the Clipboard

The key to creating links from the clipboard is to know when to link and when not to. The default behavior for a Paste operation is to create an embedded object. To create a link from the clipboard, the user must select either Edit ➤Paste Link or Edit➤ Paste Special. In these situations the paste code will paste a linked object instead of an embedded object. This doesn't happen automatically, of course. In Chapter 7 we presented the code for the `Document::CreateFromDataObject()` method. This method now takes another argument that specifies whether or not to paste a link and then calls the routine `OleCreateLinkFromData()`. Then we call one of the helper routines in the User Interface Library.

Enabling the Paste Link Menu Item

To determine whether to enable the Edit ➤ Paste Link menu item, the routine –`CanPaste()` has been modified to call `OleQueryCreateLinkFromData()` to determine whether the link formats exist on the clipboard.

User Interface Support for a Link Container

The user interface requirements for a link container are relatively minor. They include the Edit Links dialog box and the Update Links indicator, as well as the ability to enable links in the Insert Object dialog.

The Edit Links Dialog Box

The Edit Links dialog box (see Figure 8.3) is one of the most difficult to implement, even with the support provided by the OLE 2 User-Interface Library. To support all the necessary functionality, you must supply a custom interface called `IOleUI-LinkContainer`. This interface allows the OLE 2 User-Interface Library to enumerate through all the links in your document and manipulate the status of the link in various ways, including toggling the link type between automatic and manual, modifying the link source, and even breaking the link.

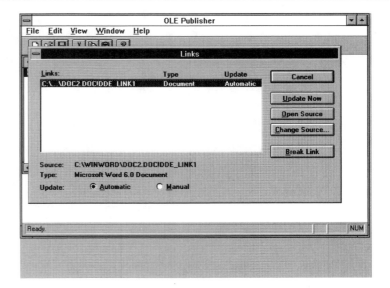

The IOleUILinkContainer Interface

Implementation of the IOleUILinkContainer interface should be handled carefully, but it isn't necessary to understand all the details of how this interface works. After you have spent a little time working with OLE and implementing support for OLE in your applications, you will begin to understand what is going on. This section provides an overview and some tips on this interface, but it is best to use the sample code provided with this book.

The IOleUILinkContainer should have easy access to the objects in your container. The reason is that the IOleUILinkContainer::GetNextLink() method is essentially an enumerator that allows the OLE 2 UI Library to enumerate the links that exist. The GetNextLink() method takes a DWORD parameter called dwLink that is initially set to 0. This is your cue to return a DWORD result that represents the first link object. On successive calls to GetNextLink(), you will be passed the previous value of `dwLink`, and it will be up to you to return the next link in your container. Since the library never actually examines the `dwLink` value, you can use it any way you like. In OLE Publisher we actually cast this value into the pointer to the `Object` class instance that represents the link we want to manipulate. This is extremely convenient since we have references to most other interfaces and information we need contained inside our `Object` class.

The `IOleUILinkContainer::GetLinkUpdateOptions()` and `IOleUILinkContainer::SetLinkUpdateOptions()` simply call the `IOleLink::GetUpdateOptions ()` and `IOleLink::SetUpdateOptions()` methods for the `Object` pointer that is passed in through `dwLink`. Of course, we also have to mark the document as modified.

The most complicated methods of this interface are the `IOleUILinkContainer::GetLinkSource()` and `IOleUILinkContainer::SetLinkSource()`. The job they perform is simple in spite of the amount of code required: they get and set the source of the link, which includes the file as well as the item information.

Finally, the `IOleUILinkContainer::OpenLinkSource()`, `UpdateLink()`, and `CancelLink()` methods activate, update, and break the link, respectively.

The Update Links Progress Indicator

The `IOleUILinkContainer` interface was designed to update the automatic links when the document is loaded so you won't have done all this work to implement a single dialog. The `OleUIUpdateLinks()` routine performs this function for you and places the dialog on the screen. After you have called this routine, if for some reason all the links were not able to be updated, you should give the user the option of opening the Edit Links dialog to fix the problem and restore the link that was causing the problem. The following code performs this function in OLE Publisher:

```
if( numLinks && !OleUIUpdateLinks( &m_linkContainer,
                    theApp.m_hWnd,
                    theApp.m_szAppName,
                    numLinks ) ) {
    if( OleUIPromptUser( IDD_CANNOTUPDATELINK,
        theApp.m_hWnd ) == ID_PU_LINKS )
        OnEditLinks() ;
}
```

If the call to OleUIUpdateLinks() fails for some reason, we call the OleUIPrompt-User() routine to display a dialog informing the user that some links could not be updated and asking whether the Edit Links dialog should be displayed. We handle this by simply calling our single implementation of this routine in Document::OnEditLinks().

The numLinks variable is initialized when we iterate through all the objects as we are loading them. After successfully loading each object, we execute this code:

```
if( pObj->m_isLink ) {
        LPOLELINK pOleLink =
                (LPOLELINK)OleStdQueryInterface(
                                (LPUNKNOWN)pObj->m_pOleObj,
                                IID_IOleLink ) ;
        DWORD linkStatus ;
        pOleLink->GetUpdateOptions( &linkStatus ) ;
        if( linkStatus == OLEUPDATE_ALWAYS )
                numLinks++ ;

        pOleLink->Release() ;
}
```

This code first determines whether the loaded object is a link by examining the saved flag m_isLink. We then obtain a pointer to the IOleLink interface by calling OleStdQueryInterface() on the object.

NOTE   The OleStdQueryInterface() routine is simply a shorthand method of obtaining interfaces. You can always call QueryInterface() on the object directly. The only real saving provided by using the OleStdQueryInterface() routine is that you do not have to check an HRESULT. OleStdQueryInterface() returns NULL if the interface is not available.

Implementing the View ➤ Objects Command

The View ➤ Objects menu command is handled by the document and maintains a BOOL value in the Document class called m_showObjects to indicate whether the

OleUIShowObject() routine should be called when drawing the objects. Whenever this menu item is toggled, we invalidate the entire visible document window to force a redraw so this routine will be called. When calling this routine, you must pass the object RECT, which we store in the Object::m_objRect member variable (the device context for drawing), and a BOOL to indicate whether or not it is a link. We store a flag called Object::m_isLink to indicate an object's link status. The following code draws the object and calls the OleUIShowObject() routine to implement this feature:

```
void Object::Draw( HDC hDC, BOOL fSelected )
{
    // First check to see if the item is in the clip region
    if( !RectVisible( hDC, &m_objRect ) ) return ;

    // Draw the item
    RECTL rectl ;
    rectl.top = m_objRect.top ;
    rectl.bottom = m_objRect.bottom ;
    rectl.left = m_objRect.left ;
    rectl.right = m_objRect.right ;
    m_pView2->Draw( m_dvAspect,
                -1,
                NULL,
                NULL,
                NULL,
                hDC,
                &rectl,
                NULL,
                NULL,
                OL ) ;

    // If the object was selected, then draw the handles
    if( fSelected )
        OleUIDrawHandles( &m_objRect, hDC,
            OLEUI_HANDLES_INSIDE,
            6, TRUE ) ;

    // If the object is currently being shown
    // then draw the show object effect
    if( m_objWinOpen )
        OleUIDrawShading( &m_objRect, hDC,
            OLEUI_SHADE_FULLRECT, 1 ) ;

    if( m_pDoc->m_showObjects )
```

```
            OleUIShowObject( &m_objRect, hDC, m_isLink ) ;

    // Update the clipping region
    ExcludeClipRect( hDC, m_objRect.left,
                m_objRect.top,
                m_objRect.right,
                m_objRect.bottom ) ;
}
```

The OleUIShowObject(&m_objRect, hDC, m_isLink) takes care of the details of this command. All we have to do is make sure that the menu toggle is handled properly and that we force a repaint when the state of the View Objects toggle is changed.

Allowing Links to Embedded Objects

Supporting links to your embedded objects is a little more involved. The first step is to add the supporting interfaces at the appropriate level of your application. These interfaces include IClassFactory, IPersistFile, and IOleItemContainer. You must also add the code to create and manage the monikers that will be needed by the system to handle links to your embedded objects.

Notice that we added the IClassFactory at the application level. It is not required that the class factory be available from the application object, although, like certain other interfaces, this seems the appropriate level to place it. The class factory creates Document objects that support the IPersistFile interface that will initialize the document using the IPersistFile::+- method.

Creating the File Monikers

For our document we will create the monikers when we open or save the file. When we do not have a file name, such as when a new document is created, we will not be able to create a moniker. After creating the moniker, we will have to register the moniker with the running object table to inform the system that the file is currently loaded. This avoids multiple attempts to load multiple copies of the file, as well as

179

saving load time if the file is already in memory. The following code is used to create the monikers for the compound documents in OLE Publisher:

```
HRESULT Document::OpenFile( LPCSTR lpszFileName )
{
    ...

    // Create and load the moniker
    CreateFileMoniker( m_fileName, &m_pMoniker ) ;
    OleStdRegisterAsRunning( this, m_pMoniker,
                &m_monikerToken ) ;
    ...
}
```

The `CreateFileMoniker()` method takes care of all the details of creating the moniker that we store in the `Document::m_pMoniker` member variable. After creating the moniker we call the `OleStdRegisterAsRunning()` method, which is a helper function provided by the OLE 2 UI Library, although registering a moniker without this function is not very complicated. The function calls `GetRunningObjectTable()`, which returns a pointer to the `IRunningObjectTable` interface. This interface is used to register the moniker in the table, after which the interface pointer is released. Since the running object table is a paired entry table, we must also supply a pointer to the `Document` object that implements the `IOleItemContainer` interface. The `m_monikerToken` parameter stores a token value we can use to remove the entry from the running object table whenever we need to change the name of the document or shut down the document.

The following code deletes the registered moniker from the running object table and creates a new moniker for the new file name. This code is executed for a File ➤ Save Aso…operation.

```
// Save the relevant information for the file
if( m_pMoniker != NULL ){
    OleStdRevokeAsRunning( &m_monikerToken ) ;
    m_pMoniker->Release() ;
}
CreateFileMoniker( m_fileName, &m_pMoniker ) ;
OleStdRegisterAsRunning( this, m_pMoniker,
            &m_monikerToken ) ;
```

Creating the Item Monikers to Support Links to Embedded Objects

Creating the item monikers is similar to creating file monikers. The differences are that the item monikers do not bind to files and that they are not registered directly by the container in the running object table. When an item moniker is created, an artificial name is generated. (For OLE Publisher, this is the same name as the child storage and is based on the ID number we assign to objects.) This name should be sufficient to locate the object through the `IOleItemContainer` that we supplied with our `Document` class. The following code creates and registers the item moniker:

```
if( m_pDoc->m_pMoniker != NULL )
    m_pOleObj->SetMoniker( OLEWHICHMK_CONTAINER,
                           m_pDoc->m_pMoniker ) ;

if( m_pMoniker != NULL ) m_pMoniker->Release() ;
char stgName[34] ;
wsprintf( stgName, "Obj%u", m_objID ) ;
CreateItemMoniker( "!", stgName, &m_pMoniker ) ;

m_pOleObj->SetMoniker( OLEWHICHMK_OBJREL,
                       m_pMoniker ) ;
```

Notice in the preceding code that we first call the `IOleObject::SetMoniker()` interface pointer that we cached in the `Object::m_pOleObj` member variable for the document's file moniker. We do this to tell the object where it is being stored. The constant value `OLEWHICHMK_CONTAINER` specifies the type of moniker being passed to the `IOleObject::SetMoniker()` method. (See Table 8.1 for a description of these constants.) This is required for containers that support linking to objects regardless of whether or not you actually support links to embedded objects; OLE uses this information to help reconstruct broken links. The second call to `SetMoniker()` specifies the relative path to the item within the container. This is why we use the `OLEWHICHMK_OBJREL` constant.

TABLE 8.1: Moniker Type Constants

Constant	Description
OLEWHICHMK_CONTAINER	Specifies that the moniker represents the container's storage. This is usually a file moniker, except in the case where a class of objects may also support embedded and linked objects
OLEWHICHMK_OBJREL	Specifies that the moniker represents the object's relative path. This is the portion of the path that locates the object within the container but does not include the container itself. This is usually an item moniker, but in some cases it may be a composite moniker for complex containers
OLEWHICHMK_OBJFULL	The full moniker for the object. It is usually a composite moniker composed of a file moniker and one or more item monikers. This constant is used in calls to the IOle-ClientSite::GetMoniker()

Updating the IOleClientSite Interface

One of the methods we ignored in the IOleClientSite interface in Chapter 7 is the IOleClientSite::GetMoniker() method. The object uses this method to request the various monikers that our container is responsible for supplying. The following code uses the monikers we previously built for the container and the items to respond to the different requests this method can receive.

```
STDMETHODIMP Object::ObjClientSite::GetMoniker(
    DWORD dwAssign,
    DWORD dwWhichMoniker,
    LPMONIKER FAR *ppmk )
{
    HRESULT hErr = NOERROR ;
    *ppmk = NULL ;

    switch( dwWhichMoniker ) {
    case OLEWHICHMK_CONTAINER:
        if( m_pObj->m_pDoc->m_pMoniker != NULL )
            *ppmk = m_pObj->m_pDoc->m_pMoniker ;
        break ;

    case OLEWHICHMK_OBJREL:
```

```
            if( m_pObj->m_pMoniker != NULL )
                *ppmk = m_pObj->m_pMoniker ;
            break ;

        case OLEWHICHMK_OBJFULL:
            if( m_pObj->m_pMoniker != NULL &&
                m_pObj->m_pDoc->m_pMoniker != NULL )
                CreateGenericComposite(
                        m_pObj->m_pDoc->m_pMoniker,
                        m_pObj->m_pMoniker, ppmk ) ;
            break ;
    }

    if( *ppmk == NULL )    hErr = ResultFromScode( E_FAIL ) ;
    else (*ppmk)->AddRef() ;

    return hErr ;
}
```

The constants for the dwAssign parameter for this method are listed in Table 8.2. (They are provided for symmetry, even though we do not use them in our implementation.) Since the monikers in OLE Publisher exist at all times, we will have no problem complying with any of the OLEGETMONIKER_constant requests.

TABLE 8.2: Get Moniker Constants

Constant	Description
OLEGETMONIKER_ONLYIFTHERE	Informs the called function that if the moniker is not already assigned, it should not create it
OLEGETMONIKER_FORCEASSIGN	Informs the called function that it should assign a moniker if one does not already exist
OLEGETMONIKER_UNASSIGN	Provided as an optimization. It informs the container that it no longer needs to hold onto the moniker
OLEGETMONIKER_TEMPFORUSER	Specifies that a temporary moniker should be created. It is used for drag-and-drop and clipboard operations

The Registration File

The registration file for our object is very simple and only serves the purpose of registering a class ID for the container so the system can load it on demand.

WARNING For the purposes of this book, lines in the following code have been limited to 65 characters. However, for this code to compile correctly, there need to be no artificial line breaks.

```
REGEDIT

Registration info for OLE Publisher

Local Server Definition

HKEY_CLASSES_ROOT\OlePublisher = Ole Publisher
HKEY_CLASSES_ROOT\OlePublisher\Clsid = {00026202-0000-0000-
    C000-000000000046}
HKEY_CLASSES_ROOT\CLSID\{00026202-0000-0000-C000-
    000000000046} = Ole Publisher
HKEY_CLASSES_ROOT\CLSID\{00026202-0000-0000-C000-
    000000000046}\ProgID = OlePublisher
HKEY_CLASSES_ROOT\CLSID\{00026202-0000-0000-C000-
    000000000046} \LocalServer = C:\DEV\OLEAPP\OLEAPP.EXE
```

This is a minimal registration file that does nothing more than provide the system with access to our OLE system. We have to specify all entries in the registration database at the root-level key, which is explicitly specified using HKEY_CLASSES_ROOT. First, we add a main key that uses a short name (with no embedded spaces) to indicate our application's entry in this database. Under this main key is a single entry for our class ID. The remaining keys are under HKEY_CLASSES_ROOT\Clsid\, which specifies the class ID of the application, an entry for the ProgID, and, finally, an entry for the path to our container, which, by virtue of not being a DLL, is a Local-Server. Having the dual entries allows the system to locate an entry either by an application's short name or by its class ID.

The IPersistFile Interface for OLE Publisher

The IPersistFile interface is required to support linking to embedded objects just to provide a method for loading and unloading documents. This interface contains methods to load, save, and obtain the currently open file name, as well as the modified status of the current file. It also contains a method to determine the class ID for the document. The following code implements this interface in OLE Publisher:

```
#include "appl.h"
#include "doc.h"
#include "obj.h"

Document::DocPersistFile::DocPersistFile( Document *pDoc )
{
    m_pDoc = pDoc ;
    m_refCount = 0
}

STDMETHODIMP Document::DocPersistFile::QueryInterface(
            REFIID riid,
            LPVOID FAR *lpVoid )
{
    return m_pDoc->QueryInterface(riid,lpVoid) ;
}

STDMETHODIMP_(ULONG) Document::DocPersistFile::AddRef()
{
    m_refCount ++
    return m_pDoc->AddRef() ;
}

STDMETHODIMP_(ULONG) Document::DocPersistFile::Release()
{
    m_refCount --
    return m_pDoc->Release() ;
}

// *** IPersist methods ***
STDMETHODIMP Document::DocPersistFile::GetClassID(
        LPCLSID lpClassID)
{
    *lpClassID = CLSID_OlePublisher ;
    return NOERROR ;
}

// *** IPersistFile methods ***
STDMETHODIMP Document::DocPersistFile::IsDirty()
{
```

```
        if( m_pDoc->IsDirty() )
            return ResultFromScode( S_OK ) ;
        return ResultFromScode( S_FALSE ) ;
    }


    STDMETHODIMP Document::DocPersistFile::Load(
            LPCSTR lpszFileName, DWORD grfMode)
    {
        if( lpszFileName == NULL || lpszFileName[0] == 0 )
            return ResultFromScode( E_UNEXPECTED ) ;

        theApp.HourGlassOn() ;
        HRESULT hErr = m_pDoc->OpenFile( lpszFileName ) ;
        theApp.HourGlassOff() ;
        return hErr ;
    }


    STDMETHODIMP Document::DocPersistFile::Save(
            LPCSTR lpszFileName, BOOL fRemember)
    {
        // if document not loaded yet, then abort
        if( !m_pDoc->m_init )
            return ResultFromScode( E_UNEXPECTED ) ;

        theApp.HourGlassOn() ;
        HRESULT hErr = m_pDoc->SaveFile( lpszFileName,
            fRemember ) ;
        theApp.HourGlassOff() ;

        return hErr ;
    }


    STDMETHODIMP Document::DocPersistFile::SaveCompleted(
        LPCSTR lpszFileName)
    {
        return NOERROR ;
    }


    STDMETHODIMP Document::DocPersistFile::GetCurFile(
        LPSTR FAR* lplpszFileName)
    {
        LPMALLOC pMalloc ;
        LPSTR lpsz ;
        HRESULT hErr ;
```

```
        CoGetMalloc(MEMCTX_TASK, &pMalloc ) ;

        if( m_pDoc->m_newDoc ) {
            lpsz = (LPSTR)pMalloc->Alloc( 6 ) ;
            lstrcpy( lpsz, "*.DFL" ) ;
            hErr = ResultFromScode( S_FALSE ) ;
        }else{
            lpsz = (LPSTR)pMalloc->Alloc(
                lstrlen( m_pDoc->m_fileName ) + 1 ) ;
            lstrcpy( lpsz, m_pDoc->m_fileName ) ;
            hErr = ResultFromScode( S_OK ) ;
        }

        pMalloc->Release() ;
        return hErr ;
    }
```

As illustrated in Figure 8.2, this interface is implemented from the Document class. When the IClassFactory creates a document, this is the interface that ends up being used. The methods on this interface are relatively simple since we take advantage of a lot of internal code for OLE Publisher. The GetClassID() method is actually part of the IPersist interface that IPersistFile is derived from because, for any type of persistent storage, you must know and be able to store the class ID of the server that created the data. The IPersistFile::LoadFile() method is fairly straightforward since it simply loads a file into the uninitialized Document object that was obtained through our class factory. It delegates the details to the Document::OpenFile() method, which takes care of loading the document and creating the window. Of course, we must set the cursor so that the user realizes that a potentially time-intensive process is running.

The IPersistFile::Save() method is a little more involved. The first parameter is, of course, the file name to save the document to. If this parameter is NULL, the current document should be saved to the same file. If it is not NULL, either a Save As... or a Save Copy As... operation is intended, depending on the fRemember switch, which indicates whether to remember the file name that is passed in lpszFileName. If the fRemember switch is FALSE, we should save the file to the new file name but not actually switch over to that file.

Finally, the IPersistFile::GetCurFile() method returns the current file name in a block of memory allocated by the current memory allocator, as obtained from CoGetMalloc(). (The memory allocator was discussed in more detail in Chapter 2 in the section "The IMalloc Interface."). If we do not have a current file name, perhaps because it is a completely new file, we are required to return the default file name mask.

Putting Links to Embedded Objects on the Clipboard

Putting links to embedded objects is similar to putting an embedded object on the clipboard—you place the CF_LINKSOURCE and CF_LINKSOURCEDESCRIPTOR. These two formats must be available to allow an application to paste a link. The CF_LINK-SOURCE actually contains a serialized version of the moniker that represents the link. The CF_LINKSOURCEDESCRIPTOR is a structure that describes the link source, including the type of link, the display aspect, and the link status. The link status is interesting in that it can tell us whether we are dealing with an inside or outside link. Since OLE Publisher is a container and does not have its own native data, we must allow the servers for the embedded objects to handle all the editing for these objects. This means that before we copy a link to the clipboard, we must check to see whether the object supports inside linking, as shown here:

```
pObj->m_pOleObj->GetMiscStatus( pObj->m_dvAspect,
                    &dwStatus ) ;
if( dwStatus & OLEMISC_CANTLINKINSIDE )
    // this object supports inside links
```

The OLEMISC_CANTLINKINSIDE flag gives us the go-ahead to place a link on the clipboard. The code in Listing 8.1 puts a link source on the clipboard by adding the appropriate formats to our IDataObject.

Listing 8.1

```
If it is an embedded object and it supports inside links
// then add CF_LINKDESCRIPTOR and CF_LINKSOURCE formats
// Set the CF_EMBEDDEDOBJECT
DWORD dwStatus ;
m_pOleObj->GetMiscStatus( m_dvAspect, &dwStatus ) ;
if( !m_isLink && !(dwStatus & OLEMISC_CANTLINKINSIDE) ) {

    LPMONIKER pMoniker ;
    CLSID classID ;
```

```
m_pOleObj->GetUserClassID( &classID ) ;
hErr = m_pOleObj->GetMoniker(0,
    OLEWHICHMK_OBJFULL, &pMoniker ) ;
if( FAILED( hErr ) ) {
    Error( "Failed to obtain moniker!" ) ;
    return NULL ;
}

pformats[fmtidx].cfFormat = RegisterClipboardFormat(
    CF_LINKSOURCE ) ;
pformats[fmtidx].dwAspect = DVASPECT_CONTENT ;
pformats[fmtidx].ptd = NULL ;
pformats[fmtidx].lindex = -1 ;
pformats[fmtidx].tymed = TYMED_ISTREAM ;
pmediums[fmtidx].tymed = TYMED_NULL ;
pmediums[fmtidx].pstg = NULL ;
pmediums[fmtidx].pUnkForRelease = NULL ;

// Now create the link source data
hErr = OleStdGetLinkSourceData( pMoniker, &classID,
        &pformats[fmtidx],
        &pmediums[fmtidx] ) ;

if( FAILED( hErr ) ) {
    Error( "Failed to create the link source!" ) ;
    return NULL ;
}
fmtidx++ ;

// Set the CF_LINKSRCDESCRIPTOR
pformats[fmtidx].cfFormat = RegisterClipboardFormat(
    CF_LINKSRCDESCRIPTOR ) ;
pformats[fmtidx].ptd = NULL ;
pformats[fmtidx].dwAspect = m_dvAspect ;
pformats[fmtidx].lindex = -1 ;
pformats[fmtidx].tymed = TYMED_HGLOBAL ;
XformSizeInPixelsToHimetric( NULL,
            (LPSIZEL)&pointl, (LPSIZEL)&pointl ) ;
pmediums[fmtidx].hGlobal =
    OleStdGetObjectDescriptorDataFromOleObject( m_pOleObj,
        m_pDoc->m_windowTitle,
        m_dvAspect,
        pointl,
```

```
            NULL ) ;
    pmediums[fmtidx].tymed = TYMED_HGLOBAL ;
    pmediums[fmtidx].pUnkForRelease = NULL ;
    fmtidx++ ;
}
```

The two formats we add are the CF_LINKSOURCE and the CF_LINKSOURCEDESCRIP-
TOR. The CF_LINKSOURCE is created when we call the OleStdGetLinkSourceData()
routine from the OLE 2 Library. The CF_LINKSOURCEDESCRIPTOR is created exactly
the same way as CF_OBJECTDESCRIPTOR. The OLE 2 UI Library provides the OleSt-
dGetObjectDescriptorFromOleObject() routine that does the work of creating
this structure for us. These formats are provided along with the standard embed-
ded-object formats described in Chapter 7. This code is in the file OBJDATA.CPP as
part of the Object:: CreateTransferDataObject() method.

Handling Saves with Links Using IAdviseSink2

In version 2.0 of OLE, when a link was updated, no notifications took place to indicate that the link source was changed. This meant that the only way to determine
whether the link source was changed was a call to IPersistStorage::IsDirty().
This problem has been fixed in the latest version of OLE. A new interface is provided that allows for notification of link source changes. This interface is called
IAdviseSink2. It is simply an extension of the IAdviseSink interface with a single
new method named, IAdviseSink2::OnLinkSrc Change(). Do we need to implement two advise sinks for each object? No; we can simply support returning the
same interface from the main IUnknown, as demonstrated by the following code:

```
HRESULT Object::QueryInterface( RIID riid,
    LPVOID *ppvObj )
{
    ...
    }else if( riid == IID_IAdviseSink ||
            riid == IID_IAdviseSink2 ) {
        *lpVoid = &m_adviseSink ;
        (LPUNKNOWN)*lpVoid) -> Addref();
        return NOERROR ;
    }
    ...
}
```

For applications that support toolbars with Save buttons on them, such as OLE Publisher, this notification is important because it lets us know when to trigger the toggling of this button between enabled and disabled. In OLE 2 you simply had to wait until there was some reason to iterate through all the objects, such as on a WM_INITMENUPOPUP message.

Summary

Adding support for simple linking to a container is easy. There is almost no difference between the way you paste a link from the clipboard and the way you paste an embedded object, except for calling OleCreateLinkFromData() instead of OleCreateFromData(). Of course, before this can happen you need to determine that there is a link on the clipboard, as represented by the presence of the CF_LINKSOURCE and CF_LINKSOURCEDESCRIPTOR format. This can be easily determined if you call the OleQueryLinkFromData() routine passing the IDataObject you obtained by calling OleGetClipboard(). After this, the most significant work you have to do is implementing the OLE 2 User-Interface requirements. Although there is still some work left to do, the OLE 2 UI Library takes care of the majority of the details for you.

Allowing other containers to link to the objects that are embedded in your container involves several steps. First you have to create and register monikers for both the open documents, as well as for the objects. Second, you must implement the IOleItemContainer and the IPersistFile interfaces to support locating and binding to the objects in your container's documents. Third, you must register the container with the registration database with its class ID. After these steps, all that remains is to provide the extra clipboard formats so that when a Copy operation is performed, your container puts the appropriate clipboard formats on the clipboard.

The next chapter introduces the concepts and techniques you can use to add in-place activation to your container.

CHAPTER
NINE

In-Place Containers

- Supporting in-place activation in a container

- Implementing the in-place container interfaces

- Activating an object in place

- How the container and server share user-interface components

In-place activation is the Holy Grail of object linking and embedding. With in-place activation, the user is truly working on a compound document and does not ever have to exit or otherwise leave the document to edit an embedded object.

What actually happens is that when the user selects an object inside a container and causes it to be activated, the container and the server go through a negotiation phase to determine how to share the user-interface components of the workspace in which the user is currently editing the compound document. These components include menus, toolbars, and the status bar. Although this feature is wonderful for the user, it is not trivial to implement. This chapter is devoted to implementing in-place activation in containers.

How In-Place Activation Works

In-place activation involves the integration of a good portion of the interface into the container. Because of this integration of interfaces, adding support to your container for in-place activation will probably not be as easy as implementing support for other aspects of OLE. Before we get into the specifics, let's take a look at the details of what happens to the interface.

First of all, objects usually reside in a document window of some sort in your container. The object in Figure 9.1 actually resides inside a document window that is an MDI child window. The frame window is the MDI application's main window and is usually the parent of the document window. When an object is in-place activated by the container, it must be able to communicate with all levels of the interface. The frame window is asked to merge menus from the activated object. After the object server merges its menus with the container's menus, it may also occasionally request that the status bar display text that is relevant to the in-place active object. The object may also request toolbar space from the frame window. At the level of the document window, the object may request space for interface adornments, such as a ruler or even a document-level toolbar.

Finally, there is the pane window, which applies when the application has more than one view of an active object. This usually happens in situations in which the container supports split-pane windows.

FIGURE 9.1:

Conceptual diagram of an
in-place container

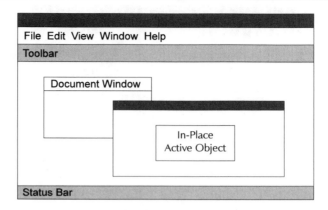

SDI (single-document interface) applications use the same model, with the exception that only one document window can be open at once. This helps to simplify the code required to handle the situation only when two or more document windows are open, each with in-place active objects.

Activating an In-Place Object

The container does not explicitly request that an object be activated in place. The container actually activates the object in almost the same manner that it normally would, but once the object takes over, differences occur. The object starts by asking the container if it supports in-place activation by querying the container's `IOle-ClientSite` interface for the `IOleInPlaceSite` interface. The moniker is responsible for loading the server and resolving the data required to specify the linked object. From here the object goes on to negotiate for its various interface requirements, as discussed earlier in this chapter. If the negotiation is successful—that is, if the container is able to support all the interface space requirements for merged menus, toolbars, and space around the object—it will in-place activate itself. Otherwise, it will open-activate itself in the manner of OLE 1 objects.

Merging Menus on In-Place Activation

For merging menus, OLE has defined a collection of six menu groups that the applications will use when building the combined menu for in-place activation. A *menu group* is a related set of menus that appear on the menu bar during in-place activation. Three of the six menu groups are filled by the container, and the other three are built by the server. These groups are as follows:

Group	Description
File (container)	Provides a File menu
Edit (server)	Provides an Edit menu
Container (container)	Provides any specific container-related menus that should still be available during in-place activation
Server (server)	Provides any specific server menus that are needed for manipulating the in-place activated object
Window (container)	Used for MDI containers that need to provide a Window menu
Help (server)	Supplies any help-related menus, such as the standard Help menu

During menu negotiation both the container and the server get a chance to put their menu items in their respective groups. The File group belongs to the container since it contains all the logic and code for saving and loading the documents in the container. The Edit and Server groups supply all the menus needed for supporting the in-place activated object. The Container group provides any extra container menus that are still needed during in-place activation. The Window and Help groups are supplied by the container and the server, respectively, to complete the support for merged menus.

Figure 9.2 is a screen snapshot of Microsoft Word with an in-place activated Equation Editor 2.0 object. Word has hidden all the toolbars that are normally supplied, and its menus are merged with the menus that are supplied by the Equation Editor applet. The File menu and Window menu belong to Word, and the rest of the menus

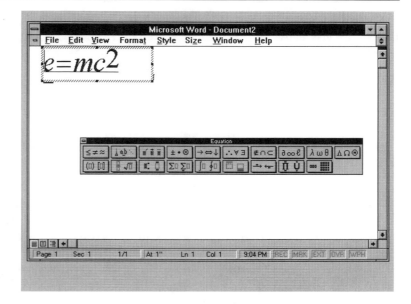

FIGURE 9.2:

Screen snapshot of an in-place activation

belong to Equation Editor. Notice in this example that Word does not supply any menus for the Container group since none of the menus directly relate to the object being edited in place.

Making Room for the Object's Toolbars

Adding a toolbar involves a process called *border-space negotiation*. This occurs when the object asks the container for space on one or more of its windows. In most cases the object will want to put a toolbar on the frame window, but this is not a requirement, and the container should try to be as flexible as possible in allowing for toolbars to be placed on any border of its frame window, as well as allowing for toolbars and other adornments on the document window.

Toolbar negotiation starts when the object requests space on the border of one of the windows in the application. If the object's request is successful, it can allocate up to the requested amount of space for use by one of its toolbars. The border space an object can negotiate for at the different user interface levels is illustrated in Figure 9.3.

FIGURE 9.3:

Border space for an in-place container

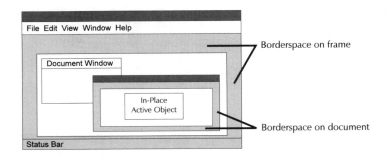

Sharing the Status Bar

Status bars are a common feature in many Windows applications, and because of their popularity they are directly supported by OLE. The container can provide a method that allows the object to pass status bar text. The status bar text can be used for many things, but mainly it is used for displaying the help text associated with menu items.

Context-Sensitive Help

Context-sensitive help is another important feature in a lot of applications. OLE handles support for this feature by providing a method through which an in-place active object can inform the container that the system has entered context-sensitive help mode. When the container is notified of this, it is responsible for informing the other active objects so that, regardless of which object receives the next command message, the object can handle the message by presenting the appropriate help for the object. This happens only for objects that support context-sensitive help. Even if the container does not support help, it must handle the context-sensitive help support so an in-place active object that supports help can react properly.

The In-Place Interfaces

The interfaces that relate to in-place activation are illustrated in Figure 9.4.

The interfaces that relate to the container and the portions of the user interface they correlate to are illustrated in Figure 9.5.

FIGURE 9.4:
In-place interfaces

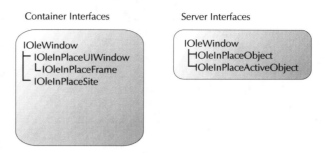

FIGURE 9.5:
Structure of an application interface

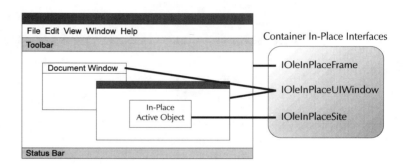

The IOleWindow Interface

One of the things you will notice is that all the interfaces are based on the IOleWindow interface. This interface is responsible for doing nothing but returning a window handle associated with each level of the interface. This interface is used all the time, but you will probably never explicitly create an instance of it.

The IOleWindow interface has two methods, which are described in Table 9.1. These methods include the IOleWindow::GetWindow() method, which is responsible for returning the HWND associated with the specific implementation of the IOleWindow interface. For the frame window, the GetWindow() method returns the HWND of the frame window. For a document window, the HWND of that window is returned. For the in-place client site, this method returns the parent window of the object, which in some cases is actually the same as the document window.

TABLE 9.1: The IOleWindow Interface

Method	Description
HRESULT GetWindow(lphwnd)	Returns the HWND for the window associated with the implementation of the interface
HRESULT ContextSensitiveHelp (fEnterHelpMode)	Notifies the object or container that it should enter context-sensitive help mode

The IOleWindow interface is also used as the base for the object's in-place interfaces. In the case of the object, the GetWindow( ) method returns the window in which the object is in-place activated.

The IOleInPlaceUIWindow Interface

The IOleInPlaceUIWindow interface is the basis for the support of both frame and document windows in OLE. This interface contains the methods for setting an active in-place object for a window and for negotiating for border space.

The methods listed in Table 9.1 are also supported by the IOleInPlaceUIWindow interface since it is derived from IOleWindow. The methods for the IOleIn-PlaceUIWindow interface are listed in Table 9.2.

TABLE 9.2: The IOleInPlaceUIWindow Interface

Method	Description
HRESULT GetBorder (lprectBorder)	Called by the object to determine whether a container's document or frame window has any space available on the border of its windows. The lprectBorder argument is returned, containing the size in pixels of the available space at the border of the window
HRESULT RequestBorderSpace (lpBorderWidths)	Called by the object to preapprove the space that is required on the border
HRESULT SetBorderSpace (lpBorderWidth)	Allocates the border space on either the document window or the frame window of the container
HRESULT SetActiveObject (lpActiveObject, lpszObjName)	Called by the object to provide the container window with a pointer to the active in-place object

This interface contains the GetBorder() method, which informs the object of the amount of border space available to the object. The RequestBorderSpace() and SetBorderSpace() methods query and allocate border space on either the document window or the frame window. And the SetActiveObject() method informs the document window or frame window of the pointer to the object's IOleIn-PlaceActiveObject interface.

The IOleInPlaceFrame Interface

The IOleInPlaceFrame interface is derived from the IOleInPlaceUIWindow interface and adds the specific routines for supporting the frame window. The container must implement the methods described in Table 9.3 to support in-place activation properly.

TABLE 9.3: The IOleInPlaceFrame Interface

Method	Description
HRESULT InsertMenus (hmenuShared, lpMenuWidths)	Called by the object to request that the container insert its menus into the new shared menu that will be used for the in-place activation. The lpMenuWidths argument is filled out by the container to let the object know how many menus were inserted and where those menus should be placed in the final menu structure
HRESULT SetMenu(hMenuShared, holemenu, hwndActiveObject)	Called by the object after the menu has been constructed to request that the container set the menu as the main menu bar for the window. The holemenu parameter is used by the container to provide the OLE system with enough information to dispatch the messages to the appropriate windows. The hwndActiveObject parameter is the HWND of the active object's window
HRESULT RemoveMenus(hmenuShared)	Called by the object to provide the frame with a chance to remove its menus from the shared menu. If this is not done by the container, the object will destroy the menus that the container inserted in the hmenuShared menu in the IOleInPlaceFrame::InsertMenus() method

TABLE 9.3: The IOleInPlaceFrame Interface (continued)

Method	Description
HRESULT SetStatusText (lpszStatusText)	Called by the object to set the text that should be displayed in the container's status bar. The text in lpszStatusText should be copied to a local buffer
HRESULT EnableModeless (fEnable)	Called by the in-place active object to enable or disable the container's modeless dialogs
HRESULT Translate-Accelerator(lpmsg,wID)	Called by OleTranslateAccelerator() to allow the frame to process any accelerators it may be using

The methods for this interface support adding the menus to the frame window of your container and setting the status bar text.

When an object is in-place activated, it can determine the pointer to the frame window for the container by calling IOleInPlaceSite::GetWindowContext(). Once the object has determined that it can in-place activate, it begins building the shared menu by calling IOleInPlaceFrame::InsertMenu() with an empty menu. When InsertMenu() is called, it is the container's responsibility to add the menus it wants to provide in its groups. When this routine returns, the server will add its own menus to the menu and then call the IOleInPlaceFrame::SetMenu() method. This method should call the Windows SDK function SetMenu() to associate the shared menu with the frame window. OLE takes care of the details of dispatching the menu command messages to either the container or the server, as appropriate.

The IOleInPlaceSite Interface

The IOleInPlaceSite interface represents the container's state as it relates to the in-place object. It also determines whether a container supports in-place activation. When an object is activated using the OLEIVERB_SHOW verb, it is passed a pointer to an IOleClientSite interface that is implemented by the container. An object that supports in-place activation will call QueryInterface() on this pointer to obtain an IOleInPlaceSite interface. If the container supports in-place activation, the object will attempt to continue the in-place activation by using the methods supplied by this interface to begin negotiation for the object's interface requirements. The methods for this interface are described in Table 9.4.

TABLE 9.4: The IOleInPlaceSite Interface

Method	Description
HRESULT CanInPlace-Activate()	Called by the object to determine whether the container will allow an in-place activation. One situation in which this is not possible is when the object is displayed in an aspect other than DVASPECT_CONTENT, such as DVASPECT_ICON
HRESULT OnInPlace-Activate()	Called by an object when the object is activated in place for the first time
HRESULT OnUIActivate()	Called just before the object installs its own menu on the container's frame window using the IOleInPlace Frame interface
HRESULT GetWindowCon-text(ppFrame,ppDoc, prcPosRect,prcClip Rect, lpFrameInfo)	Called by the object to determine specific information about a container, including pointers to the IOleInPlaceFrame and IOleInPlaceUIWindow interfaces for the container. The IOleInPlaceFrame interface must be returned in the ppFrame parameter. The IOleInPlaceUIWindow parameter is returned in ppDoc if the container has a concept of a document, such as in an MDI application. The container returns the object's position rectangle in pixels to the object in prcPosRect. The prcClipRect is the rectangle, in pixels, of the object's frame window or document window. The visible portion of the object is the intersection of these two rectangles. Finally, the lpFrameInfo structure is filled out by the container with information about the application, such as whether it is an MDI application, the HWND of the frame window, and information about the application's accelerators
HRESULT Scroll(scroll-Extent)	Called by the object when it wants to scroll the container's document window. The scrollExtent parameter contains the number of pixels to scroll the window from its current position
HRESULT OnUIDeactivate(fUndoable)	Called by the object to notify the container that the object is deactivating itself and that the container should reinstall its user interface and take the focus. The fUndoable parameter indicates whether the object supports undoing the changes that were made by calling IOleInPlaceObject::Reactivate AndUndo()

TABLE 9.4: The IOleInPlaceSite Interface (continued)

Method	Description
HRESULT OnInPlace Deactivate()	Called by an object when it is fully deactivated. At this point, any undo state that the object had supported has been flushed
HRESULT DiscardUndoState()	Called by an object to indicate that the undo state it had been maintaining is no longer valid
HRESULT DeactivateAnd-Undo()	Called when the user invokes Edit ➤ Undo right after the object has been activated. At this point the command does not apply to the object and is a signal to the container to deactivate the object by calling IOleInPlaceObject::UIDeactivate() and then performing the appropriate action to respond to the undo request
HRESULT OnPosRectChange()	Called to inform the container that its extents have changed. Even though the object knows what the new extents are, it will not change its physical appearance until the container responds by calling IOleInPlace-Object::SetObjectRects()

The IOleInPlaceSite interface is also derived from the IOleWindow interface. In this case the IOleWindow::GetWindow() method should return the parent window of the object. This allows the object server to create a window for the object and call the Windows SDK SetParent() function to specify the document window as the parent window.

After determining whether the container supports this interface, the object being activated calls the CanInPlaceActivate() method. If the container will allow the activation, it returns S_OK and the object calls GetWindowContext() to obtain the interfaces for the frame and document windows. The GetWindowContext() method is also responsible for informing the object of its position in the document window, as well as in the client area of the document window. The other methods for this interface are a mix of notifications and utility methods for updating visual information about the in-place object.

The IOleInPlaceActiveObject and IOleInPlaceObject Interfaces

The IOleInPlaceActiveObject and IOleInPlaceObject interfaces are used extensively throughout in-place activation and are implemented by the server (see Figure 9.4). The `IOleInPlaceActiveObject` interface represents an object that is currently active and has its interface installed in its container. The `IOleInPlaceObject` is a more general interface used to communicate with an in-place object regardless of whether or not it is currently active.

NOTE When an object becomes in-place active, its toolbars and menus are installed in the container. If it is then deactivated, the server is not unloaded. This allows the container to reactivate the object quickly, since the server does not need to be reloaded.

NOTE Although various aspects of these interfaces are discussed throughout this chapter, they are not discussed for their own sake until Chapter 12.

Adding In-Place Activation to OLE Publisher

Adding support for in-place activation (see Figure 9.6) to OLE Publisher required fairly extensive additions to the program. We implemented the `IOleInPlaceSite` interface on the `Object` class, the `IOleInPlaceUIWindow` interface on our `Document` class, and the `IOleInPlaceFrame` interface on our `Application` class. These changes were then supplemented by changes to such things as our message-handling code for the application and the document window, as well as some subtler changes to the way we handle the toolbar and our menus. Figure 9.7 illustrates where the new interfaces were added into the architecture for OLE Publisher.

At each level of the application, we have made changes to support the addition of in-place editing.

FIGURE 9.6:

Screen snapshot of OLE Publisher
with in-place active WordArt object

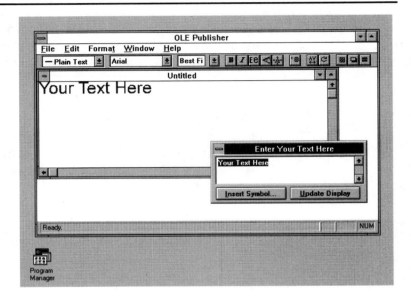

FIGURE 9.7:

Class architecture for OLE Publisher
as an in-place container

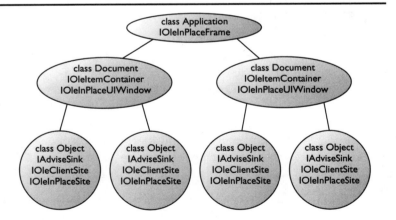

The Support Code for the In-Place Interfaces

There is more to adding in-place editing than just implementing the interfaces. Once you have done that, extra logic must be added to fully support in-place editing, including

- The translation of accelerator messages for the in-place object
- Extra handling of activation messages (especially in an MDI application)
- Informing the in-place activated object of window size changes
- Handling undo

Handling Activation Messages Properly

An object needs to be informed of the Windows activation messages because the object will need to know the activation state of the windows in which it resides, as well as the moment a change in this state occurs. This is a requirement for several reasons. If an MDI document window has an in-place activated object and is deactivated when another MDI document window is activated, the object should be able to remove any tools it previously placed on the frame, as well as its menus. When a document window in an MDI application is activated (or deactivated), the container should call the `IOleInPlaceActiveObject::OnDocWindowActivate()` method if there is an active object. This method takes a `BOOL` argument that specifies whether or not the document is being activated. The following code demonstrates the usage of `OnDocWindowActivate()`:

```
case WM_MDIACTIVATE:
    if( m_inPlaceWindow.m_pActObj != NULL )
        m_inPlaceWindow.m_pActObj->
            OnDocWindowActivate( !!wParam ) ;
    else if( wParam )
        AddFrameUI() ;

    OnMDIActivate( (BOOL)wParam,
            (HWND)LOWORD(lParam),
            (HWND)HIWORD(lParam) ) ;
break ;
```

When the document window does not have an active in-place object, it calls the `Document::AddFrameUI()` method on activation. This is because we might be activating from a situation in which the previous document window had an in-place active object and the frame's user interface was hidden for that document. This method will reinstall the toolbar and menus as needed. Here is the code for this method (located in DOCIPWIN.CPP):

```
void Document::AddFrameUI()
{
    theApp.m_inPlaceFrame.SetMenu( NULL, NULL, NULL ) ;

    BORDERWIDTHS bw = {0,0,0,0} ;
    theApp.m_inPlaceFrame.SetBorderSpace( &bw ) ;
    theApp.m_toolBar.ShowBar( theApp.m_fToolbar ) ;
    theApp.AdjustClientWindow() ;
}
```

The call to the `IOleInPlaceFrame::SetMenu()` method restores the menu when it is called with NULLs. The `IOleInPlaceFrame::SetBorderSpace()` method deallocates the border space that was required by any previous object. The call to `theApp.ShowBar()` resets the toolbar to its original visual state (as saved in the `m_fToolbar` member variable). The size of the client window is recalculated and repainted by `theApp.AdjustClientWindow()`.

The other situation in which the activation of a window must be communicated to the active object is with the frame window. It is the in-place container's responsibility to call the `IOleInPlaceActiveObject::OnFrameWindowActivate()` method to pass this information to the object. This method is usually called from the `WM_ACTIVATEAPP` message handler in the container.

Examine the following code:

```
switch( msg ) {
...
case WM_ACTIVATEAPP:
    // Check for an in-place active object
    if( m_inPlaceFrame.m_pActObj != NULL ) {
        HRESULT hErr ;
        hErr = m_inPlaceFrame.m_pActObj->
                OnFrameWindowActivate( !!wParam ) ;
    }
    ...
    }
    break ;
```

Handling Resize Messages to the Application and Document Windows

In-place objects actually create a new window to provide the editing site for the object itself. This window is created inside your document window and is actually a child window. For this reason, when the document window is moved or resized, the object must be informed of the changes so it can adjust itself accordingly. This is done when the container calls the IOleInPlaceActiveObject::ResizeBorder() method for the object on a WM_SIZE message. The following code demonstrates how this is done in the Document class for OLE Publisher:

```
case WM_SIZE:
    if( m_inPlaceWindow.m_pActObj != NULL ) {
        RECT newRect ;
        GetClientRect( hWnd, &newRect ) ;
        m_inPlaceWindow.m_pActObj->ResizeBorder(
            &newRect, &m_inPlaceWindow, FALSE ) ;
    }
    ResetScrollBars() ;
    break ;
```

Implementing Context-Sensitive Help

Since context-sensitive help is an important feature to a lot of Windows applications, OLE provides support for this feature even when objects are in-place active in a container. In the case of SDI containers, the only thing you have to do is set a flag when your implementation of the IOleInPlaceClientSite::ContextSensitiveHelp() is called and handle the next mouse event or WM_COMMAND message in an appropriate manner. If you support context-sensitive help, you must first remove all objects from the context-sensitive help mode. Do this by simply calling the IOleInPlaceActiveObject::ContextSensitiveHelp() method for the in-place active object with the mode parameter set to FALSE. Then provide the appropriate help, as defined by your application. If the object receives a mouse-click or a WM_COMMAND message first, you don't have to do anything. The object will call the IOleInPlaceActiveObject::ContextSensitiveHelp() method again to turn off help mode.

For MDI applications the requirements are a little more stringent, but not much. Initially, when the object first informs your container that it should enter help mode, you must also inform all other documents in the system that help mode should be entered. Examine the MDI application depicted in Figure 9.8. Both Document A and Document B contain active in-place objects. Only the in-place object that is active in the top-level document can have menus and toolbar support. When the other document becomes active, it takes over the interface.

With context-sensitive help we have a slightly more complicated situation. Suppose the user requests the in-place object in Document A to enter context-sensitive help mode by pressing Shift+F1. Then, when the user clicks on some portion of the interface, the application is supposed to respond by providing help, since we set a flag indicating that the next mouse event would be a help request. But what about the object in Document B? If the user clicks this object and it is not aware that we are in help mode, it will not respond properly. This is why it is imperative that we inform all active objects—even objects in inactive MDI document windows—of the help mode.

Finally, if your container supports help mode, everything should be handled as if you were in one of the first two situations just described (depending on whether you are implementing an MDI or SDI application), with this exception: upon entering help mode you must inform all in-place active objects to enter help mode.

FIGURE 9.8:

MDI application with two active in-place objects

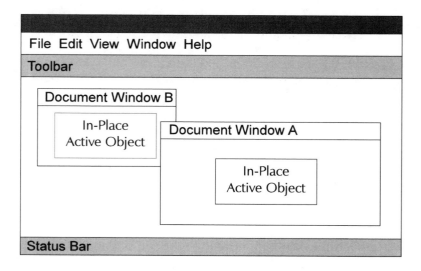

Implementing the IOleInPlaceSite Interface

Listing 9.1 contains the IOleInPlaceSite interface for OLE Publisher.

Listing 9.1

```
#include "appl.h"
#include "doc.h"
#include "obj.h"

Object::ObjInPlaceSite::ObjInPlaceSite(Object *pObj)
{
    m_pObj = pObj ;
    m_refCount = 0 ;
    m_pInPlaceObj = NULL ;
}

STDMETHODIMP Object::ObjInPlaceSite::QueryInterface(
        REFIID riid,
        LPVOID FAR *lpVoid )
{
    return m_pObj->QueryInterface(riid,lpVoid) ;
}

STDMETHODIMP_(ULONG) Object::ObjInPlaceSite::AddRef()
{
    m_refCount++ ;
    return m_pObj->AddRef() ;
}

STDMETHODIMP_(ULONG) Object::ObjInPlaceSite::Release()
{
    m_refCount-- ;
    return m_pObj->Release() ;
}

// *** IOleWindow methods ***
STDMETHODIMP Object::ObjInPlaceSite::GetWindow(
        HWND FAR* lphwnd)
{
    *lphwnd = m_pObj->m_pDoc->m_hWnd ;
    return NOERROR ;
}
```

```
STDMETHODIMP Object::ObjInPlaceSite::ContextSensitiveHelp(
                            BOOL fEnterMode)
{
    m_pObj->m_pDoc->m_helpMode = fEnterMode ;
    theApp.m_inPlaceFrame.
        ContextSensitiveHelp( fEnterMode ) ;
    return NOERROR ;}


// *** IOleInPlaceSite methods ***
STDMETHODIMP Object::ObjInPlaceSite::CanInPlaceActivate()
{
    if( m_pObj->m_dvAspect == DVASPECT_CONTENT )
        return NOERROR ;
    return ResultFromScode( E_FAIL ) ;
}


STDMETHODIMP Object::ObjInPlaceSite::OnInPlaceActivate()
{
    HRESULT hErr = m_pObj->m_pOleObj->QueryInterface(
            IID_IOleInPlaceObject,
            (LPVOID *)&m_pInPlaceObj ) ;
    if( FAILED( hErr ) )
        return ResultFromScode( E_FAIL ) ;
    return NOERROR ;
}


STDMETHODIMP Object::ObjInPlaceSite::OnUIActivate()
{
    m_pObj->m_pDoc->m_addMyUI = FALSE ;
    return NOERROR ;
}


STDMETHODIMP Object::ObjInPlaceSite::GetWindowContext(
    LPOLEINPLACEFRAME FAR* lplpFrame,
    LPOLEINPLACEUIWINDOW FAR* lplpDoc,
    LPRECT lprcPosRect,
    LPRECT lprcClipRect,
    LPOLEINPLACEFRAMEINFO lpFrameInfo)
{
    // Get the interfaces
    m_pObj->m_pDoc->QueryInterface(
            IID_IOleInPlaceUIWindow,
            (LPVOID *)lplpDoc ) ;
    theApp.QueryInterface( IID_IOleInPlaceFrame,
```

```
            (LPVOID *)lplpFrame ) ;

    // Get the position rect for the object
    // and the clip rect
    // and the document
    *lprcPosRect = m_pObj->m_objRect ;
    m_pObj->m_pDoc->VirtualToClientRect( lprcPosRect ) ;
    GetClientRect( m_pObj->m_pDoc->m_hWnd,
                lprcClipRect ) ;

    // Get frame information
    lpFrameInfo->fMDIApp = TRUE ;
    lpFrameInfo->hwndFrame = theApp.m_hWnd ;
    lpFrameInfo->haccel = NULL ;
    lpFrameInfo->cAccelEntries = 0 ;

    return NOERROR ;
}

STDMETHODIMP Object::ObjInPlaceSite::Scroll(
            SIZE scrollExtent)
{
    m_pObj->m_pDoc->ScrollDocument(
            scrollExtent.cx,
            scrollExtent.cy ) ;
    return NOERROR ;
}

STDMETHODIMP Object::ObjInPlaceSite::OnUIDeactivate(
        BOOL fUndoable)
{
    BOOL fDblClk = FALSE ;
    MSG msg ;
    if( PeekMessage( &msg,
        m_pObj->m_pDoc->m_hWnd,
        WM_LBUTTONDBLCLK,
        WM_LBUTTONDBLCLK,
        PM_NOREMOVE ) ) fDblClk = TRUE ;

    if( fDblClk )
        m_pObj->m_pDoc->m_addMyUI = TRUE ;
    else
        m_pObj->m_pDoc->AddFrameUI() ;
```

```
        m_pObj->Invalidate() ;
        m_pObj->m_inPlaceActive = FALSE ;

        return NOERROR ;
}

STDMETHODIMP Object::ObjInPlaceSite::OnInPlaceDeactivate()
{
        if( m_pInPlaceObj != NULL )
                return ResultFromScode( E_UNEXPECTED ) ;

        m_pInPlaceObj->Release() ;
        m_pInPlaceObj = NULL ;
        return NOERROR ;
}

STDMETHODIMP Object::ObjInPlaceSite::DiscardUndoState()
{
        return NOERROR ;
}

STDMETHODIMP Object::ObjInPlaceSite::DeactivateAndUndo()
{
        return NOERROR ;
}

STDMETHODIMP Object::ObjInPlaceSite::OnPosRectChange(
                                LPCRECT lprcPosRect)
{
        if( EqualRect( lprcPosRect, &m_pObj->m_objRect ) )
                return NOERROR ;

        RECT newObjRect = *lprcPosRect ;
        m_pObj->m_pDoc->ClientToVirtualRect( &newObjRect ) ;
        m_pObj->Move( &newObjRect ) ;

        RECT docWinRect ;
        GetClientRect( m_pObj->m_pDoc->m_hWnd,
                &docWinRect ) ;
        m_pInPlaceObj->SetObjectRects( &m_pObj->m_objRect,
                &docWinRect ) ;

        return NOERROR ;
}
```

The code starts with the `IOleWindow` base interface methods supporting the `GetWindow()` and `ContextSensitiveHelp()` methods. In the `GetWindow()` method OLE requires that you pass whatever window should be the parent window of the object. In our case this is the same as the document window. For the `ContextSensitiveHelp()` method, we simply pass this up to the frame window. Setting the help flag on our document window prevents the system from recursing back down to this object and trying to set its help mode again.

The `CanInPlaceActivate()` method informs the system as to whether the object can in-place activate. For OLE Publisher the only requirement is that the object be in the `DVASPECT_CONTENT` display mode. If this method returns `S_OK` (or `NOERROR`), the object will call `OnInPlaceActivate()` to inform the container that it is activating in place. At this point you should obtain a reference to the object's `IOleInPlaceObject` interface and cache this pointer for the duration of the object's active state. The `OnUIActivate()` method is called by the object to indicate that it is about to install its user interface. OLE Publisher simply sets a flag to indicate that we should remove it when the object starts to install its own interface.

The `GetWindowContext()` method is how the object obtains information about the other in-place interfaces supported by the container. The following code demonstrates how this method should return the information requested by the object:

```
STDMETHODIMP Object::ObjInPlaceSite::GetWindowContext(
    LPOLEINPLACEFRAME FAR* lplpFrame,
    LPOLEINPLACEUIWINDOW FAR* lplpDoc,
    LPRECT lprcPosRect,
    LPRECT lprcClipRect,
    LPOLEINPLACEFRAMEINFO lpFrameInfo)
{
    // Get the interfaces
    m_pObj->m_pDoc->QueryInterface(
            IID_IOleInPlaceUIWindow,
            (LPVOID *)lplpDoc ) ;
    theApp.QueryInterface( IID_IOleInPlaceFrame,
        (LPVOID *)lplpFrame ) ;

    // Get the position rect for the object
    // and the clip rect
    // and the document
    *lprcPosRect = m_pObj->m_objRect ;
    m_pObj->m_pDoc->VirtualToClientRect( lprcPosRect ) ;
```

```
GetClientRect( m_pObj->m_pDoc->m_hWnd,
            lprcClipRect ) ;

// Get frame information
lpFrameInfo->fMDIApp = TRUE ;
lpFrameInfo->hwndFrame = theApp.m_hWnd ;
lpFrameInfo->haccel = NULL ;
lpFrameInfo->cAccelEntries = 0 ;

return NOERROR ;
}
```

The first portion of OLE Publisher's implementation of the `GetWindowContext()` method returns the in-place interfaces for the frame window and the document window in which the object resides. The next few lines of code return the position and clipping rectangle for the object, in pixels. Even though most of the other interfaces in OLE require coordinates in `HIMETRIC`, all the in-place routines require the coordinates in pixels. Finally, we fill out the `OLEINPLACEFRAMEINFO` structure and return.

The `OnUIDeactivate()` and `OnInPlaceDeactivate()` methods are notifications called by the object to inform that application that the object is deactivating. The `OnUIDeactivate()` notification is called when the object is removing its user interface, and the `OnInPlaceDeactivate()` method is called when the object is fully deactivating itself. In our implementation of `OnUIDeactivate()`, we reinstall the interface for our object. For optimizing the container for repaints, we check to see whether the system has a pending double-click. If it does, we set a flag and wait until the double-click is handled to reinstall our toolbar. This allows for the possibility that the double-click will activate another object and cause it to install its own interface. That way we avoid the flashing caused by removing the current object's supporting interface, reinstalling our own, and then removing it again to install the interface for a new object.

The `OnPosRectChange()` method is called when the object needs to change its size or position. After repositioning and invalidating the object, we call the `IOleInPlaceObject::SetObjectRects()` method to make the new size and position permanent.

Implementing the IOleInPlaceUIWindow Interface

Listing 9.2 contains the IOleInPlaceUIWindow interface for OLE Publisher.

Listing 9.2

```
DOCIPWIN.CPP
#include "appl.h"
#include "doc.h"
#include "obj.h"

void Document::AddFrameUI()
{
    theApp.m_inPlaceFrame.SetMenu( NULL, NULL, NULL ) ;

    BORDERWIDTHS bw = {0,0,0,0} ;
    theApp.m_inPlaceFrame.SetBorderSpace( &bw ) ;
    theApp.m_toolBar.ShowBar( theApp.m_fToolbar ) ;
    theApp.AdjustClientWindow() ;
}

void Document::RemoveFrameUI()
{
    theApp.m_toolBar.ShowBar( FALSE ) ;
    theApp.AdjustClientWindow() ;
}

Document::DocInPlaceWindow::DocInPlaceWindow( Document *pDoc )
{
    m_pDoc = pDoc ;
    m_pActObj = NULL ;
}

STDMETHODIMP Document::DocInPlaceWindow::QueryInterface(
    REFIID riid,
LPVOID FAR *lpVoid )
{
    return m_pDoc->QueryInterface(riid,lpVoid) ;
}

STDMETHODIMP_(ULONG) Document::DocInPlaceWindow::AddRef()
{
    return m_pDoc->AddRef() ;
```

```
}

STDMETHODIMP_(ULONG) Document::DocInPlaceWindow::Release()
{
    return m_pDoc->Release() ;
}

// *** IOleWindow methods ***
STDMETHODIMP Document::DocInPlaceWindow::GetWindow(
                HWND FAR* lphwnd)
{
    *lphwnd = m_pDoc->m_hWnd ;
    return NOERROR ;
}

STDMETHODIMP Document::DocInPlaceWindow::ContextSensitiveHelp(
                BOOL fEnterMode)
{
    if( m_pDoc->m_helpMode != fEnterMode ) {
        m_pDoc->m_helpMode = fEnterMode ;
        if( m_pActObj != NULL )
            m_pActObj->ContextSensitiveHelp( fEnterMode ) ;
    }
    return NOERROR ;
}

// *** IOleInPlaceUIWindow methods ***
STDMETHODIMP Document::DocInPlaceWindow::GetBorder(
                LPRECT lprectBorder)
{
    if( IsRectEmpty( lprectBorder ) ) return NOERROR ;

    return ResultFromScode( INPLACE_E_NOTOOLSPACE ) ;
}

STDMETHODIMP Document::DocInPlaceWindow::RequestBorderSpace(
                LPCBORDERWIDTHS lpborderwidths)
{
    return ResultFromScode( INPLACE_E_NOTOOLSPACE ) ;
}

STDMETHODIMP Document::DocInPlaceWindow::SetBorderSpace(
    LPCBORDERWIDTHS lpborderwidths)
{
    return ResultFromScode( OLE_E_INVALIDRECT ) ;
```

```
   }

   STDMETHODIMP Document::DocInPlaceWindow::SetActiveObject(
       LPOLEINPLACEACTIVEOBJECT lpActiveObject,
       LPCSTR lpszObjName)
   {
       if( m_pActObj != NULL )
           m_pActObj->Release() ;

       // Save new active object pointer
       m_pActObj = lpActiveObject ;

       if( m_pActObj != NULL )
           m_pActObj->AddRef() ;

       return NOERROR ;
   }
```

The first two routines in Listing 9.2 are helper routines to aid in removing the toolbar for the application when an object becomes active. Since documents have a concept of an active object, the document will control whether or not the toolbar is visible. This can change at any time when the user activates another document.

The `IOleInPlaceUIWindow::GetWindow()` method simply returns the HWND for the MDI child window. The `ContextSensitiveHelp()` method first must check to see whether it is already in the requested help mode by checking the `m_helpMode` member variable; if it is not, it saves this mode. If there is an active object, it also calls the `ContextSensitiveHelp()` method for that object.

The border negotiation methods for this interface, `GetBorder()`, `RequestBorderSpace()`, and `SetBorderSpace()`, are simple for our document window. Since we do not support tools on our document window, they simply return `INPLACE_E_NOTOOLSPACE`.

All that is left is to keep track of the active object by saving and releasing it as a result of calls to `SetActiveObject()`.

Implementing the IOleInPlaceFrame Interface

Listing 9.3 contains the `IOleInPlaceFrame` interface for OLE Publisher.

Listing 9.3

```
APPIPFRM.CPP
#include "appl.h"

Application::AppInPlaceFrame::AppInPlaceFrame()
{
    m_pActObj = NULL ;
}

STDMETHODIMP Application::AppInPlaceFrame::QueryInterface( REFIID riid,
                                    LPVOID FAR *lpVoid )
{
    return theApp.QueryInterface( riid, lpVoid ) ;
}

STDMETHODIMP_(ULONG) Application::AppInPlaceFrame::AddRef()
{
    return theApp.AddRef() ;
}

STDMETHODIMP_(ULONG) Application::AppInPlaceFrame::Release( )
{
    return theApp.Release() ;
}

// *** IOleWindow methods ***
STDMETHODIMP Application::AppInPlaceFrame::GetWindow(
             HWND FAR* lphwnd)
{
    *lphwnd = theApp.m_hWnd ;
    return NOERROR ;
}

STDMETHODIMP Application::AppInPlaceFrame::ContextSensitiveHelp(
             BOOL fEnterMode)
{
    if( theApp.m_helpMode != fEnterMode ) {
        theApp.m_helpMode = fEnterMode ;

        /* Loop through all of the documents in the application */
        HWND hWnd = ::GetWindow( theApp.m_hClientWnd, GW_CHILD ) ;
        while( hWnd != NULL ) {
            Document *pDoc = DocFromHWND( hWnd ) ;
            if( pDoc != NULL ) {
```

```
                    if( pDoc->m_inPlaceWindow.m_pActObj != NULL )
                        pDoc->m_inPlaceWindow.m_pActObj->
                            ContextSensitiveHelp( fEnterMode ) ;
                }
                hWnd = ::GetWindow( hWnd, GW_HWNDNEXT ) ;
            }
        }
        return NOERROR ;
}


// *** IOleInPlaceUIWindow methods ***
STDMETHODIMP Application::AppInPlaceFrame::GetBorder(
                LPRECT lprectBorder)
{
    GetClientRect( theApp.m_hWnd, lprectBorder ) ;
    lprectBorder->bottom -= theApp.m_statusBar.BarHeight() ;

    return NOERROR ;
}

STDMETHODIMP Application::AppInPlaceFrame::RequestBorderSpace(
                LPCBORDERWIDTHS lpborderwidths)
{
    m_borderWidths = *lpborderwidths ;
    return NOERROR ;
}

STDMETHODIMP Application::AppInPlaceFrame::SetBorderSpace(
                LPCBORDERWIDTHS lpborderwidths)
{
    if( lpborderwidths != NULL )
        m_borderWidths = *lpborderwidths ;
    return NOERROR ;
}

STDMETHODIMP Application::AppInPlaceFrame::SetActiveObject(
        LPOLEINPLACEACTIVEOBJECT lpActiveObject,
        LPCSTR lpszObjName)
{
    if( m_pActObj != NULL ) {
        m_pActObj->Release() ;
    }

    // Save new active object pointer
    m_pActObj = lpActiveObject ;
```

```
        if( m_pActObj != NULL ) {
            m_pActObj->AddRef() ;
        }

        return NOERROR ;
    }



    // *** IOleInPlaceFrame methods ***
    STDMETHODIMP Application::AppInPlaceFrame::InsertMenus(
                HMENU hmenuShared,
                LPOLEMENUGROUPWIDTHS lpMenuWidths)
    {
        HMENU hmenu ;

        // Insert menus
        hmenu = GetSubMenu( theApp.m_appMenu, FILE_MENU ) ;
        InsertMenu( hmenuShared, -1,
                    MF_POPUP|MF_BYPOSITION, (UINT)hmenu, "&File" ) ;
        hmenu = GetSubMenu( theApp.m_appMenu, WINDOW_MENU ) ;
        InsertMenu( hmenuShared, -1,
            MF_POPUP|MF_BYPOSITION, (UINT)hmenu, "&Window" ) ;

        // Add menus to hmenuShared
        lpMenuWidths->width[0] = 1 ;
        lpMenuWidths->width[2] = 0 ;
        lpMenuWidths->width[4] = 1 ;
        return NOERROR ;
    }

    STDMETHODIMP Application::AppInPlaceFrame::SetMenu(
                HMENU hmenuShared, HOLEMENU holemenu,
                HWND hwndActiveObject)
    {
        if( holemenu == NULL ) {
            hmenuShared = theApp.m_appMenu ;
        }

        HMENU hmenu = GetSubMenu( theApp.m_appMenu, WINDOW_MENU ) ;

        SendMessage( theApp.m_hClientWnd, WM_MDISETMENU, FALSE,
                    MAKELPARAM( hmenuShared, hmenu ) ) ;
        SendMessage( theApp.m_hClientWnd, WM_MDISETMENU, TRUE, OL ) ;
```

```
        ::SetMenu( theApp.m_hWnd, hmenuShared ) ;

    HRESULT hErr = NOERROR ;
    if( holemenu != NULL )
        hErr = OleSetMenuDescriptor( holemenu, theApp.m_hWnd,
                        hwndActiveObject, NULL, NULL ) ;
    else
        OleSetMenuDescriptor( NULL, theApp.m_hWnd, NULL, NULL, NULL ) ;
    DrawMenuBar( theApp.m_hWnd ) ;
    return hErr ;
}

STDMETHODIMP Application::AppInPlaceFrame::RemoveMenus(
            HMENU hmenuShared)
{
    HMENU fileMenu, windowMenu ;
    int menusLeft = 2, pos = 0 ;
    fileMenu = GetSubMenu( theApp.m_appMenu, FILE_MENU ) ;
    windowMenu = GetSubMenu( theApp.m_appMenu, WINDOW_MENU ) ;
    while( GetMenuItemCount( hmenuShared ) && menusLeft ) {
        if( fileMenu == GetSubMenu( hmenuShared, pos ) ||
            windowMenu == GetSubMenu( hmenuShared, pos ) ) {
            RemoveMenu( hmenuShared, pos, MF_BYPOSITION ) ;
            menusLeft -- ;
        }else pos++ ;
    }
    return NOERROR ;
}

STDMETHODIMP Application::AppInPlaceFrame::SetStatusText(
            LPCSTR lpszStatusText)
{
    theApp.m_statusBar.SetText( lpszStatusText ) ;
    return NOERROR ;
}

STDMETHODIMP Application::AppInPlaceFrame::EnableModeless(
        BOOL fEnable)
{
    return NOERROR ;
}
```

```
STDMETHODIMP Application::AppInPlaceFrame::TranslateAccelerator(
              LPMSG lpmsg, WORD wID)
{
    return NOERROR ;
}
```

Just like the other interfaces, the `IOleInPlaceFrame` interface has to support the `GetWindow()` and `ContextSensitiveHelp()` methods. The `GetWindow()` again just returns the `HWND` of the frame window saved in the `App.m_hWnd`. The `ContextSensitiveHelp()` method is a little more involved than it was in the other in-place interfaces. For the frame window for an MDI application, you must iterate through all the open documents and call the `IOleInPlaceUIWindow::ContextSensitiveHelp()` methods for each of these interfaces.

In the border-space negotiation methods, we added support for allocating border space around our MDI client window. This requires keeping track of how much space is being used by the current in-place active object and making sure this is accounted for in the `WM_SIZE` handlers for the frame window. The allocated border widths are stored in a member variable called `m_borderWidths`. The `GetBorder()` method returns the available client window space on the frame window, minus the space used by the status bar.

The `InsertMenus()` method adds the File menu and the Window menu using the `GetSubMenu()` and `InsertMenu()` SDK routines. The menus are the same as the ones in OLE Publisher's main menu, which is stored in the `Application::m_appMenu` member variable. Notice that we put menus in only two of the menu groups that are available to the container. We communicate this information to the object by setting the entries for the `lpMenuWidths` structure to the number of menus that will be placed in each group. The `IOleInPlaceFrame::SetMenu()` method must install the shared menu that is passed in the `hmenuShared` parameter on the frame window. We do this by using the Windows SDK `SetMenu()` routine. Since OLE Publisher is an MDI application, we also take the extra steps required to inform the MDI client window that a new menu is being installed and that it should take the appropriate actions to handle the Window menu. The `OleSetMenuDescriptor()` routine takes care of the details of installing a message filter that passes the messages for your container's menus to your frame window. For the object, these messages are passed the window specified in hwndActiveObject, which was passed to OleSetMenuDescriptor(). It is for this purpose that this window handle is passed to IOleInPlaceFrame::SetMenu() in the first place. The IOleInPlaceFrame::SetMenu() method must also handle the scenario in which the menu is being uninstalled. This is indicated by NULLs for all the parameters. In this case the container's main menu is restored and the message filter is removed when you call OleSetMenuDescriptor() with NULLs.

Summary

Adding support for in-place activation touches almost every portion of your application. You must add the IOleInPlaceSite interface to your objects, the IOleInPlaceUIWindow to your document (usually only for MDI applications), and the IOleInPlaceFrame interface for the frame window for your application. After implementing these interfaces, you must make modifications to your message loop to add support for the translation of accelerators for in-place objects. The frame and document windows must make calls to the active object when they are moved, scrolled, or resized. Also, support must be added for activation and deactivation of in-place objects at the appropriate times, such as when a mouse event takes place outside the in-place active object.

In the next chapter we will discuss the details of drag-and-drop for the application.

CHAPTER
TEN

Supporting Drag-and-Drop

- User interface issues with drag-and-drop

- Drop targets for OLE objects

- Drag sources for OLE objects

- Implementing Autoscroll

One interface feature that has come from the widespread adoption of window- and mouse-oriented interfaces is drag-and-drop. The idea is simple: instead of clicking an object to select it at the source, using the Cut command to move it to the clipboard, switching to the target, and then pasting the object from the clipboard (whew!), you can simply grab it with the mouse and drop it on the target.

Unfortunately, most applications do not implement drag-and-drop, even though it is only slightly more difficult to implement than cutting, copying, and pasting. The most recent versions of the Windows File Manager do support the ability to drag-and-drop files from directory to directory and even into some applications that support the messages the File Manager sends to the application. When a file from the File Manager is dropped into one of these applications, the application opens the dropped file. This is a step in the right direction. Now it's time to take the technique the rest of the way—to drag-and-drop almost anything from one application (or at least any OLE 2 application) to another.

For users to be able to apply the drag-and-drop technique, it must be consistently implemented, and this requires guidelines for the way the user obtains feedback while performing a drag operation. This chapter discusses both the user-interface aspects of drag-and-drop and its technical aspects.

User Feedback for Drag-and-Drop

The user needs feedback in two areas when performing a drag-and-drop: a representation of the object being dragged from a specific source and a representation of the result of dropping on a specific target.

Source Feedback

To drag an object, the user points to it, presses the left mouse button, and continues to hold down the button while moving the object to a valid target (see Figure 10.1). To drop the object, the user releases the left mouse button. While the drag operation is in progress, the cursor changes to indicate the different states of the drag operation.

FIGURE 10.1:

Sample screen for drag-and-drop

Spreadsheet document →

Dragged object →

Word processor document →

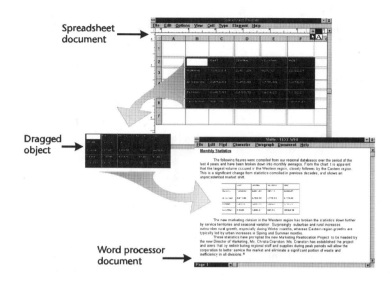

The OLE specification uses the shape of the mouse cursor to indicate the type and state of the object being dragged (as well as to indicate whether a given target can accept the object being dropped, as described in the next section). The standard drag-and-drop cursors are illustrated in Figure 10.2. Note, though, that the shape of the cursor during a drag operation can be specific to the application. All of these cursors are similar in that each is an arrow with some sort of attachment representing the object. This is the cursor the user sees when the object is over any target window that can accept the drop. When the user moves the object over a target window that cannot accept the object being dragged, the cursor changes to the "No" cursor.

The default type of drop operation may be either a move or a copy. In most applications the default should be a move, but there are exceptions. To change the type of operation that takes place, the user can use a keyboard modifier to change the default behavior. The cursor then changes to indicate the operation that will take place, as shown in Figure 10.2.

FIGURE 10.2:

Standard drag-and-drop cursors

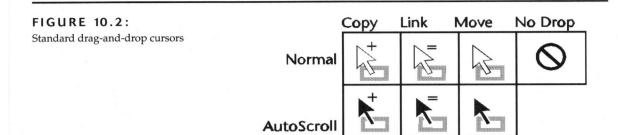

Target Feedback

The user also needs layout feedback for potential drop sites. In a word processor, for example (see Figure 10.3), a thick gray insertion point might be used to show where graphics or text will land if dropped. This feedback allows the user to fine-tune the drop operation.

FIGURE 10.3:

Drag-and-drop with a word processor

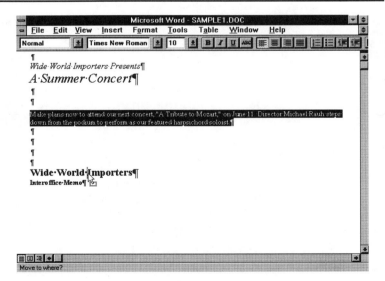

Is It a Move or a Copy?

The usual default behavior when dragging an object from one place to another, to *move* the object from the source to the target, is equivalent to a cut-and-paste operation. To *copy* an object from the source to the destination by dragging, which is equivalent to a copy-and-paste operation, the OLE user interface has specified the Shift key as the keyboard modifier.

Automatic Scrolling

Another aspect of drag-and-drop is the scrolling of document windows as the user is dragging the object. For example, what if the user wants to place the object being dragged to a location on the document that is not visible? To accommodate the user you could write your application so the document window scrolls automatically whenever the user is at or past the edge of the document. The user could then drop the item anywhere within the document. But what if the user wanted to move the object to another window on the screen? OLE provides a solution for this situation. When the cursor is within a fixed region at the edge of the document window for longer than a certain amount of time, the document window automatically scrolls. But if the user moves outside this area, the object can be dropped in any other window that can act as a drop target.

The autoscroll region of a document window is illustrated in Figure 10.4. According to the OLE user-interface specifications, if the cursor remains in this area for more than 50 milliseconds, the window should autoscroll in the direction indicated by the border the cursor is closest to.

FIGURE 10.4:
Autoscroll region of a drop target document window

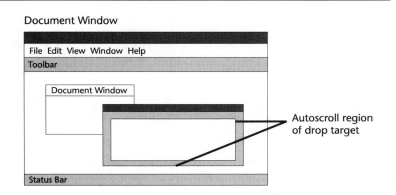

231

The Drag-and-Drop Interfaces

Two interfaces define the drag-and-drop support for OLE: IDropSource and IDropTarget. The relationship between the two interfaces is one in which the drop source ultimately makes the decision to perform a drop or not, but it must first ask the drop target whether it can accept the data object to be dropped.

The IDropSource Interface

The IDropSource interface defines the behavior of a drop source when an object is being dragged. Table 10.1 contains the IDropSource methods. The main job of the IDropSource interface is to control the cursor changes. The easiest way to deal with the cursor is to return a result value of DRAGDROP_S_USEDEFAULTCURSORS from IDropSource::GiveFeedback( ), indicating that you want OLE to control the cursor for you. This works for most cases of drag-and-drop unless you want to display a special cursor.

TABLE 10.1: IDropSource Methods

Method	Description
HRESULT QueryContinueDrag(fEscapePressed, grfKeyState)	Called by OLE during the drag operation to determine whether the drag should continue. This method returns S_OK to continue the drag, DRAGDROP_S_DROP to cause a drop to happen, or DRAG-DROP_S_CANCEL to abort the drag operation
HRESULT GiveFeedback(dwEffect)	Called to give the drop source a chance to set the cursor feedback for the drag operation. If the standard drag-and-drop cursors are acceptable, the method can return DRAGDROP_S_USEDEFAULT-CURSORS and OLE will handle the cursor changes automatically

The other method, `QueryContinueDrag()`, returns a result value that indicates whether the drag operation is to continue, abort, or cause a drop over the current target.

The IDropTarget Interface

The `IDropTarget` interface in turn defines the target's responses to the drop request, such as drop feedback and autoscrolling. This interface contains methods for when a drag operation enters the area of the target's window, for all movement inside the window, and for when the drag leaves the window. The `IDropTarget` interface is listed in Table 10.2.

TABLE 10.2: IDropTarget Methods

Method	Description
`HRESULT DragEnter( lpDataObj, grfKeyState, pt, pdwEffect )`	Called when a drag operation enters a given drop target. The `lpDataObj` parameter points to the data object for the drop operation. If the drop target wants to hold onto this object, it should call `AddRef()` on the data object. For the purpose of providing feedback, though, it should be enough to obtain the object size by using the `CF_OBJECTDESCRIPTOR` and `CF_LINKDESCRIPTOR` data formats from the data object. The `grfKeyState` parameter indicates the state of the keyboard and the `pt` indicates the current mouse location in screen coordinates. (Note that all drag-and-drop mouse points are in screen coordinates.) `pdwEffect` is an output parameter that communicates the type of operation that the drop target thinks would be appropriate. This method is called once each time the drag enters a given target window
`HRESULT DragOver( grfKeyState, pt, pdwEffect )`	Called while a drag operation is passing over a drop target. You can use this method to provide target feedback to indicate the effect the drop operation will have on the target, such as the appearance of the cursor. Use the parameters for this routine in the same manner as for the `DragEnter()` method

TABLE 10.2: IDropTarget Methods (continued)

Method	Description
HRESULT DragLeave()	Called once before a drag operation leaves a window or even if a drop is occurring in the window. This gives the target a chance to remove any visual feedback
HRESULT Drop(lpDataObj, grfKeyState, pt, pdwEffect)	Called when the drop source indicates that a drop should take place over a given target. This will be called only if the drop target indicated that it would accept a drop by the settings returned in pdwEffect in the Drag-Enter() and DragOver() methods. The lpDataObj is passed again and is used by the target to actually perform the drop

Each of the methods in this interface has a dwEffect parameter as an argument. The three methods DragEnter(), DragOver(), and DragLeave() are responsible for determining the operation that will be performed by setting this parameter to appropriate DROPEFFECT values. These constants are listed in Table 10.3.

TABLE 10.3: Drop Effect Constants

Constant	Description
DROPEFFECT_NONE	Indicates that the target will not accept the drop operation
DROPEFFECT_MOVE	Indicates that a move operation will be accepted
DROPEFFECT_COPY	Indicates that a copy operation will be accepted
DROPEFFECT_LINK	Indicates that a link to the dragged object will be accepted
DROPEFFECT_SCROLL	Is set when the drop target is autoscrolling

The drop target decides what these actions should be by examining the other arguments to the methods, which include the key state (MK_ALT, MK_CONTROL, MK_SHIFT, and the mouse button indicators MK_LBUTTON, MK_MBUTTON, and MK_RBUTTON), as well as the current mouse location in screen coordinates. This information, when combined with the extent information in the CF_OBJECTDESCRIPTOR data format (you have a pointer to the data object and are free to request this data as needed), is enough to provide even more feedback, such as a drop area rectangle to indicate the object's placement if it were dropped in a specific location. As a matter of fact, the way the methods are defined actually encourages this sort of feedback. When your drop target is notified of a drag operation entering the window by a call to `IDropTarget::DragEnter()`, it should draw the original feedback graphics. On each call to `IDropTarget::DragOver()`, you can remove the original feedback and draw the new feedback to account for the new mouse position. Finally, on `IDrop-Target::DragLeave()`, you should remove the feedback for the final time. OLE makes sure that the calls to these routines always follow this pattern so you can easily support this extra visual feedback for the user.

Drag, Drop, and the Clipboard

Drag-and-drop is very similar to clipboard operations in that it requires an `IDataObject` interface to manipulate the data being dragged. The only major difference in function between using the clipboard and drag-and-drop is that you have a concept of position with drag-and-drop—you can specify where the object should be dropped with the mouse.

Other than that, you create the data object in a similar manner (in fact, we use the same code as for the copy operation), and you should insert the code into your document similarly to a paste operation (yes, we use the same paste code here, too).

Adding Drag-and-Drop
Support to OLE Publisher

The structure of OLE Publisher after adding the drag-and-drop interfaces has changed only slightly (see Figure 10.5). We added the `IDropTarget` interface to the document level to allow each document to be a drop target. And we defined an `IDropSource` interface that is not associated with any application object but stands alone to support the drop source aspect of drag-and-drop.

FIGURE 10.5:

Class architecture for OLE Publisher with support for drag-and-drop

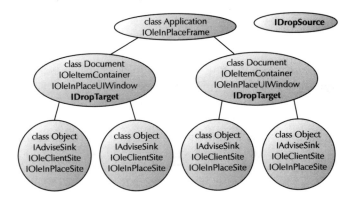

Building a Drop Source

Building a drop source is easy if you already have the code to create your data object. The code originally presented in Chapter 7 for the `Object::CreateTransfer-DataObject()` method is used here to create a data object to be used for the drag operation. To add a drop source, we first have to define our drop source interface. Listing 10.1 is the code for our implementation of the `IDropSource` interface.

Listing 10.1

```
/////////////////////////////////////////////////////////////
// IDropSource Class Source: IDROPSRC.CPP
//
#include "appl.h"
#include "idropsrc.h"

// Constructor/Destructor
GenericDropSource::GenericDropSource()
{
    m_refCount = 0 ;
}

GenericDropSource::~GenericDropSource()
{
}
```

```
// IUnknown methods
STDMETHODIMP GenericDropSource::QueryInterface(
        REFIID riid,
        LPVOID FAR *ppvObj )
{
    if( riid == IID_IDropSource || riid == IID_IUnknown ) {
        *ppvObj = this ;
        AddRef( ) ;
        return NOERROR ;
    }
    *ppvObj = NULL ;
    return ResultFromScode(E_NOINTERFACE) ;
}


STDMETHODIMP_(ULONG) GenericDropSource::AddRef()
{
    return ++m_refCount ;
}


STDMETHODIMP_(ULONG) GenericDropSource::Release()
{
    if(--m_refCount == 0 ) {
        delete this ;
        return 0 ;
    }
    return m_refCount ;
}


STDMETHODIMP GenericDropSource::QueryContinueDrag(
    BOOL fEscapePressed,
    DWORD grfKeyState )
{
    if( fEscapePressed ) {
        return ResultFromScode( DRAGDROP_S_CANCEL ) ;
    }

    if( !( grfKeyState & MK_LBUTTON ) ) {
        return ResultFromScode( DRAGDROP_S_DROP ) ;
    }

    return ResultFromScode( S_OK ) ;
}
```

```
STDMETHODIMP GenericDropSource::GiveFeedback(
    DWORD dwEffect)
{
    return
        ResultFromScode( DRAGDROP_S_USEDEFAULTCURSORS ) ;
}
```

The `IDropSource::QueryContinueDrag()` determines when the drop should actually happen.

All that is left is to actually initiate the drag operation at the proper time. When a `WM_LBUTTONDOWN` message is received by your document window, your hit-testing code will determine whether it was on an object, and if it was, which object. Once you have this information you must create your data object, instantiate your `IDropSource` interface, and call `DoDragDrop()`. The code for handling this in OLE Publisher is listed here:

```
void Document::OnLButtonDown( POINT pt )
{
    // OTHER MOUSE HANDLING CODE OMITTED HERE
    // FOR CLARITY

    // Drag and drop the object
    ClientToVirtualPoint( &pt ) ;
    LPDROPSOURCE pDropSrc = new GenericDropSource ;
    LPDATAOBJECT pDataObj = pObj->
            CreateTransferDataObject( pt ) ;
    pDataObj->AddRef() ;
    pDropSrc->AddRef() ;

    DWORD dwEffect = DROPEFFECT_COPY |
                     DROPEFFECT_LINK |
                     DROPEFFECT_MOVE ;
    HRESULT hErr = DoDragDrop( pDataObj, pDropSrc,
        dwEffect, &dwEffect ) ;

    pDataObj->Release() ;
    pDropSrc->Release() ;

    // If the drop was a move
    // then delete the current object
    if( GetScode( sc ) == DRAGDROP_S_DROP ) {
        if( dwEffect & DROPEFFECT_MOVE )
```

```
            OnEditDelete() ;
    }else
        Error( "Drag/Drop Error!" ) ;

    // OTHER MOUSE HANDLING CODE OMITTED HERE
    // FOR CLARITY

}
```

The call to DoDragDrop() takes care of all the details of tracking the mouse, determining the window the mouse cursor is over, and calling the drop source and drop target methods at the appropriate time. This routine also provides the appropriate cursor feedback for windows that are not registered as drop targets (the "No" cursor again).

Building a Drop Target

The drop operation, of course, will use the same Document::CreateFromDataObject() method that we used for the paste operation discussed in Chapter 7. After defining the drop target as an interface that is available from our Document's IUnknown, we must register and unregister the drop target with OLE.

NOTE It is not a requirement that the IDropTarget interface be another interface that can be queried from the Document's IUnknown, but the IDropTarget interface and the Document class are related enough for this to be appropriate since the Document is the drop target. Other than that, there is no technical reason that the IDropTarget needs to be associated with the Document class.

When the Document's window is created, a call to RegisterDragDrop() associates the HWND for the document with our IDropTarget interface. The following code registers the OLE Publisher drop target:

```
// Register the drop target here
RegisterDragDrop(m_hWnd, &m_dropTarget ) ;
```

When an application starts a drag operation, OLE takes over, using the Windows SDK to determine the HWND that the mouse pointer is over. OLE then does a lookup in an internal table to determine whether the window is a drop target. If it is, OLE starts a dialog with the drop target to determine how the target will react to the data being dragged. When the document is closed, the RevokeDragDrop() routine is called to unregister the window as a drop target. If it is determined that a drop operation should take place, OLE will call our IDropTarget::Drop() method, passing the data object.

Listing 10.2 contains the source code for the implementation of this interface in the Document class for OLE Publisher.

Listing 10.2

```
//////////////////////////////////////////////////////////////////
// IDropTarget Class Source: DOCDTARG.CPP
//
#include "appl.h"
#include "doc.h"
#include "obj.h"

Document::DocDropTarget::DocDropTarget( Document *pDoc )
{
    m_refCount = 0 ;
    m_pDoc = pDoc ;
}

STDMETHODIMP Document::DocDropTarget::QueryInterface(
    REFIID riid,
    LPVOID FAR *lpVoid )
{
    if( riid == IID_IDropTarget ||
        riid == IID_IUnknown ) {
        AddRef() ;
        *lpVoid = this ;
        return NOERROR ;
    }
    *lpVoid = NULL ;
    return ResultFromScode( E_NOINTERFACE ) ;
}
```

```
STDMETHODIMP_(ULONG) Document::DocDropTarget::AddRef()
{
    m_refCount++ ;
    return m_refCount ;
}

STDMETHODIMP_(ULONG) Document::DocDropTarget::Release()
{
    m_refCount-- ;
    if( m_refCount == 0 )
        return 0 ;
    return m_refCount ;
}

// auto-scroll variables
static int defScrollInset ;
static int defScrollDelay ;
static int defScrollInterval ;
static DWORD startDelay, currDelay ;
static BOOL fAutoScrolling ;
static RECT clientRect, scrollRect ;

STDMETHODIMP Document::DocDropTarget::DragEnter(
    LPDATAOBJECT pDataObject,
    DWORD grfKeyState, POINTL pt, LPDWORD pdwEffect)
{
    // initialize scroll constants
    defScrollInset = GetProfileInt( "windows",
            "DragScrollInset",
            DD_DEFSCROLLINSET ) ;
    defScrollDelay = GetProfileInt( "windows",
            "DragScrollDelay",
            DD_DEFSCROLLDELAY ) ;
    defScrollInterval = GetProfileInt( "windows",
            "DragScrollInterval",
            DD_DEFSCROLLINTERVAL ) ;

    // init start delay, scrollRect and clientRect
    startDelay = 0 ;
    currDelay = 0 ;
    GetClientRect( m_pDoc->m_hWnd, &clientRect ) ;
    scrollRect = clientRect ;
    InflateRect( &scrollRect,
        -defScrollInset, -defScrollInset ) ;
```

```
        // init effect
        DWORD dwEffect = *pdwEffect ;

        // Save the pointer to the data object on enter
        if( m_pDoc->CanDrop( pDataObject ) ) {
            m_pDataObject = pDataObject ;
            m_pDataObject->AddRef( ) ;
        }else m_pDataObject = NULL ;

        // Determine whether we can drop
        if( m_pDataObject != NULL ) {
            *pdwEffect = OleStdGetDropEffect( grfKeyState ) ;
            if( *pdwEffect == DROPEFFECT_NONE )
                *pdwEffect = DROPEFFECT_MOVE ;
        }else
            *pdwEffect = DROPEFFECT_NONE ;

        // Verify that we have not asked
        // the source to do something that it can't do
        *pdwEffect = *pdwEffect & dwEffect ;

        return NOERROR ;
    }

STDMETHODIMP Document::DocDropTarget::DragOver(
    DWORD grfKeyState,
    POINTL pt,
    LPDWORD pdwEffect )
{
    DWORD dwEffect = *pdwEffect ;

    // Determine whether we can drop
    if( m_pDataObject != NULL ) {
        *pdwEffect = OleStdGetDropEffect( grfKeyState ) ;
        if( *pdwEffect == DROPEFFECT_NONE )
            *pdwEffect = DROPEFFECT_MOVE ;
    }else
        *pdwEffect = DROPEFFECT_NONE ;

    // Verify that we have not asked the source
    // to do something that it can't do
    *pdwEffect = *pdwEffect & dwEffect ;
```

```
    // check for the scroll effect
    POINT pts ;
    pts.x = (int)pt.x ;
    pts.y = (int)pt.y ;
    ScreenToClient( m_pDoc->m_hWnd, &pts ) ;

    if( PtInRect( &clientRect, pts ) &&
        !PtInRect( &scrollRect, pts ) ) {

        if( ( fAutoScrolling &&
            (currDelay-startDelay)<defScrollInterval) ||
            (currDelay-startDelay)>=defScrollDelay ) {
            m_pDoc->AutoScrollDocument(
                pts, &scrollRect ) ;
            *pdwEffect |= DROPEFFECT_SCROLL ;
            fAutoScrolling = TRUE ;
            startDelay = (int)GetTickCount() ;
        }

        currDelay = (int)GetTickCount() ;

    }else{

        fAutoScrolling = FALSE ;
        currDelay =
        startDelay = 0 ;

    }

    return NOERROR ;
}

STDMETHODIMP Document::DocDropTarget::DragLeave()
{
    // Release the data object that we have been holding
    if( m_pDataObject != NULL ) {
        m_pDataObject->Release( ) ;
        m_pDataObject = NULL ;
    }
    return NOERROR ;
}

STDMETHODIMP Document::DocDropTarget::Drop(
        LPDATAOBJECT pDataObject,
        DWORD grfKeyState,
```

```
            POINTL pt,
            LPDWORD pdwEffect)
{
    // Release the data object that we have been holding
    m_pDataObject->Release( ) ;

    // Update effects flag
    if( m_pDataObject != NULL ) {
        *pdwEffect = OleStdGetDropEffect( grfKeyState ) ;
        if( *pdwEffect == DROPEFFECT_NONE )
            *pdwEffect = DROPEFFECT_MOVE ;
    }else
        *pdwEffect = DROPEFFECT_NONE ;

    // Drop it now
    // 1 - first convert the points from
    //     screen coordinates to local coordinates
    // 2 - call the drop method for the current document
    POINT pts ;
    pts.x = (int)pt.x ;
    pts.y = (int)pt.y ;

    ScreenToClient( m_pDoc->m_hWnd, &pts ) ;

    // Offset the rect by the offset of
    // the point in the object
    // Set the aspect
    HGLOBAL hMem ;
    STGMEDIUM stgMedium ;
    if( hMem = OleStdGetData( pDataObject,
        RegisterClipboardFormat( CF_OBJECTDESCRIPTOR ),
        NULL,
        DVASPECT_CONTENT,
        &stgMedium ) ) {

        LPOBJECTDESCRIPTOR pObjDesc ;
        pObjDesc =
            (LPOBJECTDESCRIPTOR)GlobalLock( hMem ) ;

        POINTL pointl ;
        XformSizeInHimetricToPixels( NULL,
            (LPSIZEL)&pObjDesc->pointl,
            (LPSIZEL)&pointl ) ;
        pts.x -= (int)pointl.x ;
        pts.y -= (int)pointl.y ;
```

```
        GlobalUnlock( hMem ) ;
        ReleaseStgMedium( &stgMedium ) ;
    }

    BOOL fLink ;
    if( *pdwEffect & DROPEFFECT_LINK ) fLink = TRUE ;
    else fLink = FALSE ;

    if( m_pDoc->m_isDragging &&
        *pdwEffect == DROPEFFECT_MOVE ) {
        RECT objRect = m_pDoc->m_dragObj->m_objRect ;
        m_pDoc->m_dragObj->Move( pts.x, pts.y,
                    objRect.right-objRect.left,
                    objRect.bottom-objRect.top ) ;
    }else{
        m_pDoc->CreateFromDataObject(
            fLink, pDataObject, pts ) ;
    }

    m_pDoc->SetModified( TRUE ) ;

    return NOERROR ;
}
```

Implementing Autoscroll

If you have already implemented scrolling support in your application, autoscrolling during a drag-and-drop operation is not as difficult as it may seem. To define the standard behavior for a drag-and-drop operation, OLE has defined three user settings for implementing autoscroll:

Setting	Description
Auto-scroll Inset	Defines the space on the inner border of a window in which the cursor must be positioned to cause autoscrolling. The default value, 11 pixels, is defined by the constant DD_DEFSCROLLINSET in the header OLE2.H

Setting	Description
Auto-scroll Delay	Defines the display in milliseconds that the cursor must remain in the autoscroll region of a window before autoscrolling begins. The default value for this setting, 50 milliseconds, is defined by the constant `DD_DEFSCROLLDELAY`
Auto-scroll Interval	Defines the interval between which the actual scrolling should take place after an autoscroll operation begins. This changes the speed of the scroll operation. The default value for this setting, also 50 milliseconds, is defined by the constant `DD_DEFSCROLLINTERVAL`

Since these settings will eventually be user definable, perhaps through the control panel, you should use the Windows profile routines to access these values. The following code illustrates how to do this for the three autoscroll settings:

```
// initialize scroll constants
defScrollInset = GetProfileInt( "windows",
        "DragScrollInset",
        DD_DEFSCROLLINSET ) ;
defScrollDelay = GetProfileInt( "windows",
        "DragScrollDelay",
        DD_DEFSCROLLDELAY ) ;
defScrollInterval = GetProfileInt( "windows",
        "DragScrollInterval",
        DD_DEFSCROLLINTERVAL ) ;
```

Listing 10.2 demonstrates how these values can be used to implement autoscrolling.

Obtaining the Mouse Offset from the Object

One more detail should be considered, just for its aesthetic value. When the user drops an object into your drop target, it should be dropped at a position relative to the point in the object where the user originally pressed the mouse button.

In Figure 10.6 the user clicked the object and dropped it in a new location. Since this example did not use the offset information that was available, we dropped the object with the top-left corner at the exact location of the button up. This causes the visual effect of dropping the object as though the user had dragged the object by the top-left corner. To make this work in a more intuitive fashion, the button up location must be combined with information about where the mouse was originally clicked inside the object. With this information we can offset the drop location so that the object is positioned as the user would expect.

The offset information is contained within the CF_OBJECTDESCRIPTOR format that can be retrieved from the IDataObject that is being dropped. The following code demonstrates how to use this information:

```
// Offset the rect by the offset of the point in the object
HGLOBAL hMem ;
STGMEDIUM stgMedium ;
if( hMem = OleStdGetData( pDataObject,
        RegisterClipboardFormat( CF_OBJECTDESCRIPTOR ),
        NULL,
        DVASPECT_CONTENT,
        &stgMedium ) ) {
```

FIGURE 10.6:

Offset from top-left corner of object

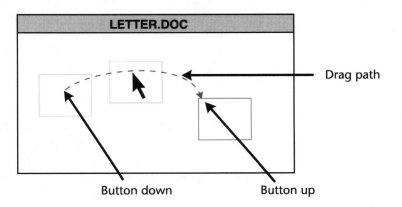

LETTER.DOC

Drag path

Button down

Button up

```
        LPOBJECTDESCRIPTOR pObjDesc ;
        pObjDesc = (LPOBJECTDESCRIPTOR)GlobalLock( hMem ) ;

        POINTL pointl ;
        XformSizeInHimetricToPixels( NULL,
                (LPSIZEL)&pObjDesc->pointl,
                (LPSIZEL)&pointl ) ;
        pts.x -= (int)pointl.x ;
        pts.y -= (int)pointl.y ;

        GlobalUnlock( hMem ) ;
        ReleaseStgMedium( &stgMedium ) ;
    }
```

Since the offset saved in the CF_OBJECTDESCRIPTOR is saved in HIMETRIC, it must be converted to whatever coordinate system is appropriate for your container. In this case the offset is converted to client coordinates and then used to offset the button up location in pts to properly offset the drop location.

Optimizing Drag Operations

One of the difficulties with implementing drag-and-drop is that when your container detects a click on an object, it may be the first click of a double-click or simply a mouse down that is going to be the start of a drag operation. There is absolutely no way to distinguish between these two operations based on the information that is available at the time of the first click. When a drag operation starts, there is a lot of overhead in constructing a data object to begin the operation, so if your can somehow avoid this overhead when the user only intends to double-click an object, you will improve the response time.

To accommodate this sort of optimization, OLE defines two more constants in the same fashion in which the autoscroll constants are used: DD_DEFDRAGDELAY and DD_DEFDRAGMINDIST. These two constants define the delay in milliseconds that must pass before dragging starts and the minimum distance the cursor must move before dragging starts. The idea is that if both of these settings are not satisified, a drag-and-drop operation should not be initiated.

These settings should be determined in exactly the same fashion as the autoscroll constants. The following code demonstrates how to determine the values of these settings:

```
// Get drag settings
ddDragDelay = GetProfileInt( "windows",
    "DragDelay",
    DD_DEFDRAGDELAY ) ;

ddDragDist = GetProfileInt( "windows",
    "DragMinDist",
    DD_DEFDRAGMINDIST ) ;
```

Examine the source file DOCMOUSE.CPP for an example of how to use this in your mouse-handling code.

Using the Drag-and-Drop Interfaces for Normal Data Transfer

Up to this point we have talked about drag-and-drop in terms of dragging and dropping OLE objects. This is not a requirement by any means. Since a data object is used to encapsulate the clipboard, you are free to use the IDataObject interface clipboard format that your application needs. You can use the IDataObject::Get-Data() and IDataObject::GetDataHere() methods to obtain any clipboard format that is available. If you utilize this information and add your private formats to the data object, OLE drag-and-drop can be used for just about anything. Your IDropTarget::Drop() method could look for bitmaps, metafiles, or even text, if for some reason you did not want to implement container support. Figure 10.7 shows the clipboard formats that are available from the IDataObject that was dropped onto the DataObject Viewer from Microsoft Word 6.0. If you examine the available formats, you will see that all the OLE formats are there, but standard formats such as the CF_METAFILEPICT and CF_TEXT exist as well. You can use these to support drag-and-drop from OLE 2 applications even if your application is not a full container.

FIGURE 10.7:

Clipboard formats available in
drag-and-drop

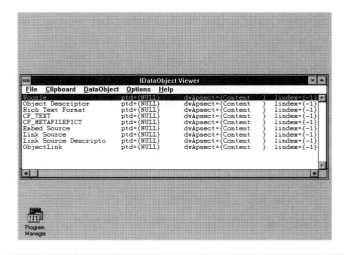

> **NOTE** The DataObject Viewer is available in the OLE 2 SDK. This application
> allows you to examine the contents of data objects that are
> transferred on the clipboard or by drag-and-drop.

Summary

This chapter has covered details of implementing the IDropSource and IDropTarget interfaces on the OLE Publisher container to enable the OLE drag-and-drop feature. If you want your application or its document to be a drop target, you simply implement the IDropTarget interface and call RegisterDragDrop() to associate the IDropTarget interface with the HWND that is to be the drop target. The IDropTarget is responsible for performing the actual drop operation after the drop source determines that a drop operation will take place. The IDropTarget::Drop() method is called with a pointer to an IDataObject to actually perform the drop.

You must implement an IDropSource to act on behalf of the drop source to set the drop cursor feedback. You use the IDropSource::QueryContinueDrag() method to tell OLE whether to continue the drag operation and when to perform the actual drop.

After you have implemented the IDropSource interface, you must also have an implementation of the IDataObject interface that contains the data to be dragged. When your application detects a mouse-click that would begin a drag operation, you should call DoDragDrop() with the IDataObject and your IDropSource implementations.

This chapter used the OLE container as the example for implementing the drag-and-drop interfaces, but the same techniques apply for implementing drag-and-drop in any application. This includes OLE object servers, which are discussed in Chapter 11.

PART IV

Servers

This section covers the interface specifications for building a server. This includes support for in-place, as well as the details of adding various types of support for linking to your server. Also included is a sample server called OLE Draw that implements the concepts explained in this section.

Chapter 11 describes the techniques and interfaces you use to create a basic server. The chapter covers the `IOleObject`, `IDataObject`, and `IPersistStorage` interfaces.

Chapter 12 presents the issues involved in creating an in-place server. It discusses the user-interface issues involved in activating an object in-place, as well as the details of the required OLE interfaces. It covers the `IOleInPlaceObject`, `IOleInPlaceActiveObject`, and `IOleWindow` interfaces.

Chapter 13 discusses the issues involved in adding linking support to your server. The chapter contains a conceptual explanation of the linking process that will allow you to determine the best approach to use in your applications. It explains concepts such as notifications, cache updating, and pseudo-objects in detail.

CHAPTER

ELEVEN

Designing a Simple Object Server

- Building the OLE Draw object

- Implementing the basic object interfaces

- Implementing object verbs

- Handling and managing notifications

- Registering the object in the registration database

Chapter 7 discussed what it would take to design a container that could handle any type of graphics object. You saw how OLE provided exactly the interfaces that were needed to do just that. This chapter shows you how to build OLE objects. It discusses the required object interfaces and, finally, builds a simple object server.

The Three Basic Server Interfaces

Creating a simple object server requires you to implement a component object that supports three basic interfaces. These interfaces are the IOleObject interface, the IPersistStorage interface, and the IDataObject interface (see Figure 11.1). They are described in the following sections.

FIGURE 11.1:

OLE interfaces used in the basic server

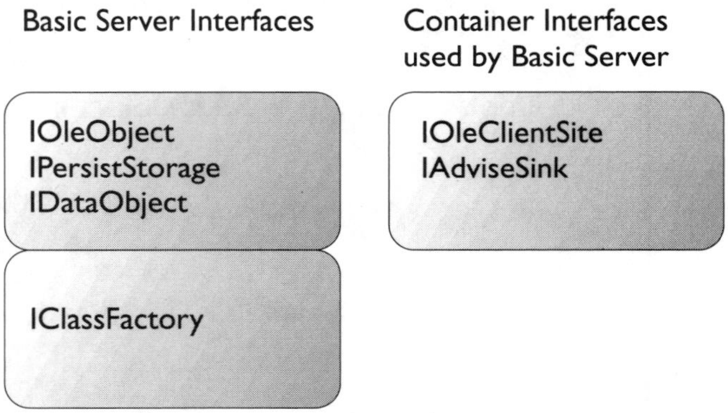

Basic Server Interfaces

Container Interfaces used by Basic Server

IOleObject
IPersistStorage
IDataObject

IOleClientSite
IAdviseSink

IClassFactory

The IDataObject Interface

The IDataObject interface is always used as the mechanism for transferring data. In Chapter 7 you saw how to use it for extracting data from the clipboard. In Chapter 10 you saw how to use it to transfer data in a drag-and-drop operation. Here the IDataObject interface provides access to an object server's data. The IDataObject interface that must be implemented for an object server is different from the implementation we used for the OLE Publisher container. The `IDataObject` interface used for the clipboard and for drag-and-drop merely provided an encapsulation of data that already existed in various forms. The object server must be able to synthesize different data formats when they are requested, as well as to send advise notifications. Table 11.1 lists the `IDataObject` methods, along with a brief description of the functionality the method serves in an object server.

TABLE 11.1: IDataObject Methods

Method	Description
HRESULT GetData (pformatetcIn, pmedium)	Requests data of the type specified by the pformatetcIn parameter that is then returned in the pmedium output parameter. The STGMEDIUM pointed to by the pmedium parameter is uninitialized and must be allocated by the data object HRESULT GetDataHere(pformatetc, pmedium). This method is similar to the GetData() method, with the exception that the STDMEDIUM pointed to by pmedium is preallocated. The allocated storage medium must be used. If there is not enough room in the allocated storage medium, this method returns the STG_E_MEDIUMFULL result code
HRESULT Query GetData(pformatetc)	Returns S_OK if the specified format can be retrieved from this data object. It returns S_FALSE if the format is not available
HRESULT GetCanonical-FormatEtc(pformatetc, pformatetcOut)	Since a number of formats can actually return the same data, you can use this method to reduce the format specified in pformatetc to the common format specification it will be reduced to when the GetData() or GetDataHere() method is called
HRESULT SetData (pformatetc, pmedium, fRelease)	Called to add the specified format and its data to the data object
HRESULT EnumFormatEtc(dwDirection, ppenumFormatEtc)	Returns a pointer to an IEnumFORMATETC interface that you can use to enumerate the available formats for this data object
HRESULT DAdvise (pFormatetc, advf, pAdvSink, pdw Connection)	Sets up an advise connection between the data object and the IAdviseSink passed in the pAdvSink parameter. The formatetc specifies the format the advise connection is interested in. The advf constant indicates the type of advise connection.

TABLE 11.1: IDataObject Methods (continued)

Method	Description
HRESULT DUnadvise (dwConnection)	Removes the advise connection specified by the dwConnection parameter
HRESULT EnumDAdvise (ppenumAdvise)	Obtains a pointer to the IEnumSTATDATA interface to enumerate all the existing advise connections for the object. The STATDATA structure contains all the details about a given advise connection, including the pointer to the IAdviseSink, the data format for the advise, the type of advise, and the connection token that represents the specific connection

For an object server, the GetData() and GetDataHere() methods must at least provide the following visual formats: CF_METAFILEPICT, CF_BITMAP, and CF_DIB. If you want to be able to paste or drag objects from your server, you must also provide the CF_EMBEDSOURCE format to provide access to the actual object data. Finally, you must provide the CF_OBJECTDESCRIPTOR format to describe the object you have embedded. This format is a structure that is stored in an HGLOBAL; it contains related information about the object. The OLE2UI library contains a routine called OleStd-GetObjectDescriptorData() to assist in creating this data structure. The fields for the CF_OBJECTDESCRIPTOR data structure are described in Table 11.2.

TABLE 11.2: Fields for the CF_OBJECTDESCRIPTOR data format

Field	Description
cbSize	Size of the object descriptor structure
clsid	Contains the CLSID of the object
dwDrawAspect	Indicates the visual aspect of the object that is available. This can be either DVASPECT_CONTENT or DVASPECT_ICON
sizel	Contains the extents of the object in HIMETRIC units
pointl	Used for drag-and-drop operations. It contains the offset from the top-left corner of the object of the mouse pointer location
dwStatus	Contains the status flags for the object. These flags are the same constants returned by the IOleObject::GetMiscStatus() method (see Table 11.5)

TABLE 11.2: Fields for the CF_OBJECTDESCRIPTOR data format (continued)

Field	Description
dwFullUser-TypeName	Contains the offset from the beginning of the data structure to a null-terminated string that specifies the full user type name of the object
dwSrcOfCopy	The offset to a string describing the object's source. This is used for display in the Paste Special… dialog

The IPersistStorage Interface

You use the IPersistStorage interface to make sure an object sticks around. Its sole purpose is to load and save the object's data to a storage. The only thing that makes this interface tricky is that it must be able to guarantee that the object can be saved in a low-memory situation. This means you cannot allocate any memory during a save operation. Table 11.3 lists the IPersistStorage methods that must be implemented for a basic object server.

TABLE 11.3: IPersistStorage Methods

Method	Description
HRESULT GetClassID (lpClassID)	Returns the class ID of the object in the lpClassID parameter
HRESULT IsDirty()	Returns S_OK if the object has changed since the last save and S_FALSE if it has not
HRESULT InitNew(pStg)	Called to request that the container initialize the storage passed in the pStg parameter
HRESULT Load(pStg)	Loads an object's data from the storage passed in the pStg parameter
HRESULT Save(pStgSave, fSameAsLoad)	Saves an object's data to the storage passed in the pStg parameter. You use the fSameAsLoad parameter to indicate to the server that the passed storage is the same as the storage used to load the object's data
HRESULT HandsOffStorage()	Called by the container to indicate that the server should not write to the storage until the SaveCompleted() method is called
HRESULT Save-Completed(pStgNew)	Called to indicate that the Save operation is complete and the server can now safely access its storage again

The Load() and Save() methods are the workhorse functions that load and save the object to and from an IStorage. When the object is first created, as when the user selects the object server from the "Insert Object..." dialog, the InitNew() method is called to give the server a chance to initialize the passed storage. When this happens, the server should at least call WriteClassStg() to write the object's class ID to the storage. The system later uses this class ID to determine the object's type and which server to load when an object is loaded or activated.

OLE has very strict memory requirements for this interface. Since OLE guarantees that a Save operation will not fail in low-memory situations, the IPersistStorage::Save() method cannot perform any memory allocations. This means that all streams and substorages required by your object's storage format will have to be opened and saved in either the IPersistStorage::InitNew() or the IPersistStorage::Load() method.

The storage models that were discussed in Chapter 4 apply very well to object servers. You can maintain all the object's data in memory while the server is running, only writing to the object's storage when the IPersistStorage::Save() method is called. The alternative is that you can write the data directly to the storage that was provided for your object's use and simply commit the changes when you are asked to save the data. This requires the server to monitor calls to the HandsOffStorage() method, which you use to indicate that the server should not modify the storage unless it is explicitly requested to do so by a call to the Save() method. The Save-Completed() method is called by the container to indicate that the server can again access the storage freely as well as to signify the end of the Save operation.

The IOleObject Interface

You can look at the IOleObject interface in one of two ways. You can see it as the command central for manipulating an object, or you can see it as the place to stick all the methods that didn't fit into one of the other two interfaces. Regardless, it is the biggest single interface in terms of the number of methods. Don't let this intimidate you. As you will see, many of the methods are implemented by the system. The main purpose of this interface is to allow the system and the container to query the object's properties and attributes. Since the OLE system implements many of the methods for you, most of these methods can return the result code OLE_S_USEREG. The data that would normally be returned by one of these methods is stored in the registration database and is returned by the OLE system. Only under special situations will you need to provide an implementation that does more than the default behavior the system provides.

Table 11.4 lists the `IOleObject` methods that need to be implemented for a basic object server. Table 11.5 lists the constants that are returned from the `GetMisc-Status()` method.

TABLE 11.4: IOleObject Methods

Method	Description
HRESULT SetClient-Site(pClientSite)	Called by the container to inform the object of its client site
HRESULT GetClient-Site(ppClientSite)	Returns a pointer to the current client site for the object
HRESULT SetHost-Names(szContainer-App, szContainer-Obj)	Used to set the name information for the container. The szContainerApp parameter will be set to the name of the container application, and the szContainerObj parameter will contain the name of the container's document
HRESULT Close(dwSaveOption)	Forces the object to close if it is running. The dwSaveOption parameter specifies how the Close operation should handle any changed data. It can be one of the following values: OLECLOSE_SAVEIFDIRTY, OLECLOSE_NOSAVE, OLECLOSE_PROMPTSAVE
HRESULT SetMoniker (dwWhichMoniker, pmk)	Informs the object of the container's moniker. The dwWhichMoniker specifies the type of moniker being passed. The values for dwWhichMoniker are described in Table 8.1 in Chapter 8
HRESULT GetMoniker (dwAssign, dwWhich-Moniker, ppmk)	Requests the moniker from the object. The dwAssign parameter lets the object know how to proceed in situations in which a moniker may not be available. The values for the dwAssign parameter are listed in Table 8.2 in Chapter 8
HRESULT Init-FromData(pData-Object, fCreation, dwReserved)	Initializes a new object from a data object. The fCreation parameter indicates whether the object is just being created
HRESULT GetClip-boardData(dwReserved, ppData-Object)	Obtains a data object pointer that contains a snapshot of the current state of the object. This is different from just performing QueryInterface() on the object for an IDataObject interface since a data object obtained in this manner would reflect any changes made to an object instead of remaining static

TABLE 11.4: IOleObject Methods (continued)

Method	Description
HRESULT DoVerb(iVerb, lpmsg, pActiveSite, lindex, hwndParent, lprcPosRect)	Causes the object to execute the verb passed in iVerb. The lpmsg parameter contains a pointer to the current message that caused the call to DoVerb(). The values that can be passed for the iVerb parameter are listed in Table 7.5 in Chapter 7
HRESULT EnumVerbs(ppenumOleVerb)	Returns an IEnumOLEVERB interface you can use to determine the available verbs for an object
HRESULT Update()	Called to update any cached information that an object may have. It is usually used for linked objects, but when it is called on an embedded object, the embedded object recursively calls IOleObject::Update() for any embedded or linked objects it contains
HRESULT IsUpToDate()	Returns S_OK if the object is up to date and S_FALSE if it is not
HRESULT GetUser-ClassID(pClsid)	Returns the class ID of the object server
HRESULT GetUserType (dwFormOfType, pszUserType)	Returns a name that can be displayed to the user. The dwFormOfType parameter can be one of the following values: The USERCLASSTYPE_FULL constant indicates that the full name of the object class should be returned. The USERCLASSTYPE_SHORT constant indicates that the short name of the class should be returned (fewer than 15 characters). The USERCLASSTYPE_APPNAME constant indicates that the name of the server application should be returned. The pszUserType parameter is an output parameter that should be allocated using the current memory allocator
HRESULT SetExtent(dwDrawAspect, lpsizel)	Sets the extents for an object. The dwDrawAspect parameter contains the aspect that is being used, and the lpsizel parameter contains the new extents in HIMETRIC
HRESULT GetExtent(dwDrawAspect, lpsizel)	Gets the extents for an object. The dwDrawAspect parameter contains the aspect for which the extents are being requested, and the lpsizel parameter should be filled with the new extents in HIMETRIC on output
HRESULT Advise(pAdvSink, pdw Connection)	Sets up an advise connection with the object. The pdwConnection parameter is an output that will contain a token value that can be used when calling IOleObject::Unadvise() to sever an advise link
HRESULT Unadvise(dwConnection)	Severs the advise link specified by dwConnection

TABLE 11.4: IOleObject Methods (continued)

Method	Description
HRESULT EnumAdvise(ppenumAdvise)	Obtains a pointer to the IEnumSTATDATA interface to enumerate all the existing advise connections for the object. The STATDATA structure contains all the details about a given advise connection, including the pointer to the IAdviseSink, the data format for the advise, the type of advise, and the connection token that represents the specific connection
HRESULT GetMisc Status(dwAspect, pdwStatus)	Returns the status contstants for the object. These constants are returned for the object aspect specified in dwAspect. The pdwStatus parameter is an output that will contain one or more of the constant flags listed in Table 11.5
HRESULT SetColor-Scheme(lpLogpal)	Informs the object of any special palette requirements a container may have

TABLE 11.5: IOleObject Status Constants

Constant	Description
OLEMISC_RECOMPOSE-ONRESIZE	Indicates that the container needs to do more than simply scale cached representations on resize
OLEMISC_ONLYICONIC	Indicates that the object had no useful content view. It supports only iconic views
OLEMISC_INSERT-NOTREPLACE	Indicates that the object does not want the current selection replaced when the object is inserted into a container document. You can use this constant when objects are created using the IOleObject::InitFromData() method
OLEMISC_STATIC	Indicates that the object is a static object. It was created by the OleCreateStaticFromData() method
OLEMISC_CANT-LINKINSIDE	Indicates that the object cannot be linked to if it is already embedded inside a container
OLEMISC_CAN-LINKBYOLE1	Indicates that the object can be linked to by an OLE 1 container
OLEMISC_IS-LINKOBJECT	A link object. It is not usually set by the object server and is instead set by OLE when an application calls GetMisc-Status() on a linked object

TABLE 11.5: IOleObject Status Constants (continued)

Constant	Description
OLEMISC_INSIDEOUT	An inside-out object. It can be active in place without requiring menus or toolbars to run. It is useful for objects that wish to behave similarly to VBX controls
OLEMISC_ACTIVATE-WHENVISIBLE	Indicates that the container should activate the object when it is visible. You can use this constant in conjunction with the OLEMISC_INSIDEOUT constant. Noted that some containers will always ignore this constant
OLEMISC_RENDERING-ISDEVICE INDEPENDENT	Does not handle device-specific renderings of its data. The cache data will be the same regardless of the device for which it is being requested

You use the methods in the IOleObject interface to set up general advise connections, set the names of the container and the container's document for display by the server, and get and set various aspects of the object's state.

Using CoLockObjectExternal

The Component Object Model relies heavily on reference counting. For each time AddRef() is called on an object, a corresponding call to Release() is required to decrement the reference count. When the reference count reaches 0 for a component object, the object is automatically destroyed. This is true for an object server, as well, since servers are component objects too. There are situations in which a server needs to be closed, regardless of the number of active references—for example, when the user selects the Exit menu item in the object server's menu. At this point the server will have a number of outstanding references to the object, including, among others, the references on the IOleObject interface. This situation requires a mechanism to release all external references to the object so it can shut down cleanly. The CoLockObjectExternal() method provides just such a mechanism.

The declaration for `CoLockObjectExternal()` looks like this:

```
HRESULT CoLockObjectExternal( LPUNKNOWN lpUnk, BOOL fLock,
    BOOL fRelease ) ;
```

The `lpUnk` parameter is a pointer to any `IUnknown` interface for the object to be locked. The `fLock` parameter indicates whether an external lock or an external unlock is being applied to an object, and the `fRelease` parameter indicates whether the specific call is to be the one that causes a release on the object. Obviously, this parameter is applicable only if the `fLock` parameter is FALSE. It is important to realize that this does not cause any calls to `IUnknown::AddRef()` or `IUnknown::Release()` on the object. This method works by trapping any external calls (external to the object application) to the `AddRef()` or `Release()` method. If you call `CoLockObjectExternal()` with `fLock` set to TRUE, it will not be possible for a container to call `Release()` so that the reference count goes to 0. The reference count will not be allowed to go to 0 until a corresponding call is made to `CoLockObjectExternal()` with `fLock` set to FALSE. In a similar situation, when the user wants to exit the server, the object calls `CoLockObjectExternal()` with the `fLock` parameter set to FALSE and the `fRelease` parameter set to TRUE. This causes all external references to the object to be released so that object can begin a controlled shutdown. In short, `CoLockObjectExternal()` allows the server to maintain control of the reference counting even in cases in which a container has problems with its reference counting.

Notifying the Container

In Chapter 7 you saw that a number of methods are called on a container to notify it of changes in the various states of the object. For example, the `IAdviseSink::OnViewChange()` method is called when the cached visual representation of the object changes, and the `IAdviseSink::OnDataChange()` method is called when the object's data changes. The object server and the OLE system share the responsibility for calling these notification methods. Any process that you want notified of changes for a specific object need only call the appropriate registration routine, passing a pointer to an `IAdviseSink` interface. For example, if you want a container to receive data change notifications, you have it call the object's `IDataObject::DAdvise()` method to register an `IAdviseSink` interface to receive the notifications. Table 11.6 is a list of the different notifications a server is responsible for handling.

TABLE 11.6: Advise Notifications

IAdviseSink Method	Notification Sent By	Description
OnDataChange()	Object Server	Sent by the server whenever the data changes for the object
OnViewChange()	OLE Default Handler	Indicates that the visual aspect of the object has changed and that the object should be redrawn
OnRename()	Object Server/Link Container	Sent when the file name of an object server or container's document that contains active links changes
OnSave()	Object Server	Sent when the object saves itself
OnClose()	Object Server	Sent to notify the system that the object is shutting down

Since there are no limits to the number of IAdviseSinks that can be registered to receive a specific notification, the server must be able to track and manage an unlimited number of IAdviseSink references. To make this easier to implement, OLE provides a facility called IAdviseHolder to manage sending the notifications to multiple IAdviseSinks. The IDataAdviseHolder interface is used for managing the IAdviseSinks for the server's IDataObject interface. The CreateDataAdvise-Holder() routine creates a new instance of this interface for use by the object server. The IOleAdviseHolder interface manages notifications for the IOleObject interface and is created by calling the CreateOleAdviseHolder() routine. Your server calls this function to create an IOleAdviseHolder to handle calls to the IOleObject.

The Server's Registration File

All object servers are registered in the registration database. As discussed in Chapter 2, the registration database is hierarchical. Each object server will have an entry in the root (also known as HKEY_CLASSES_ROOT) of the registration database that is referred to as the ProgID key. The ProgID key is a short programmatic name for the component object. The value of this key is always a human-readable name for the object. One of the important pieces of information contained in the subkeys for an object's `ProgID` key is the `CLSID` subkey. This subkey contains as its value the actual class ID of the object. The other relevant information stored as a subkey of the `ProdID` key is the `Insertable` subkey. This key does not have an associated value. If this key is present, the object is insertable into the Insert Object dialog. An example of this portion of the registration database for our simple object follows:

```
OLEDraw = OLE Draw 1.0
    Insertable
    CLSID = {00026204-0000-0000-C000-000000000046}
```

There will also be a subkey entry for each object under the root key `CLSID`. This entry will be the actual class ID of the object. It is under this subkey that the majority of the registration information for an object is provided. The following information can be stored under this key:

- The type of server (local server or in-process server)
- The server status as returned by the `IOleObject::GetMiscStatus()` method
- The verbs supported by the object and the flags to indicate how these should be displayed on the verb menu
- The human-readable names for the object under the `AuxUserType` subkey
- An entry for the `ProgID` to locate the `ProgID` root key for the object
- Whether the object is insertable using the `Insertable` subkey (Yes, this information is usually stored twice, once here and again under the `progID` root key.)
- The default icon to use for displaying the object with `DVASPECT_ICON` using the `DefaultIcon` subkey
- The information OLE needs to supply a default `IEnumFORMATETC` for the `IDataObject` interface on your object is supplied by the `DataFormats` subkey

A lot of the information listed above is not required. However, since OLE uses most of it when you request that OLE handle one or more of the `IOleObject` methods for you by returning `OLE_S_USEREG`, it is less work to provide it in the registration database than to write the code for your `IOleObject` interface to supply the information instead.

The OLE Draw Object Server

For our object server we will implement a mini-server called OLE Draw (see Figure 11.2). This is not the most sophisticated drawing program, but it suffices to demonstrate the techniques needed to implement an OLE server. For applications that have the luxury of being designed to accommodate OLE, adding support for objects is not difficult. If you are adding server support to an existing application, you should plan your changes thoroughly before beginning to implement them. Adding server support touches more of the application than adding container support. OLE Draw was designed with OLE support in mind, as Figure 11.3 illustrates. When adding server support to an existing application, you should know where the logical boundaries are between the object, the document, and the application.

FIGURE 11.2:

Screen snapshot of OLE Draw

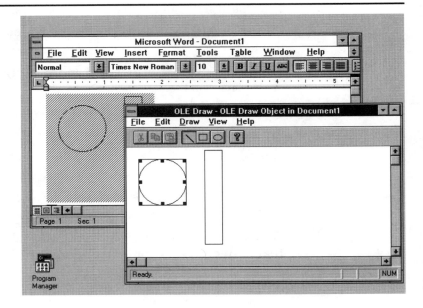

As you can see in Figure 11.3, OLE Draw does not have an Object class like the OLE Publisher container application presented in Part III of this book. For OLE Draw, the document is the object. This is why all the server interfaces are implemented at the Document class level.

FIGURE 11.3:

Class architecture for OLE Draw
with supported interfaces

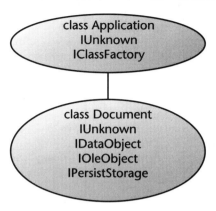

Implementing IDataObject

The IDataObject implemented here is different from the implementation used to put data on the clipboard. This implementation is primarily used by OLE to request specific data types from your object in order to support the caching mechanism that is built into OLE. OLE takes care of all the details, but you still must provide the original data. You must support at least one of the graphics formats, such as CF_METAFILEPICT or CF_BITMAP. Also, the application must support and generate the CF_EMBEDSOURCE and CF_OBJECTDESCRIPTOR formats. Listing 11.1 is the source code for the IDataObject interface in OLE Draw.

Listing 11.1

```
// DOCDOBJ.CPP
//
// This file contains the IDataObject implementation for
// the Document class.
//
#include "appl.h"
#include "doc.h"
#include "shape.h"

Document::DocDataObject::DocDataObject( Document *pDoc )
{
    m_refCount = 0 ;
    m_pDoc = pDoc ;
```

```
        m_pAdvHolder = NULL ;
}

Document::DocDataObject::~DocDataObject()
{
}

STDMETHODIMP Document::DocDataObject::QueryInterface(
    REFIID riid,
    LPVOID FAR *lpVoid )
{
    return m_pDoc->QueryInterface( riid, lpVoid ) ;
}

STDMETHODIMP_(ULONG) Document::DocDataObject::AddRef()
{
    return m_pDoc->AddRef() ;
}

STDMETHODIMP_(ULONG) Document::DocDataObject::Release()
{
    return m_pDoc->Release() ;
}

STDMETHODIMP Document::DocDataObject::GetData(
    LPFORMATETC pformatetcIn,
    LPSTGMEDIUM pmedium )
{
    HRESULT hErr = NOERROR ;

    pmedium->pUnkForRelease = NULL ;
    pmedium->tymed = NULL ;
    pmedium->hGlobal = NULL ;

    if( pformatetcIn->cfFormat == CF_METAFILEPICT ) {
        if( pformatetcIn->dwAspect &
            ( DVASPECT_CONTENT | DVASPECT_DOCPRINT ) ) {

            pmedium->tymed = TYMED_MFPICT ;
            pmedium->hGlobal =
                m_pDoc->CreateMetaFilePict() ;

            if( pmedium->hGlobal == NULL )
                hErr = ResultFromScode( DATA_E_FORMATETC ) ;
        }else
```

```
            hErr = ResultFromScode( DATA_E_FORMATETC ) ;

}else if( pformatetcIn->cfFormat == CF_BITMAP ) {
    if( pformatetcIn->dwAspect &
        ( DVASPECT_CONTENT | DVASPECT_DOCPRINT ) ) {

        pmedium->tymed = TYMED_GDI ;
        pmedium->hGlobal =
            m_pDoc->CreateBitmap() ;

        if( pmedium->hGlobal == NULL )
            hErr = ResultFromScode( DATA_E_FORMATETC ) ;
    }else
        hErr = ResultFromScode( DATA_E_FORMATETC ) ;

}else if( pformatetcIn->cfFormat ==
    RegisterClipboardFormat( CF_EMBEDSOURCE ) ) {

    pmedium->tymed = TYMED_ISTORAGE ;
    pmedium->pstg = OleStdCreateStorageOnHGlobal(
                NULL,
                TRUE,
                STGM_SALL ) ;

    if( pmedium->pstg != NULL )
        hErr = m_pDoc->m_pStorage.Save(
            pmedium->pstg,
            FALSE ) ;
    else
        hErr = ResultFromScode( E_OUTOFMEMORY ) ;

}else if( pformatetcIn->cfFormat ==
        RegisterClipboardFormat(
        CF_OBJECTDESCRIPTOR ) ) {

    SIZEL sizel ;
    POINTL pointl ;
    RECT rect ;

    m_pDoc->GetMaximumRect( &rect ) ;
    sizel.cx = rect.right ;
    sizel.cy = rect.bottom ;
    pointl.x = 0 ;
    pointl.y = 0 ;
```

```
                pmedium->tymed = TYMED_HGLOBAL ;
                pmedium->hGlobal = OleStdGetObjectDescriptorData(
                                    CLSID_OleDraw,
                                    DVASPECT_CONTENT,
                                    sizel, pointl,
                                    0,
                                    "OLE Draw",
                                    NULL ) ;
            if( pmedium->hGlobal == NULL )
                hErr = ResultFromScode( E_OUTOFMEMORY ) ;
        }else
            hErr = ResultFromScode( DATA_E_FORMATETC ) ;

        return hErr ;
    }


    STDMETHODIMP Document::DocDataObject::GetDataHere(
        LPFORMATETC pformatetc,
        LPSTGMEDIUM pmedium )
    {
        HRESULT hErr = NOERROR ;

        if( pformatetc->cfFormat ==
            RegisterClipboardFormat( CF_EMBEDSOURCE ) ) {

            if( pmedium->pstg != NULL &&
                pmedium->tymed == TYMED_ISTORAGE )
                hErr = m_pDoc->m_pStorage.Save(
                        pmedium->pstg,
                        FALSE ) ;
            else
                hErr = ResultFromScode( E_UNEXPECTED ) ;
        }else
            hErr = ResultFromScode( DATA_E_FORMATETC ) ;

        return hErr ;
    }


    STDMETHODIMP Document::DocDataObject::QueryGetData(
        LPFORMATETC pformatetc )
    {
        if( !( pformatetc->cfFormat == CF_METAFILEPICT ||
            pformatetc->cfFormat == CF_BITMAP ||
            pformatetc->cfFormat ==
            RegisterClipboardFormat( CF_EMBEDSOURCE ) ||
```

```
            pformatetc->cfFormat ==
            RegisterClipboardFormat( CF_OBJECTDESCRIPTOR ) ) )
                return ResultFromScode( DATA_E_FORMATETC ) ;
        return NOERROR ;
}

STDMETHODIMP Document::DocDataObject::GetCanonicalFormatEtc(
    LPFORMATETC pformatetc,
    LPFORMATETC pformatetcOut)
{
    return ResultFromScode( DATA_S_SAMEFORMATETC ) ;
}

STDMETHODIMP Document::DocDataObject::SetData(
    LPFORMATETC pformatetc, STGMEDIUM FAR * pmedium,
    BOOL fRelease)
{
    return ResultFromScode( E_NOTIMPL ) ;
}

STDMETHODIMP Document::DocDataObject::EnumFormatEtc(
    DWORD dwDirection,
    LPENUMFORMATETC FAR* ppenumFormatEtc)
{
    return ResultFromScode( OLE_S_USEREG ) ;
}

STDMETHODIMP Document::DocDataObject::DAdvise(
    FORMATETC FAR* pFormatetc, DWORD advf,
    LPADVISESINK pAdvSink, DWORD FAR* pdwConnection)
{
    if( m_pAdvHolder == NULL ) {
        if( CreateDataAdviseHolder( &m_pAdvHolder ) !=
            NOERROR )
            return ResultFromScode( E_OUTOFMEMORY ) ;
    }

    return m_pAdvHolder->Advise( this,
            pFormatetc,
            advf,
            pAdvSink,
            pdwConnection ) ;
}

STDMETHODIMP Document::DocDataObject::DUnadvise(
```

```
    DWORD dwConnection)
{
    if( m_pAdvHolder == NULL )
        return ResultFromScode( E_FAIL ) ;

    return m_pAdvHolder->Unadvise( dwConnection ) ;
}

STDMETHODIMP Document::DocDataObject::EnumDAdvise(
    LPENUMSTATDATA FAR* ppenumAdvise)
{
    *ppenumAdvise = NULL ;

    if( m_pAdvHolder == NULL )
        return ResultFromScode( E_FAIL ) ;

    return m_pAdvHolder->EnumAdvise( ppenumAdvise ) ;
}
```

Since the details of managing the IAdviseSink::OnDataChange() advise registra-
tions are taken care of by the IDataAdviseHolder interface, the DAdvise(),
DUnadvise(), and EnumDAdvise() methods are simply passed to a pointer to an
IDataAdviseHolder interface that is created the first time one of these methods is
called.

Implementing IPersistStorage

A unique instance of the IPersistStorage interface must be provided for each object that is provided by the application. The code for the implementation of the
IPersistStorage interface for the OLE Draw Server is shown in Listing 11.2.

Listing 11.2

```
// DOCPSTG.CPP
//
// This file contains the IPersistStorage implementation for
// the Document class.
//
#include "appl.h"
#include "doc.h"
#include "shape.h"
BL
Document::DocPStorage::DocPStorage( Document *pDoc )
```

```
{
    m_refCount = 0 ;
    m_pDoc = pDoc ;
    m_pStg = NULL ;
    m_pStm = NULL ;
}

Document::DocPStorage::~DocPStorage()
{
}

STDMETHODIMP Document::DocPStorage::QueryInterface(
    REFIID riid,
    LPVOID FAR *lpVoid )
{
    return m_pDoc->QueryInterface( riid, lpVoid ) ;
}

STDMETHODIMP_(ULONG) Document::DocPStorage::AddRef()
{
    return m_pDoc->AddRef() ;
}

STDMETHODIMP_(ULONG) Document::DocPStorage::Release()
{
    return m_pDoc->Release() ;
}

STDMETHODIMP Document::DocPStorage::GetClassID(
    LPCLSID lpClassID)
{
    *lpClassID = CLSID_OleDraw ;
    return NOERROR ;
}

STDMETHODIMP Document::DocPStorage::IsDirty()
{
    if( !m_pDoc->m_isDirty )
        return ResultFromScode( S_FALSE ) ;
    return NOERROR ;
}

STDMETHODIMP Document::DocPStorage::InitNew(
    LPSTORAGE pStg)
{
```

```
        if( m_pStm != NULL ) m_pStm->Release() ;
        if( m_pStg != NULL ) m_pStg->Release() ;

        // Save the storage
        m_pStg = pStg ;
        m_pStg->AddRef() ;

        // Create a new stream
        HRESULT hErr ;
        hErr = m_pStg->CreateStream( "CONTENTS",
                    STGM_CREATE | STGM_SALL,
                    0, 0,
                    &m_pStm ) ;

        if( !FAILED( hErr ) ) {
            WriteClassStg( m_pStg, CLSID_OleDraw ) ;
        }

        return hErr ;
    }


STDMETHODIMP Document::DocPStorage::Load(
    LPSTORAGE pStg)
{
    if( m_pStm != NULL ) m_pStm->Release() ;
    if( m_pStg != NULL ) m_pStg->Release() ;

    // Save the storage
    m_pStg = pStg ;
    m_pStg->AddRef() ;

        // Create a new stream
    HRESULT hErr ;
    hErr = m_pStg->OpenStream( "CONTENTS",
                NULL,
                STGM_SALL,
                0,
                &m_pStm ) ;

    if( FAILED( hErr ) ) {
        m_pStg->Release() ;
        m_pStg = NULL ;
        return hErr ;
    }
```

```
        m_pDoc->DeleteContents() ;
        hErr = m_pDoc->ReadData( m_pStm ) ;

        return hErr ;
}

STDMETHODIMP Document::DocPStorage::Save(
        LPSTORAGE pStgSave, BOOL fSameAsLoad)
{
        HRESULT hErr = NOERROR ;
        LPSTORAGE pStg ;
        LPSTREAM pStm ;

        pStg = m_pStg ;
        pStm = m_pStm ;

        if( fSameAsLoad ) {

                if( pStg == NULL || pStm == NULL )
                        return ResultFromScode( E_UNEXPECTED ) ;

                LARGE_INTEGER seekpos ;
                LISet32(seekpos,0) ;
                pStm->Seek(seekpos, STREAM_SEEK_SET, NULL ) ;
                pStm->AddRef() ;

        }else
                hErr = InitNew( pStgSave ) ;

        // write out the data
        hErr = m_pDoc->WriteData( pStm ) ;

        // release the stream
        pStm->Release() ;

        m_pStg = pStg ;
        m_pStm = pStm ;

        return hErr ;
}

STDMETHODIMP Document::DocPStorage::SaveCompleted(
        LPSTORAGE pStgNew)
{
        if( m_pDoc->m_oleObject.m_pAdvHolder != NULL )
```

```
        m_pDoc->m_oleObject.m_pAdvHolder->SendOnSave() ;
    return NOERROR ;
}


STDMETHODIMP Document::DocPStorage::HandsOffStorage()
{
    if( m_pStm != NULL ) m_pStm->Release() ;
    if( m_pStg != NULL ) m_pStg->Release() ;
    m_pStg = NULL ;
    m_pStm = NULL ;
    return NOERROR ;
}
```

The InitNew() method does nothing more than write out the class ID to the passed storage and open the CONTENTS stream for saving the OLE Draw data. Even though we don't use this stream at this point, it is important to open it here since we can't allocate any memory in the Save() method.

The Load() method loads the OLE Draw data from the CONTENTS stream for the object. This method also leaves the stream open for later use by the Save() method.

The Save() method must deal with the situation in which the storage being passed is not the same as the storage that was passed during the load operation. If this is the case, we have no choice but to open the CONTENTS stream and initialize the storage by calling InitNew(). Otherwise, we can use the stream we opened during an earlier InitNew() or Load() method and write out the object's data.

Since our server is fairly simple, the implementations of the HandsOffStorage() and SaveCompleted() methods are also simple. In the HandsOffStorage() method, we simply release the pointers to the object's stream and storage. After the container calls this method, it is the container's responsibility to reload the object. The SaveCompleted() method does nothing more than send the IAdviseSink::OnSave() notification by using the IOleAdviseHolder interface.

Implementing IOleObject

Th IOleObject interface has the distinction of having more methods than any other interface in OLE. This does not mean it is difficult to implement.

If you supply the appropriate information in the registration entries for the server and return OLE_S_USEREG result code, most of the methods will be handled by OLE. A few of the methods are non-trivial and will affect how the application is structured.

Examine the implementation of the IOleObject interface for the OLE Draw mini-server shown in Listing 11.3.

Listing 11.3

```cpp
// DOCOOBJ.CPP
//
// This file contains the IOleObject implementation for
// the Document class.
//
#include "appl.h"
#include "doc.h"
#include "shape.h"
#include "resource.h"

Document::DocOleObject::DocOleObject( Document *pDoc )
{
    m_refCount = 0 ;
    m_pDoc = pDoc ;
    m_pCliSite = NULL ;
    m_pAdvHolder = NULL ;
}

Document::DocOleObject::~DocOleObject()
{
}

STDMETHODIMP Document::DocOleObject::QueryInterface(
    REFIID riid,
    LPVOID FAR *lpVoid )
{
    return m_pDoc->QueryInterface( riid, lpVoid ) ;
}

STDMETHODIMP_(ULONG) Document::DocOleObject::AddRef()
{
    return m_pDoc->AddRef() ;
}

STDMETHODIMP_(ULONG) Document::DocOleObject::Release()
{
    return m_pDoc->Release() ;
}
```

```
STDMETHODIMP Document::DocOleObject::SetClientSite(
    LPOLECLIENTSITE pClientSite)
{
    if( m_pCliSite != NULL ) m_pCliSite->Release() ;

    m_pCliSite = pClientSite ;

    if( m_pCliSite != NULL ) m_pCliSite->AddRef() ;

    return NOERROR ;
}

STDMETHODIMP Document::DocOleObject::GetClientSite(
    LPOLECLIENTSITE FAR* ppClientSite)
{
    *ppClientSite = m_pCliSite ;
    if( m_pCliSite != NULL ) m_pCliSite->AddRef() ;
    return NOERROR ;
}

STDMETHODIMP Document::DocOleObject::SetHostNames(
    LPCSTR szContainerApp,
    LPCSTR szContainerObj)
{
    // set the application title
    char titlebuf[128] ;
    wsprintf( titlebuf,
        "OLE Draw Object in %s", szContainerObj ) ;
    theApp.SetDocumentName( titlebuf ) ;

    // now set the menu item for the exit menu
    HMENU fileMenu = GetSubMenu( theApp.m_appMenu, O ) ;
    wsprintf( titlebuf,
        "E&xit and Return to %s", szContainerObj ) ;
    ModifyMenu( fileMenu, IDM_FILE_EXIT,
                MF_ENABLED, IDM_FILE_EXIT,
                titlebuf ) ;

    return NOERROR ;
}

STDMETHODIMP Document::DocOleObject::Close(
    DWORD dwSaveOption)
{
    switch( dwSaveOption ) {
```

```
        case OLECLOSE_NOSAVE:
            break ;

        case OLECLOSE_PROMPTSAVE:

            if( m_pDoc->m_isDirty ) {
                UINT id = Confirm( "OLE Draw",
                        "This document has been changed."
                        " Save the changes?" ) ;
                switch( id ) {
                case IDYES:
                    break ;

                case IDNO:
                case IDCANCEL:
                    m_pDoc->m_isDirty = FALSE ;
                    break ;
                }
            }

        case OLECLOSE_SAVEIFDIRTY:
            if(  m_pDoc->m_isDirty && m_pCliSite != NULL )
                m_pCliSite->SaveObject() ;
            break ;
    }

    // Hide the window
    DoVerb( OLEIVERB_HIDE, NULL, NULL, -1, NULL, NULL ) ;

    // Release the advise holder
    if( m_pAdvHolder != NULL ) {
        m_pAdvHolder->SendOnClose() ;
        m_pAdvHolder->Release() ;
        m_pAdvHolder = NULL ;
    }

    // Release the client site
    if( m_pCliSite != NULL )
        SetClientSite( NULL ) ;

    return NOERROR ;
}

STDMETHODIMP Document::DocOleObject::SetMoniker(
    DWORD dwWhichMoniker, LPMONIKER pmk)
```

```
{
    return ResultFromScode( E_NOTIMPL ) ;
}


STDMETHODIMP Document::DocOleObject::GetMoniker(
    DWORD dwAssign, DWORD dwWhichMoniker,
    LPMONIKER FAR* ppmk)
{
    return ResultFromScode( E_NOTIMPL ) ;
}


STDMETHODIMP Document::DocOleObject::InitFromData(
    LPDATAOBJECT pDataObject,
    BOOL fCreation,
    DWORD dwReserved)
{
    return ResultFromScode( E_NOTIMPL ) ;
}


STDMETHODIMP Document::DocOleObject::GetClipboardData(
    DWORD dwReserved,
    LPDATAOBJECT FAR* ppDataObject)
{
    return ResultFromScode( E_NOTIMPL ) ;
}


STDMETHODIMP Document::DocOleObject::DoVerb(
    LONG iVerb,
    LPMSG lpmsg,
    LPOLECLIENTSITE pActiveSite,
    LONG lindex,
    HWND hwndParent,
    LPCRECT lprcPosRect)
{
    HRESULT hErr = NOERROR ;
    switch( iVerb ) {
    case OLEIVERB_PRIMARY:
    case OLEIVERB_SHOW:
    case OLEIVERB_OPEN:

        // Show the object and its window
        if( !m_pDoc->m_hWnd ) {
            m_pDoc->DoOpenActivate() ;
        }
        theApp.Show( SW_SHOW ) ;
```

```
            SetFocus( m_pDoc->m_hWnd ) ;

            // Notify client site that the window has been
            // made visible
            if( m_pCliSite != NULL ) {
                m_pCliSite->ShowObject() ;
                m_pCliSite->OnShowWindow( TRUE ) ;
            }
            break ;

        case OLEIVERB_HIDE:
            theApp.Show( SW_HIDE ) ;

            // Notify client site that the window has been
            // hidden
            if( m_pCliSite != NULL )
                m_pCliSite->OnShowWindow( FALSE ) ;
            break ;

        default:
            hErr = ResultFromScode( OLEOBJ_S_INVALIDVERB ) ;
            break ;
    }
    return hErr ;
}

STDMETHODIMP Document::DocOleObject::EnumVerbs(
    LPENUMOLEVERB FAR* ppenumOleVerb)
{
    *ppenumOleVerb = NULL ;
    return ResultFromScode( OLE_S_USEREG ) ;
}

STDMETHODIMP Document::DocOleObject::Update()
{
    return ResultFromScode( CACHE_E_NOCACHE_UPDATED ) ;
}

STDMETHODIMP Document::DocOleObject::IsUpToDate()
{
    return NOERROR ;
}

STDMETHODIMP Document::DocOleObject::GetUserClassID(
    CLSID FAR* pClsid)
```

```
    {
        *pClsid = CLSID_OleDraw ;
        return NOERROR ;
    }

    STDMETHODIMP Document::DocOleObject::GetUserType(
        DWORD dwFormOfType, LPSTR FAR* pszUserType)
    {
        return ResultFromScode( OLE_S_USEREG ) ;
    }

    STDMETHODIMP Document::DocOleObject::SetExtent(
        DWORD dwDrawAspect, LPSIZEL lpsizel)
    {
        return ResultFromScode( E_FAIL ) ;
    }

    STDMETHODIMP Document::DocOleObject::GetExtent(
        DWORD dwDrawAspect, LPSIZEL lpsizel)
    {
        if( dwDrawAspect == DVASPECT_CONTENT ) {
            RECT rect ;
            m_pDoc->GetMaximumRect( &rect ) ;
            lpsizel->cx = rect.right ;
            lpsizel->cy = rect.bottom ;
            XformSizeInPixelsToHimetric(
                NULL, lpsizel, lpsizel ) ;
            return NOERROR ;
        }
        return ResultFromScode( E_INVALIDARG ) ;
    }

    STDMETHODIMP Document::DocOleObject::Advise(
        LPADVISESINK pAdvSink, DWORD FAR* pdwConnection)
    {
        if( m_pAdvHolder == NULL ) {
            if( CreateOleAdviseHolder( &m_pAdvHolder )
                != NOERROR )
                return ResultFromScode( E_OUTOFMEMORY ) ;
        }

        return m_pAdvHolder->Advise(
                pAdvSink, pdwConnection ) ;
    }
```

```
STDMETHODIMP Document::DocOleObject::Unadvise(
    DWORD dwConnection)
{
    if( m_pAdvHolder == NULL )
        return ResultFromScode( E_FAIL ) ;

    return m_pAdvHolder->Unadvise( dwConnection ) ;
}
STDMETHODIMP Document::DocOleObject::EnumAdvise(
    LPENUMSTATDATA FAR* ppenumAdvise)
{
    *ppenumAdvise = NULL ;

    if( m_pAdvHolder == NULL )
        return ResultFromScode( E_FAIL ) ;

    return m_pAdvHolder->EnumAdvise( ppenumAdvise ) ;
}

STDMETHODIMP Document::DocOleObject::GetMiscStatus(
    DWORD dwAspect, DWORD FAR* pdwStatus)
{
    return ResultFromScode( OLE_S_USEREG ) ;
}

STDMETHODIMP Document::DocOleObject::SetColorScheme(
    LPLOGPALETTE lpLogpal)
{
    return ResultFromScode( E_NOTIMPL ) ;
}
```

The GetClientSite() and SetClientSite() methods are trivial and do nothing more than save and return a reference to the client site application that is passed as the single argument. Along with actually saving a copy of the client site interface pointer, we call AddRef() to indicate that we are actively using the interface.

The SetHostNames() method is called by the container to provide information to be used for window titles and menu items in our server application. In keeping with the *OLE 2 Programmer's Reference,* we use the container name to set the title of the OLE Draw application window to a string of the form

OLE Draw Object in *Container Document Name*

We also change the name of the Exit menu item under the File menu to a string of the form

Exit and Return to *Container Document Name*

The `Close()` method is one of the more interesting methods in the `IOleObject` interface. This method is called either when the application closes the object or when the user closes the object. The implementation of this method can be illustrated by the pseudocode that follows:

```
HRESULT IOleObject::Close()
{
    if save flag indicates saving is needed and
        the object is dirty then
        call IOleClientSite::SaveObject()
    if object is visible then
        hide object window
        call IOleClientSite::OnShowWindow( FALSE )
    call pAdviseHolder->SendOnClose()
    call CoDisconnectObject()
    return error
}
```

The only argument to the `Close()` method is a constant indicating how the object should treat any unsaved data. The constants for this argument are listed in Table 11.7.

TABLE 11.7: OLECLOSE_constants

Constant	Description
OLE CLOSE_SAVEIFDIRTY	Indicates that the server should save the object if the data has changed since the last Save operation
OLECLOSE_NOSAVE	Indicates that the server should not save the object, regardless of whether the object's data has changed
OLEPROMPTSAVE	Indicates that the server should prompt the user to determine whether or not the object should be saved

The `DoVerb()` method is the workhorse of this interface. This is the method that is called to request the object to perform some action. For a basic server, the verb types you must support are `OLEIVERB_PRIMARY`, `OLEIVERB_SHOW`, `OLEIVERB_OPEN`, and `OLEIVERB_HIDE`. These are the minimum verbs required for basic object activations.

If we have a valid `IOleClientSite` pointer, then whenever OLE Draw is activated or hidden, we call `IOleClientSite::OnShowWindow()` to indicate whether or not our object is visible. This is important since the container uses this method to determine when to draw the hatch pattern over its representation of the object. Although it is not mandatory, we also call the `IOleClientSite::ShowObject()` method during an activation verb to force the server's object to be visible while being edited.

The `EnumVerbs()`, `GetUserType()`, and `GetMiscStatus()` methods all return `OLE_S_USEREG` to indicate that the information can be found in the registration database.

The `GetUserClassID()` method simply returns the class ID for the OLE Draw server.

The `GetExtent()` method must return the extents of the object in `HIMETRIC`. To do this we obtain the coordinates of the object in pixels and then call the OLE2UI routine `XformSizeInPixelsToHimetric()`.

The `Advise()`, `Unadvise()`, and `EnumAdvise()` methods are all passed to an `IOleAdviseHolder` interface that works similarly to the `IDataAdviseHolder` interface we used in the OLE Draw `IDataObject` interface.

The Registration File

The registration file for OLE Draw contains the information used to identify the object and locate the actual executable for the object server. This information is contained under the `OLEDraw ProdID` key and under the object's `CLSID` entry under `HKEY_CLASSES_ROOT\CLSID` using the `ProgID` and `LocalServer` subkeys. The remaining subkeys are required to allow OLE to support the `IOleObject` methods that return `IOleObject`. For more information on these registration entries, see Appendix A.

NOTE For the purposes of this book, lines in the following code have been limited to 65 characters. However, for this code to compile correctly, there need to be no artificial line breaks.

```
REGEDIT

# Registration info for OLE Draw

HKEY_CLASSES_ROOT\OLEDraw = OLE Draw 1.0
HKEY_CLASSES_ROOT\OLEDraw\CLSID = {00026204-0000-0000-C000
-000000000046}
HKEY_CLASSES_ROOT\OLEDraw\Insertable =

HKEY_CLASSES_ROOT\CLSID\{00026204-0000-0000-C000-000000000046} =
OLE Draw 1.0
HKEY_CLASSES_ROOT\CLSID\{00026204-0000-0000-C000-000000000046}
\ProgID = OLEDraw
HKEY_CLASSES_ROOT\CLSID\{00026204-0000-0000-C000-000000000046}
\LocalServer = C:\DEV\OLEDRAW\OLEDRAW.EXE
HKEY_CLASSES_ROOT\CLSID\{00026204-0000-0000-C000-000000000046}
\InprocHandler = OLE2.DLL

HKEY_CLASSES_ROOT\CLSID\{00026204-0000-0000-C000-000000000046}
\Insertable =
HKEY_CLASSES_ROOT\CLSID\{00026204-0000-0000-C000-000000000046}
\AuxUserType\3 = OLE Draw Document
HKEY_CLASSES_ROOT\CLSID\{00026204-0000-0000-C000-000000000046}
\AuxUserType\2 = Draw
HKEY_CLASSES_ROOT\CLSID\{00026204-0000-0000-C000-000000000046}
\DataFormats\GetSet\1 = Embed Source,1,8,1
HKEY_CLASSES_ROOT\CLSID\{00026204-0000-0000-C000-000000000046}
\DataFormats\GetSet\2 = 3,1,32,1
HKEY_CLASSES_ROOT\CLSID\{00026204-0000-0000-C000-000000000046}
\DataFormats\GetSet\3 = 2,1,16,1
HKEY_CLASSES_ROOT\CLSID\{00026204-0000-0000-C000-000000000046}
\Verb\0 = &Play,0,2
HKEY_CLASSES_ROOT\CLSID\{00026204-0000-0000-C000-000000000046}
\Verb\1 = &Edit,0,3
```

Figure 11.4 shows these entries after being loaded into REGEDIT.EXE.

FIGURE 11.4:

Screen snapshot of OLE Draw
entries in REGEDIT

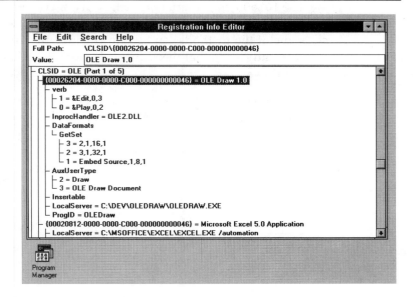

Summary

This chapter has discussed the techniques required for building a simple object server. You have seen that to build an object server, you must first build a component object with a supporting IClassFactory for creating the object, as well as the appropriate registration database entries. Then you must provide minimal implementations of the IDataObject, IPersistStorage, and IOleObject interfaces.

The IDataObject interface must be able to support OnDataChange() advises as well as supply some basic formats when requested by calls to the GetData() and GetDataHere() methods.

The IPersistStorage interface must be able to initialize, load, and save the object's data to storages that are supplied by the container. It is important that this interface be extremely sensitive to memory allocation so that a container application will be able to save the user's data to disk in low-memory situations.

The IOleObject interface executes an object's verbs, as well as obtaining miscellaneous information about the object. Even though this interface has many methods, some of the methods can be implemented by returning the OLE_S_USEREG result code indicating that the requested information can be found in the registration database.

The next chapter demonstrates how to add support for in-place activation and editing to the OLE Draw object server.

CHAPTER

TWELVE

Building an In-Place Object Server

- Supporting in-place activation in a server

- Implementing the in-place server interfaces

- Implementing the in-place object user interface

- Merging menus with containers

- Displaying the object toolbar and status bar text

- Resizing in-place objects

To the user, working with an in-place object should seem like just another feature of the application the object is contained in. This means that activating the object does not bring up another application; the user simply edits the object inside the document where it is displayed. Figures 12.1 and 12.2 display an OLE Draw object in the Microsoft Word application before and after being in-place activated.

FIGURE 12.1:

OLE Draw object embedded in an OLE Publisher document

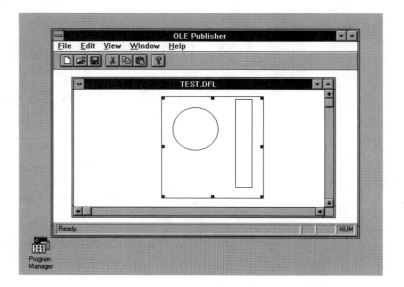

Notice that the OLE Draw object in Figure 12.2 has a hatched border around it, with black handles you can use to resize the object. Also notice that the menus and toolbars change when the object is activated. It is the responsibility of the object to modify the container's user interface to provide the appropriate menus and toolbars to allow users to effectively edit the object. This chapter discusses the OLE interfaces and the support code to add in-place support to the OLE Draw server that was described in Chapter 11.

FIGURE 12.2:

FIGURE 12.2:

OLE Draw object in-place activated
in an OLE Publisher document

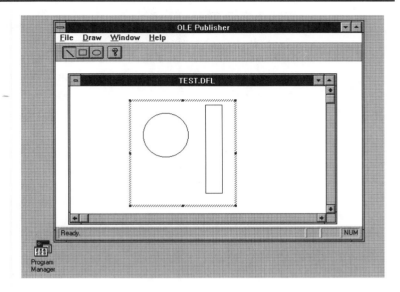

How In-Place Objects Work

In-place objects start off life as normal embedded objects. The difference is that when an in-place object is activated by a double-click or one of the other standard methods of activating an object, the in-place object starts asking the container a lot of questions to determine whether the container also supports in-place activation. Both the container and the object must support in-place activation for this to work. If either the container or the server does not implement support for in-place activation, the object should be open activated, as described in Chapter 11.

NOTE Linked objects are always open activated since the linked portion of the document can be a small portion of the actual document. Allowing in-place editing in these circumstances would cause interesting logistical problems.

293

After a container activates an in-place–capable object by calling the IOleObject::DoVerb() method, the object calls QueryInterface() on the container's client site to determine whether it supports the IOleInPlaceSite interface. If the container supports the IOleInPlaceSite interface, it supports in-place activation. Even if the container supports in-place activation, the object must still ask permission to activate in-place. You do this by calling the IOleInPlaceSite::CanInPlaceActivate() method. If this method returns a result code of S_OK, the object server can proceed with an in-place activation.

Under what conditions would the container refuse the object's request to activate in-place? If the object is being displayed in the container's document window as an icon, it would not make sense for the object to activate in-place; it would be confusing for the object to suddenly convert from an iconic display to content display. Most in-place containers (see Chapter 9) implement this method by returning S_OK if the display aspect of the object is DVASPECT_CONTENT and S_FALSE for all other display aspects.

After determining whether the container supports in-place activation and obtaining permission from the container to activate in-place, the object is ready to start constructing its interface.

The first thing it must do is create the windows required to display and edit the object in-place. Most implementations of OLE in-place servers use at least two windows to activate in-place. The first window is the *hatch window* or the *border window*, and it is responsible for drawing the hatched border and responding to the mouse messages to allow the user to resize the object. The second window is the object window itself. The *object window* is a child of the hatch window, and the hatch window is a child of the container's document window. Using two windows in this fashion allows you to isolate the code to support editing and displaying of the object from the in-place window code, which is required only when the object is in-place active.

After displaying its windows, the object must work with the container to build a combined menu bar. The menus are combined to present only the menu items that would make sense in the current context. The container supplies the menus that make sense at the document level, such as the File menu. This makes sense since the user would be saving the document by selecting the File ➤ Save menu item. The object server supplies the object-specific menus, such as the Edit menu, the Help menu, and any other relevant object-specific menus.

The final step is the negotiation to display any toolbars for the object. OLE allows the server to negotiate to place its toolbars around the border of the in-place object, the document window, or the container application's frame window. Since sharing space in another application's interface is complicated, the negotiation process takes several steps. The first step is to ask how much space is available in the container's interface. Then the object server decides how much space it needs and requests that much space from the container. If the container decides it can spare that much space, it moves or hides its toolbars as appropriate and clears the requested space for the object to use for its own toolbars. The server then creates and updates its toolbar windows.

The In-Place Object Interfaces

An object must implement two interfaces for in-place activation support (see Figure 12.3). These are the `IOleInPlaceObject` interface and the `IOleInPlaceActiveObject` interface. The distinction between the two interfaces is that the `IOleInPlaceObject` interface controls the transition to and from in-place active. The `IOleInPlaceActiveObject` interface manipulates the object while it is actually in-place active.

FIGURE 12.3:
In-place object server interfaces

In-Place Server
Interfaces

Container In-Place Interfaces
used by In-Place Server

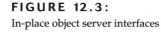

IOleInPlaceObject
IOleInPlaceActiveObject

IOleInPlaceSite

The IOleWindow Interface

The `IOleWindow` interface is the interface from which all in-place interfaces are derived. This interface has methods for obtaining the HWND for the interface that is derived from `IOleWindow` and for setting context-sensitive help mode for the interface. The methods for this interface are described in Chapter 9, in Table 9.1.

Since both of the in-place object interfaces are derived from this interface, they must fully support the methods for this interface. The `IOleWindow::GetWindow()` method should return the HWND for the in-place active object's window. The details of implementing the `IOleWindow::ContextSensitiveHelp()` method are discussed in detail in Chapter 9.

The IOleInPlaceObject Interface

The `IOleInPlaceObject` interface contains all the general-purpose methods for use by the container when working with an in-place object. These methods are listed in Table 12.1.

TABLE 12.1: IOleInPlaceObject Methods

Method	Description
HRESULT InPlaceDeactivate( )	Called by the container to deactivate an active in-place object and discard its undo state
HRESULT UIDeactivate( )	Called by the container to deactivate an in-place object. The undo state should not be discarded when this method is called
HRESULT SetObject-Rects(posRect, clipRect)	Called by the container to specify the position rect (posRect) and the clipping rectangle (clipRect) for the in-place object. These rectangles are specified in pixels using the client coordinates of the container's document window
HRESULT ReactivateAndUndo( )	Called after an object has been deactivated using UIDeactivate( ) and the user has selected the Undo menu item

The IOleInPlaceActiveObject Interface

The `IOleInPlaceActiveObject` interface is used by the container to inform an active in-place object of changes to the state of the user interface. These changes include such events as window activation and resizing for both the document window and the frame window.

Imagine the following situation. The user loads an MDI container application and activates an object in-place. The object installs its menus and toolbars and prepares to be edited by the user. Then the user changes to another open document in the container. What should happen? The in-place active object should hide its toolbars and remove its menus since they don't apply to the newly active document. When the user reactivates the first document window, the object (which is still active) should reinsert its menus and restore its toolbar. The `IOleInPlaceActiveObject` interface (see Table 12.2) contains the methods that are used by the container to notify the object of just such occurrences.

TABLE 12.2: IOleInPlaceActiveObject Methods

Method	Description
HRESULT Translate-Accelerator(msg)	Called from the container's message loop to give an in-place active object a chance to intercept keyboard commands. This is necessary only in a DLL-based object since an EXE-based object has its own message loop
HRESULT OnFrameWindow-Activate(fActivate)	Called by the container when its frame window is activated or deactivated. The object uses this method to update its toolbar. Your object should use PostMessage() to post a custom message to use for updating the toolbar. While handling this method, your application cannot call YieldMessage(), PeekMessage(), or GetMessage() or call any other functions that might call these routines, such as MessageBox() or other dialog box–related functions. You also cannot call certain OLE functions while processing this method
HRESULT OnDocWindow-Activate(fEnable)	Called by an MDI container when the document window is activated or deactivated as indicated by fEnable. On deactivation, the object should hide its hatched border and remove in-frame-level tools that it has installed. It should not call the IOleInPlaceUIWindow::SetBorderSpace() method with NULL. On activation, the object should redisplay its hatch window and reinstall any frame-level tools. This method carries the same restrictions that apply to the OnFrameWindowActivate() method
HRESULT ResizeBorder(rectBorder, lpUI-Window, fFrameWindow)	Called by the container when either the frame window or the object's document window is resized. This gives the object server a chance to resize any tools it may have installed. The rectBorder parameter contains the new size of the window, and the lpUIWindow parameter is a pointer to the IOleUIWindow interface for the window being resized. The fFrameWindow parameter simply indicates whether it is a frame window or a document window that is being resized

TABLE 12.2: IOleInPlaceActiveObject Methods (continued)

Method	Description
HRESULT Enable- Modeless(fEnable)	Called by the container to enable or disable modeless dialog windows that the object may have displayed. This is done whenever the container displays a modal dialog, to avoid any conflicts. The fEnable parameter indicates whether the call is to enable or disable the object's modeless dialog windows

Displaying the Object In-Place

Activating an object in-place involves several steps. The first is to create the object windows and the object frame window. These windows are not visible initially since more work must be done before the objects are displayed. The second step is to display the object window and the hatch border window, and the third step is to add the supporting user-interface components, such as the menu and the toolbars.

Create the Object Windows

You need to take into account a number of issues when preparing to display your object's window in-place. The first of these issues is that you must provide the hatch window border interface for your object. This is typically implemented as a separate window. The hatch window is responsible for drawing the hatched border, along with the square black resize handles that are used to modify the object's display size. This window will be a child window of the container's document window, and the in-place object window will be a child window of the hatch window. The window relationship for in-place objects is shown in Figure 12.4.

The GetWindowContext() Method

Sometime during the process of creating and showing the object window and the hatch window, you will to obtain more information about the container's environment. To obtain this information you call the IOleInPlaceSite::GetWindowContext() method. This method returns a lot of useful information about the activating container,

FIGURE 12.4:

Window relationship for in-place objects

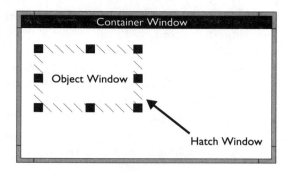

such as the position rectangle, the clipping rectangle, the `IOleInPlaceFrame` interface, the `IOleInPlaceUIWindow` interface, and an `OLEINPLACEFRAMEINFO` structure that contains general information about the container's application.

The position and clipping rectangles are used for positioning the object window and are specified in the client coordinates of the container window (see Figure 12.5).

FIGURE 12.5:

Conceptual diagram of position and clipping rectangles

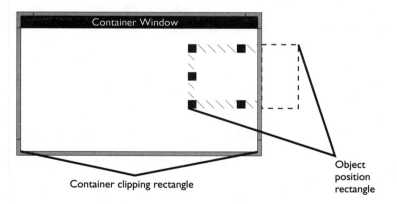

The reason there is both a clipping rectangle and a position rectangle is that the object may not be completely visible. If the object is at the border of the visible portion of the container's document, part of the object may lie off the edge of the container's window. For this reason, the clipping rect usually corresponds to the container's clipping rectangle. The object server must still know the actual position and size of the object window, so the object position is sent as a separate rectangle. It is the object server's responsibility to make sure that no portion of the object is displayed outside the clipping rectangle. You can address this requirement by sizing the hatch window so that it does not fall outside the clipping rect and setting the WS_CLIPCHILDREN style flag when the window is created.

The interfaces that are returned should be saved for later use. The IOleInPlace-Frame interface is used for performing actions on the container's frame window, such as installing and removing the object's menus and setting the status bar text. If the IOleInPlaceUIWindow interface is not NULL, this indicates that the container also has a document window that is different from the frame window. An example of this is an MDI application in which the document windows are child windows in the work space of the main application window.

Finally, the OLEINPLACEFRAMEINFO structure contains various information regarding the container application, such as whether the application is an MDI application. This structure contains the following fields:

Field	Description
cb	Size of the structure
fMDIApp	Flag to indicate whether the container is an MDI application
hwndFrame	Handle to the application's frame window
haccel	Handle to the accelerator table for the container
cAccelEntries	Number of entries in the accelerator table

Let's look at some pseudocode for creating and displaying an object in-place:

```
CreateAndShowInPlace()
{

    HWND hObjWnd, hIPWnd, hCntrWnd ;
    HRESULT hErr ;
```

```
// Does the container support in-place?
hErr = clientsite->QueryInterface(IID_IOleInPlaceSite,
                      &ipsite) ;
if( hErr != NOERROR )
    return PropagateResult( hErr, E_FAIL ) ;

// See if in-place activation is allowed.
hErr = ipsite->CanInPlaceActivate() ;
if( hErr != NOERROR )
    return PropagateResult( hErr, E_FAIL ) ;

// Ok, inform the container of the in-place
// activation
hErr = ipsite->OnInPlaceActivate() ;
if( hErr != NOERROR )
    return PropagateResult( hErr, E_FAIL ) ;

// Get the container window
ipsite->GetWindow(&hCntrWnd) ;

// Create the hatch window with the
// container window as the parent
hIPWnd = CreateHatchWindow(hCntrWnd) ;

// Create the document window with
// the hatch window as the parent
hObjWnd = CreateObjectWindow(hIPWnd) ;

// inform the container the user interface
// is being activated
m_ipSite->OnUIActivate() ;

frameInfo.cb = sizeof(frameInfo) ;
hErr = ipsite->GetWindowContext(
            &ipFrame,
            &ipUIWnd,
            &rcPos,
            &rcClip,
            &frameInfo ) ;
if( hErr != NOERROR )
    return PropagateResult( hErr, E_FAIL ) ;

// Resize the windows before displaying them
SetWindowSizes(hObjWnd,hIPWnd,&rcPos,&rcClip) ;
```

```
        ShowWindow(hIPWnd,SW_NORMAL) ;
        ShowWindow(hObjWnd,SW_NORMAL) ;
        SetFocus(hObjWnd) ;

        if( !InstallObjectMenu() )
            return ResultFromScode(E_FAIL) ;
        if( !InstallObjectToolbar() )
            return ResultFromScode(E_FAIL) ;
        return NOERROR ;
    }
```

This function creates the hatch window and the object window, making sure they are parented off the correct windows. The hatch window's parent is always the container window that was obtained by the call to the `GetWindow()` method using the `IOleInPlaceSite` interface. The object window's parent is the hatch window. After creating both windows, the `IOleInPlaceSite::GetWindowContext()` method is called to obtain the sizing information, as well as two interfaces that are used to install the menus and toolbars for the object. After the function obtains the position and clipping rectangles, an application-specific routine is called to resize these windows. After this, it is important to set the focus to the object's window so that events for the newly activated object are handled correctly.

Installing the Object's Menu

When an object is in-place active, the menu bar is a combination of menus from both the container and the server. The container supplies the File menu, the Window menu, and any other general or document-related menus. The server provides the Edit menu, the Help menu, and any other menus required by the server during in-place editing. Figure 12.6 illustrates how these menus will be combined.

To create this combined menu, the server must coordinate the process of building this menu with the container, and finally, it must request that the container install the resulting menu in its frame window.

First, you have to create a combined HMENU that contains all the menus for both the container and the server. This is easily done by a call to the Windows SDK routine `CreateMenu()`, which creates an empty menu handle. After you obtain a menu handle, the container must be asked to insert its menus into the newly created

Combined menu for in-place
containers and in-place servers

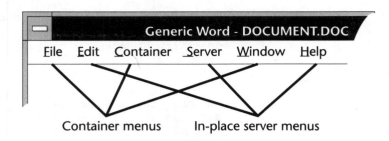

Container menus   In-place server menus

HMENU. By this stage in the object activation process, you will have already obtained a pointer to the container's `IOleInPlaceFrame` interface by calling the `IOleInPlaceSite::GetWindowContext()` method. Your server will call the `IOleInPlaceFrame::InsertMenus()` method to give the container the chance to put its menus into the new menu bar that you are creating. To call this method, your activation code must pass the HMENU handle and a pointer to an `OLEMENUGROUPWIDTHS` structure. This structure is defined as follows:

```
typedef struct tagOLEMENUGROUPWIDTHS {
    LONG widths[6] ;
} ;
```

Since the container is responsible for inserting menus at positions 0, 2, and 5, it will set the value for the `widths[]` array at these locations on return from the `InsertMenus()` routine. After this, it is up to the server to insert its menus in the spaces in between the container's items and fill out the `widths[]` data member for positions 1, 3, and 5. For the server, menu group 1 should correspond to the Edit menu item, position 5 should correspond to the Help menu item, and position 3 is where any other required menus will be inserted. Let's look at some sample code that demonstrates how this might be done.

```
BOOL InstallObjectMenu()
    HMENU hObjectMenu = CreateMenu() ;
    OLEMENUGROUPWIDTHS menuWidths ;
    HRESULT hErr ;
```

```
        // Ask the container to insert its menus
        hErr = inPlaceFrame->InsertMenus(hObjectMenu,
                                         &menuWidths) ;
        if( FAILED(hErr) ) {
            DestroyMenu(hObjectMenu) ;
            return FALSE ;
        }

        // Now insert the object menus
        int menuPos = menuWidths.widths[0] ;
        InsertMenu(hObjectEditMenu, menuPos++) ;
        menuWidths.widths[1] = 1 ;
        menuPos += menuWidths[2] ;
        InsertMenu(hDrawMenu,menuPos++) ;
        InsertMenu(hSettingsMenu,menuPos++) ;
        menuWidths.widths[3] = 2 ;
        menuPos += menuWidths.widths[4] ;
        InsertMenu(hHelpMenu,menuPos) ;
        menuWidths.widths[5] = 1 ;

        // Create the OLE Menu descriptor
        hOleMenu = OleCreateMenuDescriptor( hObjectMenu,
                                            &menuWidths ) ;
        if( hOleMenu == NULL ) {
            DestroyMenu(hObjectMenu) ;
            return FALSE ;
        }

        // Now ask the container to install the menu
        hErr = inPlaceFrame->SetMenu(hObjectMenu,
                                     hOleMenu,
                                     hObjectWnd ) ;
        if( FAILED(hErr) ) {
            DestroyMenu(hObjectMenu) ;
            OleDestroyMenuDescriptor(hOleMenu) ;
            return FALSE ;
        }
        return TRUE ;
    }
```

First, you must create an OLE menu descriptor structure of type HOLEMENU, which is used to track and coordinate the menu items for both the server and the container.

Your server can create a HOLEMENU by calling the OLE function OleCreateMenuDe-scriptor(). This function takes as an argument a combined menu and creates the HOLEMENU structure. After this, your server calls the IOleInPlaceFrame::Set-Menu() method, which actually installs the menu in the container's frame window.

Installing the Toolbar for the Object

After installing the menu, your container will install the toolbar. To do this, you must obtain a pointer to the IOleInPlaceUIWindow interface and use the Request-BorderSpace() and SetBorderSpace() methods to allocate the space your server needs to install its toolbars. The best way to describe this process is to examine some sample code:

```
BOOL InstallObjectToolbar()
{
        HRESULT hErr ;
        HWND hFrameWnd ;

        RECT rect ;
        inPlaceFrame->GetBorder(&rect) ;
        BORDERWIDTHS bw, bwTemp ;
        bw.left = bw.top = 0 ;
        bw.right = rect.right ;
        bw.bottom = TOOLBAR_HEIGHT ;
        bwTemp = bw ;
        hErr = inPlaceFrame->RequestBorderSpace( &bwTemp ) ;
        if( FAILED(hErr) ) {
                return DisplayFloatingToolbar() ;
        }
        hErr = inPlaceFrame->SetBorderSpace( &bw ) ;
        if( FAILED( hErr ) ) return FALSE ;

        HWND hToolbar = CreateToolbarWindow( objectHwnd ) ;
        inPlaceFrame->GetWindow(&hFrameWnd) ;
        SetParent( hToolbar, hFrameWnd ) ;
        return TRUE ;
}
```

The first call is to the GetBorder() method, which returns the amount of space that is potentially available for installing your toolbar. This routine is called to determine the width of the available area. A BORDERWIDTHS structure (which is exactly the same as the RECT structure) is initialized with the widths required by the server on each border. For example, you fill out the top structure member to specify that you need TOOLBAR_HEIGHT pixels in the frame. The other structure members are initialized to 0 since you do not use any space on the sides or bottom of the frame. The initialized BORDERWIDTHS structure is passed to the RequestBorderSpace() method. If the container can't support the server's space requirements, the server has the option of either displaying a floating tool palette or reverting to OLE 1–style open activation. If the request succeeds, the SetBorderSpace() method informs the container that you will be using the space immediately to install a toolbar. At this point the only thing left to do is to create the toolbar. You can obtain a handle to the frame window by calling the GetWindow() method for the frame interface. The sample code above calls the Windows SDK routine SetParent() to make the frame window the toolbar's parent window so that messages will be dispatched properly.

TIP

Remember that all the in-place interfaces are based on the IOleWindow interface. A server can obtain the window handle for the document by using the IOleInPlaceUIWindow interface returned from the IOleInPlaceSite::GetWindowContext() method. The IOleInPlaceFrame interface pointer (also obtained from GetWindow-Context()) is used to get a handle to the frame window.

WARNING

Did you notice in the InstallObjectToolbar() function described above that the temporary variable bwTemp was used to call the RequestBorderSpace() method? This is very important since some OLE containers modify the value of the BORDERWIDTHS parameter in their implementation of RequestBorderSpace().

Supporting Context-Sensitive Help

There are two situations in which you have to implement the IOleWindow::ContextSensitiveHelp() method. Obviously, the first situation is when your object server supports context-sensitive help. In this case your server should remember the state of the flag passed to this method when it is called by the container and display the appropriate help information when the user clicks on a portion of the object's interface.

The second situation is when your object is also an in-place container. In this case it should inform all in-place objects of the help state by calling the `IOleWindow::ContextSensitive()` help method for each active in-place object.

Supporting Undo in an In-Place Container

The object is responsible for all items on the Edit menu when it is in-place active. This means that if the user selects Undo from this menu, the object should undo its last action. If there is no action to undo, the most obvious thing to happen is for the last action in the container to be undone. In this case an in-place active object should call the `IOleInPlaceSite::DeactivateAndUndo()` method. This indicates to the container that it should deactivate the object and undo the last action that was stored on its Undo stack. When an object is activated and the user performs an action that is undo-able by the in-place object, it is responsible for calling the `IOleInPlaceSite::DiscardUndoState()` method to inform the container that its Undo state is no longer needed.

The flip side of this situation is when an in-place object is deactivated and the user selects Undo in the container's Edit menu before the user has performed an undo-able action. In this case the container will call the `IOleInPlaceObject::ReactivateAndUndo()` method to reactivate the object and undo the last change the user made to the object.

NOTE An in-place container will be notified of the fact that an object has an Undo state indirectly by a call to the `IOleInPlaceSite::DiscardUndoState()` method. It can use this information to determine whether to enable its Undo menu item after an in-place object is deactivated. An in-place object, however, has no way of knowing whether the container has a valid Undo state when it is first activated. Therefore, it must always leave its Undo menu item enabled while it is in-place active.

Displaying the Status Bar Text for Your Menus

The OLE system automatically determines whether to dispatch messages to the container or the server. This includes the WM_MENUSELECT message. Applications process the WM_MENUSELECT message to display the status message text while the user browses the menus. OLE in-place servers can continue to display the status bar text by calling the IOleInPlaceFrame::SetStatusText() method. The following code is an example of how to write the handler for the WM_MENUSELECT message so that it works for both open and in-place activation. It is important to note that while the WM_MENUSELECT messages are normally sent to the application frame window, when an object is in-place activated, the messages are sent to the object's window (the same window that you return from the IOleInPlaceObject::GetWindow() method).

```
void OnMenuSelect( HMENU menu, UINT fwMenu, UINT idItem )
{
        UINT rsrcID = IDS_READY ;

        // If a valid menu item was selected, then set the ID
        // otherwise display the ready resource ID.
        if( fwMenu != 0xffff || menu != 0 ) {
        if( fwMenu & MF_POPUP && fwMenu & MF_SYSMENU )
                rsrcID = IDS_SYSMENU ;
        else if( fwMenu & MF_POPUP ) return ;
                else rsrcID = idItem ;
        }

        // Now display the text
        char text[100] ;
        LoadString( hInstance, rsrcID, text, sizeof(text) ) ;
        if( server is running in place )
                inPlaceFrame->SetStatusText( text ) ;
        else
                SetStatusBarText( text ) ;
}
```

Even if your server does not support status bar text, you should still call the Set-StatusText() method with an empty string to clear the status bar when the user has selected one of the server's menu items. If you don't, the last status bar message the container displayed will still be there while the user is browsing your server's menu items.

Handling the Container Zoom Factor

The OLE in-place interface provides for containers that implement zooming. When the container changes the zoom factor (magnification) of an in-active object, it simply modifies the display rectangle of the object by the zoom factor. Things get a little more complicated when an object is in-place active. It is up to the object server to calculate the zoom factor from the container's display size for the object. The `IOleInPlaceObject::SetObjectRects()` is used by the container to change the size and position of the object. The two parameters to this method are the object's position rectangle and the clipping rectangle for the container. (For a more in-depth discussion of the position and clipping rects, see the section "The `GetWindowContext()` Method" earlier in this chapter.) When this method is called, the server should compare the requested display size to the actual size of the object. If the sizes are different, the container is requesting that the object be zoomed. If this happens and the object does not support zooming, the object server should in-place deactivate itself and reactivate itself in open mode (although it is definitely more desirable for an in-place object server to support zooming). The following code demonstrates how a server might implement this method:

```
STDMETHODIMP Document::DocIPObject::SetObjectRects(
        PCRECT lprcPosRect,
        LPCRECT lprcClipRect)
{     if( !EqualRect(&m_pDoc->m_rcPos,lprcPosRect) ||
        !EqualRect(&m_pDoc->m_rcClip,lprcClipRect) ) {
      m_pDoc->m_zoomNumX = lprcPosRect->right -
          lprcPosRect->left ;
      m_pDoc->m_zoomDenomX = m_pDoc.docRect->right -
          m_pDoc.docRect->left ;
      m_pDoc->m_zoomNumY = lprcPosRec->bottom -
          lprcPosRect->top ;
      m_pDoc->m_zoomDenomY = m_pDoc.docRect->bottom -
          m_pDoc.docRect->top ;
      m_pDoc->m_rcPos = *lprcPosRect ;
      m_pDoc->m_rcClip = *lprcClipRect ;
      m_pDoc->SetDocumentSize() ;
   }
   return NOERROR ;
}
```

The calculation of zoom factor for the X and the Y axes allows the application's drawing code to scale any drawing it does at run time. Although any in-place object should make every attempt to support in-place zooming, if it does not, the server should deactivate and reactivate OLE 1 style.

Resizing the Object In-Place

When a server needs to resize the object for some reason, it cannot just move its in-place windows to the new location. In fact, it can only ask that the container resize it and hope for the best. This is done by a call to the `IOleInPlaceSite::OnPosRectChange()` method. The desired size of the object is passed to this method in the container window's client coordinates, and the container will call the object server's `IOleInPlaceObject::SetObjectRects()` method to reposition the object.

Building an In-Place Server

The OLE Draw object server uses the architecture illustrated in Figure 12.7. Of course, the only major architectural difference between the in-place version of the OLE Draw object server and the basic version is that the two in-place object interfaces have been added at the document level for the object.

Even though we have only added two interfaces, we had to make changes throughout a large portion of the interface for the product, including adding the hatch window and the extra logic to the document window and the toolbar so that messages get processed properly. In a normal Windows application, menu commands are sent to the main window of the application. In an in-place object, the menu commands are automatically sent to the window returned by the `GetWindow()` method. For OLE Draw, this is our document window. Notice that we do not return the window handle of the hatch window. Since the OLE Draw application already forwards all relevant messages to the document window, this did require a large amount of work. The toolbar code was also changed to support passing messages to a specified window instead of its parent window. Normally, a click on the toolbar would cause a command message to be sent to the parent window, but when in-place activated, the parent window is the container application. When installing the toolbar and setting the toolbar's parent to be the container's frame window, we also call a new toolbar method to specify the window to send all commands.

Support was added for the zoom factor calculations into the mouse and the drawing code for the document window, and finally we added the extra methods we

FIGURE 12.7:

In-place architecture

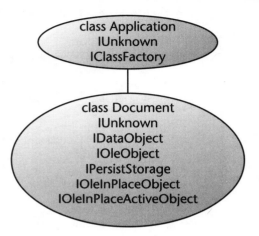

needed to create and manage the windows, menus, and toolbar. The majority of this
code is application specific, and while it follows the logic demonstrated above, it
will be implemented differently in every application.

The IOleInPlaceObject for OLE Draw

The `IOleInPlaceObject` interface contains the routines to deactivate and reactivate the object, as well as the `SetObjectRects()` method, which is responsible for
resizing and zooming the in-place object at the container's request.

```
Document::DocIPObject::DocIPObject( Document *pDoc )
{
    m_refCount = 0 ;
    m_pDoc = pDoc ;
}

Document::DocIPObject::~DocIPObject()
{
}

STDMETHODIMP Document::DocIPObject::QueryInterface(
    REFIID riid,
    LPVOID FAR *lpVoid )
```

```
    {
        return m_pDoc->QueryInterface( riid, lpVoid ) ;
    }

    STDMETHODIMP_(ULONG) Document::DocIPObject::AddRef()
    {
        m_refCount++ ;
        return m_pDoc->AddRef() ;
    }

    STDMETHODIMP_(ULONG) Document::DocIPObject::Release()
    {
        m_refCount-- ;
        return m_pDoc->Release() ;
    }

    STDMETHODIMP Document::DocIPObject::GetWindow(
        HWND FAR* lphwnd)
    {
        *lphwnd = m_pDoc->m_ipWnd->m_hWnd ;
        return NOERROR ;
    }

    STDMETHODIMP Document::DocIPObject::ContextSensitiveHelp(
        BOOL fEnterMode)
    {
        // If we supported embedded objects
        // we would want to pass the call on
        // to inform each object of the help
        // mode state
        return NOERROR ;
    }

    STDMETHODIMP Document::DocIPObject::InPlaceDeactivate()
    {
        if( !m_pDoc->m_uiActive )
            return NOERROR ;

        m_pDoc->HideUI() ;
        m_pDoc->HideInPlace() ;
        m_pDoc->m_ipSite->OnInPlaceDeactivate() ;
        return NOERROR ;
    }

    STDMETHODIMP Document::DocIPObject::UIDeactivate()
```

```
{
    m_pDoc->HideUI() ;
    return NOERROR ;
}

STDMETHODIMP Document::DocIPObject::SetObjectRects(
        LPCRECT lprcPosRect,
        LPCRECT lprcClipRect)
{
    if( !EqualRect(&m_pDoc->m_rcPos,lprcPosRect) ||
        !EqualRect(&m_pDoc->m_rcClip,lprcClipRect) ) {
        m_pDoc->m_rcPos = *lprcPosRect ;
        m_pDoc->m_rcClip = *lprcClipRect ;
        m_pDoc->SetDocumentSize() ;
    }
    return NOERROR ;
}

STDMETHODIMP Document::DocIPObject::ReactivateAndUndo()
{
    HRESULT hErr = m_pDoc->DoInPlaceActivate() ;
    if( FAILED(hErr) )
        return hErr ;
    m_pDoc->Undo() ;
    return NOERROR ;
}
```

The `OnInPlaceDeactivate()` method completely deactivates the in-place object, while the `UIDeactivate()` method simply hides the object's user-interface adornments. The `SetObjectRects()` method is responsible for resizing the object, and it uses the new position rectangle to calculate whether zooming is in effect, as described in the section "Handling the Container Zoom Factor" earlier in this chapter. Finally, the `ReactivateAndUndo()` method is responsible for reactivating the object and undoing the last change that was made by the user.

NOTE　Deactivation does not necessarily mean that the object will be unloaded. This does not happen until the `Close()` method is called explicitly by the container.

The IOleInPlaceActiveObject for OLE Draw

The main purpose of the `IOleInPlaceActiveObject` interface is to support the various interface notifications that are required to support in-place activation. The OLE Draw object server uses the methods in this interface to update its toolbar state and size, along with hiding and showing the toolbar using the `HideUI()` and `ShowUI()` methods in the `OnDocWindowActivate()` method. This method is called by MDI containers when the document window is being activated or deactivated.

```
Document::DocIPActiveObject::DocIPActiveObject(
    Document *pDoc )
{
    m_refCount = 0 ;
    m_pDoc = pDoc ;
}

Document::DocIPActiveObject::~DocIPActiveObject()
{
}

STDMETHODIMP Document::DocIPActiveObject::QueryInterface(
    REFIID riid,
    LPVOID FAR *lpVoid )
{
    return m_pDoc->QueryInterface( riid, lpVoid ) ;
}

STDMETHODIMP_(ULONG) Document::DocIPActiveObject::AddRef()
{
    m_refCount++ ;
    return m_pDoc->AddRef() ;
}

STDMETHODIMP_(ULONG) Document::DocIPActiveObject::Release()
{
    m_refCount-- ;
    return m_pDoc->Release() ;
}

STDMETHODIMP Document::DocIPActiveObject::GetWindow(
    HWND FAR* lphwnd)
{
```

```
        return m_pDoc->m_IPObject.GetWindow( lphwnd ) ;
}

STDMETHODIMP Document::DocIPActiveObject::
    ContextSensitiveHelp(BOOL fEnterMode)
{
    return m_pDoc->m_IPObject.
        ContextSensitiveHelp( fEnterMode ) ;
}

STDMETHODIMP Document::DocIPActiveObject::
    TranslateAccelerator(LPMSG lpmsg)
{
    return NOERROR ;
}

STDMETHODIMP Document::DocIPActiveObject::
    OnFrameWindowActivate(BOOL fActivate)
{
    // We need to force our toolbar to be updated
    // here, but we can't just directly update it,
    // so we post a message to ourselves to do it
    // later...
    PostMessage(m_pDoc->m_hWnd,WM_UPDATETOOLS,0,0L) ;
    return NOERROR ;
}

STDMETHODIMP Document::DocIPActiveObject::
    OnDocWindowActivate(BOOL fActivate)
{
    if( fActivate )
        m_pDoc->ShowUI() ;
    else
        m_pDoc->HideUI() ;

    return NOERROR ;
}

STDMETHODIMP Document::DocIPActiveObject::ResizeBorder(
        LPCRECT lprectBorder,
        LPOLEINPLACEUIWINDOW lpUIWindow,
        BOOL fFrameWindow)
{
    RECT rect = *lprectBorder ;
    if( fFrameWindow )
```

```
            theApp->m_toolBar.SetParentRect( &rect ) ;
        return NOERROR ;
    }

    STDMETHODIMP Document::DocIPActiveObject::EnableModeless(
            BOOL fEnable)
    {
        return NOERROR ;
    }
```

The IOleObject::DoVerb() Method

Because it is also significantly affected by the changes to support in-place activation, the IOleObject::DoVerb() method is shown here as well:

```
    STDMETHODIMP Document::DocOleObject::DoVerb(
        LONG iVerb,
        LPMSG lpmsg,
        LPOLECLIENTSITE pActiveSite,
        LONG lindex,
        HWND hwndParent,
        LPCRECT lprcPosRect)
    {

        HRESULT hErr = NOERROR ;
        switch( iVerb ) {
        case OLEIVERB_UIACTIVATE:

            if( m_pDoc->m_isOpen )
                hErr =
                    ResultFromScode( OLE_E_NOTINPLACEACTIVE ) ;
            else
                hErr = m_pDoc->DoInPlaceActivate() ;
            break ;

        case OLEIVERB_PRIMARY:
        case OLEIVERB_SHOW:

            if( m_pDoc->m_isOpen ) {
                m_pDoc->DoOpenActivate() ;
            }else {
                if( FAILED( m_pDoc->DoInPlaceActivate() ) )
                    m_pDoc->DoOpenActivate() ;
            }
```

```
            break ;

        case OLEIVERB_OPEN:
            if( m_pDoc->m_isInPlace )
                m_pDoc->m_IPObject.InPlaceDeactivate() ;

            m_pDoc->DoOpenActivate() ;
            break ;

        case OLEIVERB_HIDE:
            if( m_pDoc->m_isInPlace )
                m_pDoc->HideUI() ;
            else{
                theApp->Show( SW_HIDE ) ;
            }

            // Notify client site that the window has been
            // hidden
            if( m_pCliSite != NULL )
                m_pCliSite->OnShowWindow( FALSE ) ;

            break ;

        default:
            hErr = ResultFromScode( OLEOBJ_S_INVALIDVERB ) ;
            break ;
        }
        return hErr ;
    }
```

The changes include the attempts to in-place activate the object before attempting an "open" activation. The verb OLEIVERB_UIACTIVATE has also been added to support explicit in-place activation, although this verb will not be used often.

Summary

In this chapter you learned that to add in-place support to your object server, you must add the IOleInPlaceObject and IOleInPlaceActiveObject interfaces to the supported interfaces. When the object is initially activated, it will create its windows, including the special hatch-border window supplied by the OLE2UI library, and create its menus.

This chapter has walked you through the OLE 2 interfaces and support code for in-place activation. The techniques in this chapter combined with the techniques in Chapter 11 are all you need to build an object server. Chapter 13 covers debugging tools and techniques to help you bulletproof your OLE applications.

CHAPTER

THIRTEEN

Building a Server with Support for Linking

- **Understanding linking**

- **Types of monikers**

- **Binding monikers**

- **The running object table**

- **Linking and the clipboard**

- **Understanding pseudo-objects**

This chapter discusses the details involved in adding linking support to your server application. The interesting thing to note is that once you fully understand linking, you will realize that there is not much more to fully supporting links in a server than there is in a container. To that end, this chapter explains links so that their purpose and implementation become clear.

Understanding Linking

Links are a way to allow one or more references to a single copy of data. Some people think that links are a way of reducing the amount of disk space required by having a reference to the data instead of a copy. The assumption implied in this statement is that the reference will be much smaller than the actual data itself. This assumption by itself is almost always true. The problem is that there is another piece of the picture that people don't clearly understand. In order to display the linked data, some sort of cached representation has to be stored. This is the root of the problem.

Let's discuss an actual example. A business aquaintance once explained that he wanted to include a scanned image of his signature on each of the faxes he sent using his fax/modem. Before sending out a fax, he would create a link to the file containing the scanned signature. He explained that he had assumed this would reduce disk space, but after checking the file sizes, he realized that, in fact, the link increased the size of the file by an amount that caused it to correspond roughly to the size of the entire image file. He had not taken into account the cached representation of the linked data.

Figure 13.1 illustrates this example. The point is to give you a solid grasp of what links are and what they are not. It is possible to have a small compact representation of a link—for example, when a link is displayed as an icon.

To make links easy to use, the ideal design would make a link completely transparent to the link's client or container. Once you've thought about this for a minute, it is not difficult to do. You just have to create an object that looks and acts like an embedded object in all ways. The difference is that when it is activated by the container (perhaps when a user double-clicks on the object), it will load the application that created the linked data and ask the application to load the document that contained that data.

FIGURE 13.1:

Links to an image

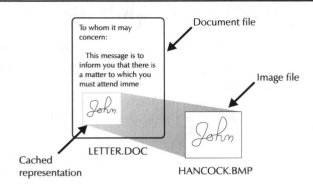

By definition, an embedded object is itself. What this means is that when an object is embedded into a container, you are actually embedding the data that represents the object. When a link is inserted into a container, what is actually being embedded is the data that describes the location of the actual object's data. By now you realize that if you wanted to, you could develop your implementation of links. In fact, the linking mechanism defined by OLE allows you to do this, as explained later in this chapter.

Let's follow what must have been the thought process of the OLE team when designing the linking subsystem. The first thing you would need is the object to act as a stand-in for your actual objects. In OLE, these stand-in objects are called *monikers*. You develop an object that stores a path name to the data and have the stand-in object (moniker) launch the application when it is activated. Designing this seems pretty straightforward. Assuming you create a mechanism for determining which application created which file and a way of asking that application to load the file, you don't really have much work to do.

But then things start getting complicated. What if the file is already open? You would want to activate the copy of the file that was already running, right? Okay, no problem. You add a table to keep track of all of the running objects. (This table is the `IRunningObjectTable` table.) You saw the rough sketch of an idea that would allow linking to whole documents, but what about linking to parts of a file? What if you want to link to objects that are already embedded in another container (as described in Chapter 8)? What about linking to parts of an object embedded in a container? What if different parts of these pieces are already running? Now you can start to understand the issues involved in linking.

The Mechanics of Linking

OLE 2 solves the linking problem by using monikers. A moniker is an object that represents the name of some other type of object. More specifically, it represents the information needed to identify and locate the object it was built to identify. Because there are different ways of storing objects, as well as different ways of linking to objects, there are many types of monikers. The three main types you need to understand are

- File monikers
- Item monikers
- Composite monikers

File monikers represent and store files and their paths. *Item monikers* represent and store items usually stored inside files. An item can be almost anything, as you will see a little later in this chapter. *Composite monikers* are two or more monikers concatenated to form a more complex moniker.

Binding Monikers

The act of resolving a moniker to get to the data it represents is called *binding*. When you bind a moniker, you are requesting that it do whatever is necessary to locate and load that object. Hence, binding a file moniker causes the moniker to locate and load the file and the application that created it. Let's take a look at a simple example (see Figure 13.2).

Step 1

A user inserts a link to a Microsoft Word 6 document into an Excel spreadsheet using the Insert Object dialog. This causes a file moniker to be created containing the path to the Word document file. This file moniker is then embedded in the Excel spreadsheet. The only thing being stored at this point is the path to the Word file.

Simple link to a file

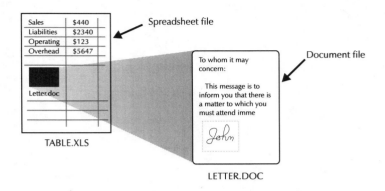

TABLE.XLS

LETTER.DOC

Step 2

The user activates the link by double-clicking on the icon.

Remember that the file moniker has no innate knowledge that the file the user specified is a Word file. The very first thing the file moniker must do is determine the application that created the file. It does this using several methods. First, it opens the file and checks to see whether the CLSID of the server was written into the root storage by the application. If the CLSID is not found, the file moniker checks the registration database to see whether the file's extension is associated with an object server. If one of these methods works, CoCreateInstance() is called to create a new object for the identified server. Then the IPersistFile interface is used to ask the server to load the file. Finally, the newly initialized object is used to obtain a pointer to the interface that Excel requested. This will probably be the IOleObject interface. At this point Excel has everything it needs to work with the object the same as it would any other.

Binding Composite Monikers

Now let's consider a more complicated example: the situation in which the user links to an object inside the Word file (see Figure 13.3).

FIGURE 13.3:

A more complicated link

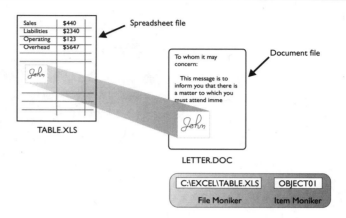

Step 1

The user selects Edit ➤ Copy when an object in the Word file is selected.

Word creates a data object and places it on the clipboard. This data object will include all the formats required to embed the object or link to the object.

Step 2

The user switchs to Excel and selects Paste Link.

At this point a link to the object is created. The moniker to represent this object will end up being a composite moniker that contains a file moniker and an item moniker. The purpose of composite monikers is to combine one or more monikers in a single wrapper.

Step 3

After closing Word, the user activates the linked object by double-clicking on it.

In this case the composite moniker is bound. Binding a composite moniker causes each of the monikers that make up the composite moniker to be bound in right-to-left order. The reason for this order is explained a little later in this chapter.

Although the item moniker is bound, before it can do anything it must obtain access to the compound file it is stored in. To do this, it binds the file moniker, which works much the same as it did in the previous example. OLE identifies the application that created the file and uses the `IPersistFile` interface to load the file. The difference, in the simple example, is that the interface requested by the application binding the moniker is the `IOleObject` interface. In this case the item moniker is binding the file moniker and will request the `IOleItemContainer` interface. Since the item moniker stores the item name, it has all the information it needs to call the `IOleItemContainer::GetObject()` method to obtain a reference to the object.

Notice that it is up to the container to implement the `IOleItemContainer` interface, which means that how the item names are interpreted is completely up to the container. When the call to `GetObject()` is made, the requested interface is the interface Excel requested when it started binding the composite moniker—probably the `IOleObject` interface.

More on the Process of Binding

Each moniker type follows a different process for binding. Table 13.1 describes the binding process for each of the moniker types.

TABLE 13.1: The Binding Process

Moniker Type	Binding Process
Composite moniker	Binds itself by asking each of its contained monikers to bind itself
File moniker	Binds itself by trying to determine which OLE application created the file, creating an object with that server, and using the `IPersistFile` interface on that object to load the file
Item moniker	Binding an item moniker requires a moniker to the left of the item moniker. This is usually a file moniker, but it can be another item moniker. When an item moniker is binding, it binds the moniker to its immediate left, requesting the `IOleItemContainer` interface. It then uses the `GetObject()` method to obtain a pointer to the specific item represented by the item moniker. The composite moniker passes the pointer to the moniker on the left as one of the parameters to the `IMoniker::BindToObject()` interface, which is how the item moniker obtains the moniker on its left
Pointer moniker	Binds itself by returning a pointer to the object that was used to create the pointer moniker. This moniker type is useful only for linking to running objects. By definition, a pointer moniker cannot be serialized (or saved) and can be used only under special conditions

To bind a moniker you must first create a binding context. A *binding context* is an object that is implemented by the system that supports the `IBindCtx` interface. Monikers use a bind context to determine the parameters of the binding operation. Since this class is not usually used directly by an OLE application, this discussion doesn't go into the details. The most important use of this class is to set a binding speed and to specify whether the bind is a full binding operation or is performed just to validate the moniker.

The binding context serves one other purpose. As objects are created during the bind operation, they are registered with the bind context using the `IBindCtx::RegisterObjectBound()` and `IBindCtx::RevokeObjectBound()` methods. The binding context is also used to release all the intermediate objects that are created if the binding operation is not successful in using the `IBindCtx::ReleaseBoundObjects()` method.

Links on the Clipboard and Persist Monikers

The process of pasting a link also deserves a more detailed explanation. You learned in Chapter 8 how links are placed on the clipboard using the Link Source and Link Source Descriptor clipboard formats.

The OLE 2 UI library function `OleStdGetLinkSourceData()` was used to create the Link Source clipboard format. This function takes care of a couple of steps you would normally have to perform. First, an `IStream` is created on an `HGLOBAL`. Second, the `CLSID` is written to the newly created `IStream`. Finally, it serializes the moniker to the `IStream` by obtaining the `IPersistStream` interface from the moniker. `OleStdGetLinkSourceData()` creates the link source format by obtaining a pointer to the `IPersistStream` interface from the moniker and calling the `Save()` method to serialize the method. When the user selects the Paste Link command, the moniker is deserialized (using the `IPersistStream::Load()` method) and then used to create a link object by calling the `OleCreateLink()` helper function. Since most container applications will use the `OleCreateLinkFromData()` function, you may never see this level of detail, but it helps to understand what is happening beneath the surface.

The Running Object Table

The *running object table* is exactly what its name states—a table of all running objects on the system. Almost. It is actually a table of all the file monikers that represent OLE compound documents that are currently in use by some application. Obviously, if the table contains only file monikers, it cannot contain all running objects. Registering file monikers is all that is needed to optimize binding. When a file moniker is bound, it first does a lookup in the running object table to see whether the file is already running. If it is, the running object is used. There is no OLE equivalent of a running object table for item monikers. The link source is responsible for implementing any caching of running objects so that the implementation of `IOleItemContainer` is as efficient as possible

Implementing Pseudo-Objects

The last area of linking you need to understand is pseudo-objects. A *pseudo-object* is a link to an arbitrary data selection in a compound document. Pseudo-objects are created using the clipboard or drag-and-drop. The item moniker for a pseudo-object is added to the end of the moniker that specifies the pseudo-object's containing document (see Figure 13.4).

FIGURE 13.4:

Pseudo-object's moniker

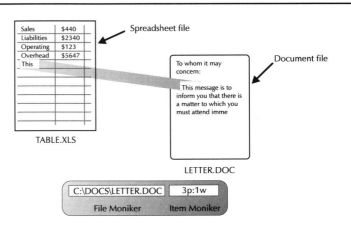

To support pseudo-objects, a server must implement the IOleItemContainer interface so that it manufactures an OLE object that represents the item when the GetObject() method is called with the text of the pseudo-object. This gets a little more complicated if the server supports both pseudo-objects and linking to embedded objects.

To help illustrate how pseudo-objects work, let's walk through an object activation example based on the moniker and link depicted in Figure 13.4. First, when the user double-clicks on the object in the spreadsheet, Excel calls IOleObject::DoVerb(). The OLE system knows the object is a link and binds the moniker so that it can pass the call to DoVerb() to the actual object. As shown in Figure 13.4, the moniker is a composite moniker composed of a file moniker that represents the LETTER.DOC file and an item moniker that represents the subset of the letter to which the link refers. When the composite moniker is bound, it will bind the item moniker, passing a pointer to the file moniker as an argument. As described earlier in this chapter, an item moniker must have another moniker in order to do its work. To obtain this interface, the item moniker binds the file moniker requesting the IOleItemContainer interface. The file moniker then loads the LETTER.DOC document and returns the requested interface. So far, this is exactly the same process that happens for linking to an embedded object. The difference is what the IOleItemContainer::GetObject() method does to return the requested object. When linking to an embedded object, most implementations of GetObject() do nothing more than return a pointer to the requested object. The GetObject() method must manufacture an object that represents the data selection. This pseudo-object will function, in most ways, exactly the same as any other object; but when DoVerb() is called, it will select only the data it represents. Also, when the cached representation is requested through the IDataObject interface, the pseudo-object will draw a representation of the selected data only, not the entire document.

Summary

This chapter has described the linking process and the moniker classes in more detail than earlier chapters in this book. At this point it should be obvious that implementing a server that supports linking is no more involved than the effort required to add support for linking in a container, with the exception of pseudo-objects. There is a little extra work if you want to add code to support pseudo-objects, but this can leverage a lot of the existing code for the standard objects supported by your server.

If you are feeling really adventurous, you might even try building your own monikers. For example, a custom moniker might be one that would allow linking to a database record. An extension of this idea might be a query moniker that executes a database query to bind or update the link. Another moniker type might be created that connects to a web page on the Internet. This would allow a limited sort of inter-linking between the web and OLE containers on a machine that was connected to the Internet.

APPENDICES

Almost all OLE applications will have to register one or more key pieces of information with the registration database. In fact, only a container that does not support linking can get away without using the registration database. Appendix A addresses the details of how to create a REG file for your application and the meanings of different keys and subkeys. Appendix B covers the details of adding support for properties, including the Summary Information property set. Due to an increasing reliance by computer users on document management tools, as well as generic file location and search utilities, it is a good idea for you to add support for the Summary Information property set. This property set, which allows the user to tag an application with useful information and attributes, can make document management much easier. For an actual example of the Summary Information property set, see the OLE Publisher product and the source code on the disk included with this book.

APPENDIX

A

Registering Database REG.DAT and REGEDIT.EXE

- Contents of the registration database file

- OLE 1 application entries

REG.DAT is the OLE registration database file that contains information about the OLE 2 libraries and specific information about all the containers and server applications installed on a system. It is located in the WINDOWS subdirectory. REG-EDIT.EXE allows additions and modifications to the REG.DAT database file. You can edit the database by running REGEDIT /v or by having information brought in from a text file. For the latter, create an XXX.REG file specific to your application, containing text entries, and invoke the command line REGEDIT /s XXX.REG to merge information from XXX.REG to the database file REG.DAT. Similarly, to add OLE 2 library information to the database, use the command line REGEDIT /s OLE2.REG.

Contents of the Registration Database File

Figure A.1 shows Microsoft Word 6.0–specific information in the REG.DAT file.

The following sections give brief descriptions of the keys and subkeys in the database.

ProgID Key

Programmable interface identifier subkeys are listed in the following sections.

Human-Readable String Subkey Entry

Example:

```
HKEY_CLASSES_ROOT\OLE2ISvrOtl = Ole 2 In-Place Server Outline
```

Information for OLE 1 Applications' Subkey Entries

```
The following entries provide compatibility with OLE 1 applications.
```

FIGURE A.1:

Microsoft Word 6.0 registration
entries

```
{00020900-0000-0000-C000-000000000046} = Microsoft Word 6.0 Document
 ProgID = Word.Document.6
 InprocHandler = ole2.dll
 LocalServer = C:\WINWORD\WINWORD.EXE
 verb
   1 = &Open,0,2
   0 = &Edit,0,2
 Insertable
 AuxUserType
   2 = Document
   3 = Microsoft Word 6.0
 DefaultIcon = C:\WINWORD\WINWORD.EXE,1
 DataFormats
   DefaultFile = MSWordDoc
   GetSet
     0 = Embed_Source,1,8,1
     1 = 1,1,1,3
     2 = 3,1,32,1
     3 = Rich Text Format,1,1,3
 MiscStatus = 0
   1 = 1
 Conversion
   Readable
     Main = WordDocument
{00010043-0000-0000-C000-000000000046} = XServer InProc No Debug
 MiscStatus = 1
   4 = 3
 DataFormats
   GetSet
     1 = 3,4,32,1
     0 = 3,1,32,1
 Conversion
   Readable
     Main = XServer
 DefaultIcon = xserver.dll,0
 AuxUserType
   3 = X No Debug Object Server
   2 = X No Debug Object
 Insertable
```

WARNING For the purposes of this book, lines of code in this appendix have been limited to 65 characters. However, for this code to compile correctly, there need to be no artificial line breaks.

Example:

```
HKEY_CLASSES_ROOT\OLE2ISvrOtl\protocol\StdFileEditing\server =
  c:\samp\isvrotl.exe
HKEY_CLASSES_ROOT\OLE2ISvrOtl\protocol\StdFileEditing\verb\0 =
  &Edit
HKEY_CLASSES_ROOT\OLE2ISvrOtl\protocol\StdFileEditing\verb\1 =
  &Open
```

Windows 3.1 Shell Subkey Entries

The following entries associate print and file open commands.

Example:

```
HKEY_CLASSES_ROOT\OLE2ISvrOtl\Shell\Print\Command =
  c:\svr\isvrotl.exe %1
HKEY_CLASSES_ROOT\OLE2ISvrOtl\Shell\Open\Command =
  c:\svr\isvrotl.exe %1
```

Insertable Subkey Entry

The Insertable subkey allows your application to appear in the Insert New dialog box.

Example:

```
HKEY_CLASSES_ROOT\OLE2ISvrOtl\Insertable
```

Entry Point Subkey

The Entry Point subkey points to the application's OLE 2 information in the registration database. Run the GUIDGEN.EXE to get a unique CLSID.

Example:

```
HKEY_CLASSES_ROOT\OLE2ISvrOtl\CLSID = {00000402-0000-0000-C000-
   000000000046}
```

CLSID (Object Class ID) Key

CLSID subkeys provide information to the OLE 2 libraries about the location of the code that services this class and the functionality of the class as it enters the loaded state. These subkeys are described in the following sections.

Immediate Subkey

The Immediate subkey of the CLSID root key is a string version CLSID. To obtain a CLSID for your application, run the GUIDGEN.EXE found in the TOOLS directory of the OLE 2 Toolkit.

Example:

```
HKEY_CLASSES_ROOT\CLSID\{00000402-0000-0000-C000-000000000046} =
   Ole 2 In-Place Server Outline
```

LocalServer Subkey

The LocalServer Subkey provides a path to the local exe server application.

InprocServer Subkey

The InprocServer subkey provides a path to the in-process server DLL.

InprocHandler Subkey

The InprocHandler subkey provides a path to the in-process handler DLL or OLE2.DLL for the default handler.

Verb Subkey

The format for the Verb subkey is

verb number = name, menu flags, verb flags

Example:

```
Verb 0: "Edit", MF_UNCHECKED | MF_ENABLED, no OLEVERATTRIB flags
HKEY_CLASSES_ROOT\CLSID\{00000402-0000-0000-C000-
   000000000046}\Verb\0 = &Edit,0,0

Verb 1: "Open", MF_UNCHECKED | MF_ENABLED, no OLEVERATTRIB flags
HKEY_CLASSES_ROOT\CLSID\{00000402-0000-0000-C000-
   000000000046}\Verb\1 = &Open,0,0
```

AuxUserType Subkey

The AuxUserType key lists the short and long names of the application.

Short name example:

```
HKEY_CLASSES_ROOT\CLSID\{00000402-0000-0000-C000-
   000000000046}\AuxUserType\2 = In-Place Outline
```

Long name example:

```
HKEY_CLASSES_ROOT\CLSID\{00000402-0000-0000-C000-
   000000000046}\AuxUserType\3 = Ole 2 In-Place Server
```

MiscStatus Subkey

Example:

```
HKEY_CLASSES_ROOT\CLSID\{00000402-0000-0000-C000-000000000046}
   \MiscStatus = 0
```

DataFormats Key

The DataFormats key lists default and main data formats.

Examples:

```
CF_METAFILEPICT DVASPECT_CONTENT, TYMED_MFPICT, DATADIR_GET
HKEY_CLASSES_ROOT\CLSID\{00000402-0000-0000-C000-
   000000000046}\DataFormats\GetSet\1 = 3,1,32,1
```

The values defined in the following entry are 2 = cfEmbedSource, DVASPECT_CON-TENT, TYMED_ISTORAGE, and DATADIR_GET.

```
HKEY_CLASSES_ROOT\CLSID\{00000402-0000-0000-C000-
   000000000046}\DataFormats\GetSet\2 = Embed Source,1,8,1
```

The values defined in the following entry are 3 = cfOutline, DVASPECT_CONTENT, TYMED_HGLOBAL, and DATADIR_GET | DATADIR_SET.

```
HKEY_CLASSES_ROOT\CLSID\{00000402-0000-0000-C000-000000000046}
   \DataFormats\GetSet\3 = Outline,1,1,3
```

The following example declares the default file format supported by this application to be CF_OUTLINE.

```
HKEY_CLASSES_ROOT\CLSID\{00000402-0000-0000-C000-000000000046}
   \DataFormats\DefaultFile = Outline
```

Insertable Subkey

See the section "Insertable Subkey" earlier in this appendix.

Example:

```
HKEY_CLASSES_ROOT\CLSID\{00000402-0000-0000-C000-000000000046}
\Insertable
```

ProgID Subkey

See the section "ProgID Subkey Entry" earlier in this appendix.

Example:

```
HKEY_CLASSES_ROOT\CLSID\{00000402-0000-0000-C000-
   000000000046}\ProgID = OLE2ISvrOtl
```

Conversion Subkey

The Convert dialog box uses the Conversion subkey entry information to determine whether the application can read and write a specific format.

Example:

```
HKEY_CLASSES_ROOT\CLSID\{00000402-0000-0000-C000-000000000046}
   \Conversion\Readable\Main = Outline,1
HKEY_CLASSES_ROOT\CLSID\{00000402-0000-0000-C000-000000000046}
   \Conversion\Readwritable\Main = Outline,1
```

DefaultIcon Subkey

The DefaultIcon subkey provides default icon information for iconic presentations of objects.

Example:

```
HKEY_CLASSES_ROOT\CLSID\{00000402-0000-0000-C000-000000000046}
    \DefaultIcon = c:\samp\isvrotl.exe,0
```

Registration Database Functions

The following functions provide direct access to the OLE code that searches the registration database. These functions are primarily used in custom handler or DLL object applications.

```
OleRegGetUserType (REFCLSID clsid, DWORD dwFormOfType,
    LPSTR FAR* pszUserType);
OleRegGetMiscStatus (REFCLSID clsid, DWORD dwAspect,
    DWORD FAR* pdwStatus);
OleRegEnumFormatEtc (REFCLSID clsid, DWORD dwDirection,
    LPENUMFORMATETC FAR* ppenumFormatetc);
OleRegEnumVerbs (REFCLSID clsid, LPENUMOLEVERB FAR* ppenumOleVerb);
```

OLE 1 Application Entries

When an OLE 1 class is inserted into an OLE 2 container for the first time, a new subkey, CLSID, is added to the original OLE 1 registration information by the OLE 2 compatibility layer.

Example:

```
OLE1ClassName = OLE1UserTypeName
    Protocol
      StdFileEditing
      Verb
    CLSID = <CLSID>
```

APPENDIX

B

Properties in Compound Files

- Property set specification

- Type indicators

- Document Summary Information property set

- Document Summary Information format

- Document Summary Information

Properties in OLE 2.0 terminology are a set of data values represented in a prede-fined format to be manipulated and expanded by any application that follows the specification. It is another way to share data among applications at the same time using the operating system code, specifically OLE 2. Compound files provide easy imple-mentation of the property set specification by taking advantage of the OLE 2 code base. Microsoft defines and implements one property known as the Document Summary In-formation property set using compound files. The Document Summary Information property set is a subset of the complete specification. Applications wanting to share a brief summary of their document without exposing the entire document can use the Document Summary Information property set.

Property Set Specification

Figure B.1 shows the format of the property set specification. The following sections provide a short description of each component of the property set format.

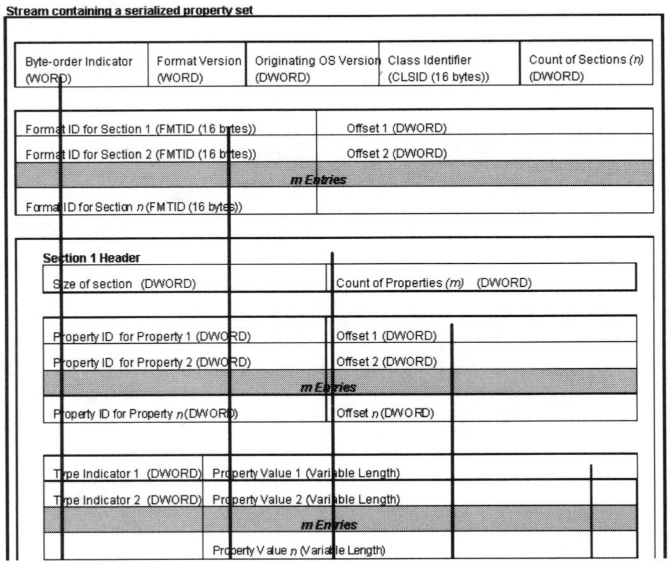

FIGURE B.1:

Property set specification

Byte-Order Indicator   The byte-order indicator is a WORD type and always holds the value 0xFFFE. The value specifies Intel byte order.

Format Version   The format version is set to 0, indicating that the stream is written according to the specification and can be read by OLE 2 code.

Originating OS Version

Operating System	Value
16-Bit Windows (Win16)	0x0000
Macintosh	0x0001
32-Bit Windows (Win32)	0x0002

For Windows, the operating system version is the low-order word of GetVersion. In Windows, the following code would correctly set the version of the originating operating system:

```
#ifdef WIN32
dwOSVer = (DWORD)MAKELONG( LOWORD(GetVersion()), 2 ) ;
#else
dwOSVer = (DWORD)MAKELONG( LOWORD(GetVersion()), 0 ) ;
#endif
```

CLSID   The value is set to CLSID_NULL or a name of an OLE class that provides access to the property values.

Count of Sections   The count of sections is the number of sections in the stream or file.

Format Identifiers   To create a unique FMTID, use the GUIDGEN.EXE program included in the OLE SDK.

Size of Section   The section size is the first 4 bytes; therefore, you can copy sections as an array of bytes.

Count of Properties   The count of properties is the count of the property values in the section.

Property ID/Offset Pairs   Property IDs are 32-bit values that uniquely identify a property within a section. The offsets indicate the distance from the start of
the section to the start of the property Type/Value Pair.

Type Indicators

Table B.1 lists the standard OLE-defined property type indicators and their meanings:

TABLE B.1: Type Indicators

Type Indicator	Code	Value Representation
VT_EMPTY	0	None. A property set with a type indicator of VT_EMPTY has no data associated with it; that is, the size of the value is 0
VT_NULL	1	None. This is like a pointer to NULL
VT_I2	2	Two bytes representing a WORD value. This value will be zero-padded to a 32-bit boundary
VT_I4	3	Four bytes representing a DWORD value
VT_R4	4	Four bytes representing a 32-bit IEEE floating-point value
VT_R8	5	Eight bytes representing a 64-bit IEEE floating-point value
VT_CY	6	Eight-byte two's complement integer (scaled by 10,000). This type is commonly used for currency amounts
VT_DATE	7	Time format used by many applications; it is a 64-bit floating-point number representing seconds since January 1, 1900. This is stored in the same representation as VT_R8
VT_BSTR	8	Counted, zero-terminated binary string; represented as a DWORD byte count (including the terminating null character) followed by the bytes of data
VT_BOOL	11	Two bytes representing a Boolean (WORD) value containing 0 (FALSE) or −1 (TRUE). This type must be zero-padded to a 32-bit boundary
VT_VARIANT	12	Four-byte indicator followed by the corresponding value. This is used only in conjunction with VT_VECTOR

TABLE B.1: Type Indicators (continued)

Type Indicator	Code	Value Representation
VT_I8	20	Eight bytes representing a signed integer
VT_LPSTR	30	Same as VT_BSTR; this is the representation of most strings
VT_LPWSTR	31	A counted and zero-terminated Unicode string; a DWORD character count (where the count includes the terminating null character) followed by that many Unicode (16-bit) characters. Note that the count is not a byte count but a WORD count
VT_FILETIME	64	64-bit FILETIME structure, as defined by Win32: typedef struct_FILETIME{ DWORD dwLowDateTime; DWORD dwHighDateTime; }FILETIME;
VT_BLOB	65	DWORD count of bytes, followed by that many bytes of data. The byte count does not include the 4 bytes for the length of the count itself; an empty BLOB would have a count of 0, followed by 0 bytes. This is similar to VT_BSTR but does not guarantee a null byte at the end of the data
VT_STREAM	66	A VT_LPSTR (DWORD count of bytes followed by a zero-terminated string that many bytes long) that names the stream containing the data. The real value for this property is stored in an IStream, which is a sibling to the CONTENTS stream. This type is valid only for property sets stored in the CONTENTS stream of an IStorage
VT_STORAGE	67	A VT_LPSTR (DWORD count of bytes followed by a zero-terminated string that many bytes long) that names the storage containing the data. The real value for this property is stored in an IStorage, which is a sibling to the CONTENTS stream that contains the property set. This type is valid only for property sets stored in the CONTENTS stream of an IStorage
VT_STREAMED_OBJECT	68	Same as VT_STREAM, but indicates that the IStream named in this property contains a serialized object, which is a CLSID followed by initialization data for the class. The named IStream is a sibling to the CONTENTS stream that contains the property set. This type is valid only for property sets stored in the CONTENTS stream of an IStorage

TABLE B.1: Type Indicators (continued)

Type Indicator	Code	Value Representation
VT_STORED_OBJECT	69	Same as VT_STORAGE, but indicates that the IStorage named in this property contains an object. This type is valid only for property sets stored in the CONTENTS stream of an IStorage
VT_BLOB_OBJECT	70	Array of bytes containing a serialized object in the same representation as would appear in a VT_STREAMED_OBJECT (VT_LPSTR). The only significant difference between this type and VT_STREAMED_OBJECT is that VT_BLOB_OBJECT does not have the system-level storage overhead that VT_STREAMED_OBJECT has. VT_BLOB_OBJECT is more suitable for scenarios involving numerous small objects
VT_CF	71	Array of bytes containing a clipboard format identifier followed by the data in that format. That is, following the VT_CF identifier is the data in the format of a VT_BLOB. This is a DWORD count of bytes followed by that many bytes of data in the following format: a LONG followed by an appropriate clipboard identifier and a property whose value is plain text should use VT_LPSTR, not VT_CF, to represent the text. Notice also that an application should choose a single clipboard format for a property's value when using VT_CF.
VT_CLSID	72	A CLSID, which is a DWORD, two WORDs, and 8 bytes
VT_VECTOR	0x1000	If the type indicator is one of the previous values in addition to this bit being set, then the value is a DWORD count of elements, followed by that many repetitions of the value. When VT_VECTOR is combined with VT_VARIANT (VT_VARIANT must be combined with VT_VECTOR), the value contains a DWORD element count, a DWORD type indicator, the first value, a DWORD type indicator, the second value, and so on

Compound Files

A compound file or docfile is an implementation of the storage scheme used in OLE 2. Basically, the data lives at the leaf nodes and a hierarchical path from the root exists to get at the data. Figures B.2 and B.3 show the compound file storage model. For more information on compound files, see Chapter 4.

FIGURE B.2:

OLE structured storage

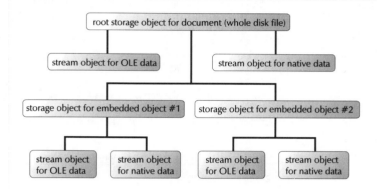

FIGURE B.3:

Compound file

```
Storage file D:\TMP\TEST.DOC
  'ICompObj', Type: Stream, Size: 98
  'ObjectPool', Type: Storage, Size: 0
  'WordDocument', Type: Stream, Size: 3022
  'ISummaryInformation', Type: Stream, Size: 844
    00000 fe ff 00 00 03 0a 00 00 00 00 00 00 00 00 00 00    ................
    00010 00 00 00 00 00 00 00 00 01 00 00 00 e0 85 9f f2    ................
    00020 f9 4f 68 10 ab 91 08 00 2b 27 b3 d9 30 00 00 00    .Oh.....+'..0...
    00030 1c 03 00 00 11 00 00 00 07 00 00 00 98 00 00 00    ................
    00040 02 00 00 00 dc 00 00 00 03 00 00 00 00 01 00 00    ................
    00050 05 00 00 00 24 01 00 00 06 00 00 00 48 01 00 00    ....$.......H...
    00060 04 00 00 00 6c 01 00 00 08 00 00 00 90 01 00 00    ....l...........
    00070 0c 00 00 00 b4 01 00 00 0b 00 00 00 d8 01 00 00    ................
    00080 0d 00 00 00 fc 01 00 00 0f 00 00 00 20 02 00 00    ................
    00090 10 00 00 00 44 02 00 00 0a 00 00 00 68 02 00 00    ....D.......h...
    000a0 12 00 00 00 8c 02 00 00 0e 00 00 00 b0 02 00 00    ................
    000b0 09 00 00 00 d4 02 00 00 13 00 00 00 f8 02 00 00    ................
    000c0 3e 16 00 24 40 16 00 00 1e 00 00 00 1f 00 00 00    >..$@...........
    000d0 43 3a 5c 57 49 4e 57 4f 52 44 5c 54 45 4d 50 4c    C:\WINWORD\TEMPL
    000e0 41 54 45 5c 4e 4f 52 4d 41 4c 2e 44 4f 54 00 00    ATE\NORMAL.DOT..
    000f0 00 00 00 00 00 00 00 00 00 00 00 00 00 00 00 00    ................
    00100 00 00 00 00 00 00 00 00 00 00 00 00 1e 00 00 00    ................
    00110 08 00 00 00 56 61 63 74 69 6f 6e 00 00 00 00 00    ....Vaction.....
    00120 00 00 00 00 00 00 00 00 00 00 00 00 00 00 00 00    ................
    00130 1e 00 00 00 0e 00 00 00 53 6e 6f 77 20 42 6f 61    ........Snow Boa
    00140 72 64 69 6e 67 00 00 00 00 00 00 00 00 00 00 00    rding...........
    00150 00 00 00 00 1e 00 00 00 0e 00 00 00 45 6e 74 65    ............Ente
    00160 72 74 61 69 6e 6d 65 6e 74 00 00 00 00 00 00 00    rtainment.......
```

OLE 2 provides the following interfaces to implement storage as a compound file:

OLE Interface	Functionality
IStorage	Instantiates a directory-like collection of storage and stream objects in which an embedded object's native data is saved
IStream	To read and write the underlying bytes of data similar to traditional file I/O
IRootStorage	To switch the underlying disk file to which IStorage objects are being saved
ILockBytes	Generally, used only by OLE to manipulate the byte array that underlies a compound file
IEnumSTATSTG	Used to enumerate IStorage objects

Document Summary Information Property Set

The Document Summary Information property set includes name, author, subject, date and time the file was created, and various other attributes for storing a brief summary of the document. Third-party applications can examine the Document Summary Information property set provided they all follow the specification. Figures B.4 and B.5 show how Microsoft displays its summary information for Word 6.0 documents.

FIGURE B.4:
Summary Info dialog box

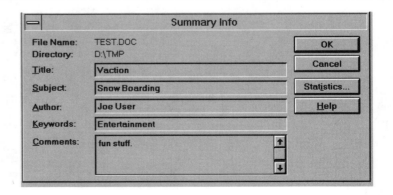

FIGURE B.5:
Document Statistics dialog box

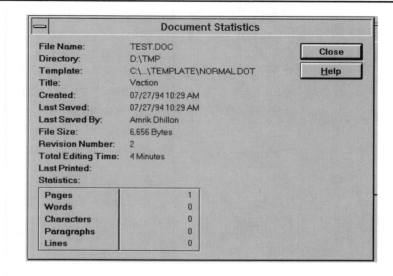

Document Summary Information Format

Use an IStream OLE 2 interface off the root IStorage interface. See Chapter 5 for more information. Table B.2 lists property names, property IDs, and type indicators for the Document Summary Information property set.

TABLE B.2: Standard OLE-Defined Property Type Indicators

Property Name	Property ID	Property ID Code	Type
Title	PID_TITLE	0x00000002	VT_LPSTR
Subject	PID_SUBJECT	0x00000003	VT_LPSTR
Author	PID_AUTHOR	0x00000004	VT_LPSTR
Keywords	PID_KEYWORDS	0x00000005	VT_LPSTR
Comments	PID_COMMENTS	0x00000006	VT_LPSTR
Template	PID_TEMPLATE	0x00000007	VT_LPSTR
Last Saved By	PID_LASTAUTHOR	0x00000008	VT_LPSTR

TABLE B.2: Standard OLE-Defined Property Type Indicators (continued)

Property Name	Property ID	Property ID Code	Type
Revision Number	PID_REVNUMBER	0x00000009	VT_LPSTR
Total Editing Time	PID_EDITTIME	0x0000000A	VT_FILETIME
Last Printed	PID_LASTPRINTED	0x0000000B	VT_FILETIME
Create Time/Date	PID_CREATE_DTM	0x0000000C	VT_FILETIME
Last saved Time/Date	PID_LASTSAVE_DTM	0x0000000D	VT_FILETIME
Number of Pages	PID_PAGECOUNT	0x0000000E	VT_I4
Number of Words	PID_WORDCOUNT	0x0000000F	VT_I4
Number of Characters	PID_CHARCOUNT	0x00000010	VT_I4
Thumbnail	PID_THUMBNAIL	0x00000011	VT_CF
Name of Creating Application	PID_APPNAME	0x00000012	VT_LPSTR
Security	PID_SECURITY	0x00000013	VT_I4

Document Summary Information

The stream that contains the Document Summary Information property set should be

```
"\005SummaryInformation"
```

The FMTID for the Document Summary Information property set is

```
F29F85E0-4FF9-1068-AB91-08002B27B3D9
```

Use the DEFINE_GUID macro to define the FMTID for the property set.

WARNING   For the purposes of this book, lines of code in this appendix have been limited to 65 characters. However, for this code to compile correctly, there need to be no artificial line breaks.

```
DEFINE_GUID(FormatID_SummaryInformation, 0xF29F85E0, 0x4FF9, 0x1068,
    0xAB,0x91, 0x08, 0x00, 0x2B, 0x27, 0xB3, 0xD9);
```

On an Intel byte-ordered machine, the FMTID has the following representation:

```
E0  85  9F  4F  68  10  AB  91  08  00  2B  27  B3  D9
```

INDEX

Note to the Reader:
Throughout this index **boldfaced** page numbers indicate primary discussions of a topic. *Italicized* page numbers indicate illustrations.

A

absolute path references, 7, *8*
accessing databases with ILockBytes
    interface, **105–106**, *105, 106*
activation. *See also* in-place activation;
    in-place containers; in-place object
    server example; in-place objects
    activating objects on double-clicks,
      159–161
    overview of, 125–126
activation messages, 207–208
adding OLE objects to existing file
    formats, 98
AddRef() method, 17–19
advise notifications for containers, **265–266**
aggregating objects, 22, *23*
allocating globally unique identification
    numbers (GUIDs), 31–32
application automation feature, 6–7
Application class, in OLE Publisher
    example, 128–129
application storage models. *See* storage
    models
automatic conversion of existing file
    formats, 98–99, *100*
automatic links, 168, 170
automatic scrolling for drag-and-drop
    operations, 231, *231*, 245–246
AuxUserType subkey in registration
    database, 338

B

Beep object server (IBeep), **40–52**. *See also*
    Component object example

BEEP.H header file, 47–49
BeepClassFactory, 49–50
BeepObject class, 51–52
    overview of, 40–41, *41*
    source code listing, 40–47
    support routines, 50–51
    using C versus C++, 48–49, *49*
Big Endian file format, 69
binding, **322–326**. *See also* link object servers;
    monikers
    composite monikers, 323–325, *324*
    file monikers, 322–323, *323*, 325
    item monikers, 325
    pointer monikers, 325
border windows, **294**
border-space negotiation for toolbars, **197**,
    198
building. *See* creating
byte swapping, 69

C

CF_OBJECTDESCRIPTOR data format,
    258–259
client applications. *See* containers
Clipboard, **119–125**, **137–156**. *See also*
    containers; link containers
    copying objects to Clipboard, 145–156,
      146
    creating links from, **174**
    drag-and-drop and, **235**, 249–250, *250*
    FORMATETC structure and, 121–122
    guidelines for using the Clipboard,
      124–125

D

L

GET A FREE CATALOG JUST FOR EXPRESSING YOUR OPINION.

Help us improve our books and get a *FREE* full-color catalog in the bargain. Please complete this form, pull out this page and send it in today. The address is on the reverse side.

Name _____   **Company** _____

Address _____   **City** _____ **State** ____ **Zip** _____

Phone (   ) _____

1. How would you rate the overall quality of this book?

❑ Excellent
❑ Very Good
❑ Good
❑ Fair
❑ Below Average
❑ Poor

2. What were the things you liked most about the book? (Check all that apply)

❑ Pace
❑ Format
❑ Writing Style
❑ Examples
❑ Table of Contents
❑ Index
❑ Price
❑ Illustrations
❑ Type Style
❑ Cover
❑ Depth of Coverage
❑ Fast Track Notes

3. What were the things you liked *least* about the book? (Check all that apply)

❑ Pace
❑ Format
❑ Writing Style
❑ Examples
❑ Table of Contents
❑ Index
❑ Price
❑ Illustrations
❑ Type Style
❑ Cover
❑ Depth of Coverage
❑ Fast Track Notes

4. Where did you buy this book?

❑ Bookstore chain
❑ Small independent bookstore
❑ Computer store
❑ Wholesale club
❑ College bookstore
❑ Technical bookstore
❑ Other _____

5. How did you decide to buy this particular book?

❑ Recommended by friend
❑ Recommended by store personnel
❑ Author's reputation
❑ Sybex's reputation
❑ Read book review in _____
❑ Other _____

6. How did you pay for this book?

❑ Used own funds
❑ Reimbursed by company
❑ Received book as a gift

7. What is your level of experience with the subject covered in this book?

❑ Beginner
❑ Intermediate
❑ Advanced

8. How long have you been using a computer?

years _____

months _____

9. Where do you most often use your computer?

❑ Home
❑ Work

❑ Both
❑ Other _____

10. What kind of computer equipment do you have? (Check all that apply)

❑ PC Compatible Desktop Computer
❑ PC Compatible Laptop Computer
❑ Apple/Mac Computer
❑ Apple/Mac Laptop Computer
❑ CD ROM
❑ Fax Modem
❑ Data Modem
❑ Scanner
❑ Sound Card
❑ Other _____

11. What other kinds of software packages do you ordinarily use?

❑ Accounting
❑ Databases
❑ Networks
❑ Apple/Mac
❑ Desktop Publishing
❑ Spreadsheets
❑ CAD
❑ Games
❑ Word Processing
❑ Communications
❑ Money Management
❑ Other _____

12. What operating systems do you ordinarily use?

❑ DOS
❑ OS/2
❑ Windows
❑ Apple/Mac
❑ Windows NT
❑ Other _____

13. On what computer-related subject(s) would you like to see more books?

_____

_____

_____

14. Do you have any other comments about this book? (Please feel free to use a separate piece of paper if you need more room)

_____

_____

_____

- - - - - - - - - - - PLEASE FOLD, SEAL, AND MAIL TO SYBEX - - - - - - - - - - -

SYBEX INC.
Department M
2021 Challenger Drive
Alameda, CA
94501

What's on the Disk?

This companion disk contains the source code and selected executables for the examples described in this book. The examples are designed to expose you to a wide range of real-world programming challenges and situations. You'll also find the full source for the OLE Publisher container application, as well as the OLE Draw object server.

What about Installation?

A high-density disk drive is required. To install the disk, type

    A:\INSTALL

A directory called MASTOLE will be created on your C drive, and the source will be copied into this directory.